Based on the Common Core State Standards (CCSS)

PARCC

SUCCESS STRATEGIES

High School Algebra II

Comprehensive Skill Building Practice for the Partnership for Assessment of Readiness for College and Careers Assessments

Written and edited by the Mometrix Test Preparation Team
Printed in the United States of America

Dear Future Exam Success Story:

Congratulations on your purchase of our study guide. Our goal in writing our study guide was to cover the content on the test, as well as provide insight into typical test taking mistakes and how to overcome them.

Standardized tests are a key component of being successful, which only increases the importance of doing well in the high-pressure high-stakes environment of test day. How well you do on this test will have a significant impact on your future, and we have the research and practical advice to help you execute on test day.

The product you're reading now is designed to exploit weaknesses in the test itself, and help you avoid the most common errors test takers frequently make.

How to use this study guide

We don't want to waste your time. Our study guide is fast-paced and fluff-free. We suggest going through it a number of times, as repetition is an important part of learning new information and concepts.

First, read through the study guide completely to get a feel for the content and organization. Read the general success strategies first, and then proceed to the content sections. Each tip has been carefully selected for its effectiveness.

Second, read through the study guide again, and take notes in the margins and highlight those sections where you may have a particular weakness.

Finally, bring the manual with you on test day and study it before the exam begins.

Your success is our success

We would be delighted to hear about your success. Send us an email and tell us your story. Thanks for your business and we wish you continued success.

Sincerely,

Mometrix Test Preparation Team

Need more help? Check out our flashcards at:
http://MometrixFlashcards.com/PARCC

TABLE OF CONTENTS

Top 15 Test Taking Tips

1. Know the test directions, duration, topics, question types, how many questions
2. Setup a flexible study schedule at least 3-4 weeks before test day
3. Study during the time of day you are most alert, relaxed, and stress free
4. Maximize your learning style; visual learner use visual study aids, auditory learner use auditory study aids
5. Focus on your weakest knowledge base
6. Find a study partner to review with and help clarify questions
7. Practice, practice, practice
8. Get a good night's sleep; don't try to cram the night before the test
9. Eat a well balanced meal
10. Wear comfortable, loose fitting, layered clothing; prepare for it to be either cold or hot during the test
11. Eliminate the obviously wrong answer choices, then guess the first remaining choice
12. Pace yourself; don't rush, but keep working and move on if you get stuck
13. Maintain a positive attitude even if the test is going poorly
14. Keep your first answer unless you are positive it is wrong
15. Check your work, don't make a careless mistake

Algebra II

The Complex Number System

Real, natural, whole, integer, rational, irrational, imaginary, and complex numbers

The set of **real numbers** contains all numbers which have distinct locations on a number line. **Natural numbers** are real numbers used for counting: 1, 2, 3, 4, ... The set of **whole numbers** includes the counting numbers along with the number zero: 0, 1, 2, 3, 4, ... The set of **integers** includes whole numbers and their opposites: ..., -4, -3, -2, -1, 0, 1, 2, 3, 4, ... **Rational numbers** include any real number which can be expressed as a fraction in which the numerator is an integer and the denominator is a non-zero integer; rational numbers include integers, fractions, terminating, and repeating decimals. **Irrational numbers,** such as $\sqrt{2}$ and π, are real numbers which are not rational; in decimal form, these numbers are non-repeating and non-terminating, so any decimal (or fractional) representations of irrational numbers are only approximations. The set of **imaginary numbers** includes all numbers whose squares are negative and therefore excludes any real number; the imaginary number i is defined as the square root of -1. The set of **complex numbers** encompasses both the real and imaginary; a complex number can be written in the form $a + bi$, where a and b are real numbers, and i is the imaginary number.

Relationships among these sets of numbers

Below is an example of a diagram which shows that natural numbers are a subset of whole numbers, which are a subset of integers, which are a subset of rational numbers. All of these together with irrational numbers comprise the set of real numbers. Complex numbers include both real and imaginary numbers.

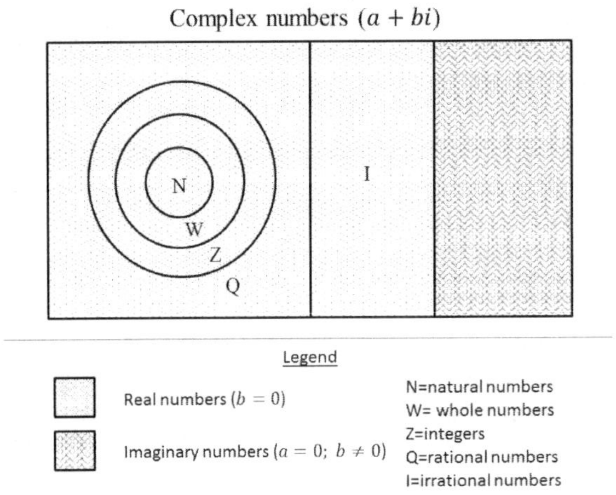

Note that the sizes of the boxes and circles do not reflect the sizes of each set. Each set contains an infinite number of elements.

Problem

Classifying each of the following numbers as a real, natural, whole, integer, rational, irrational, imaginary, and/or complex

1. π
2. −6
3. 22
4. i
5. $\frac{2}{3}$
6. $2 + 3i$

1. π is an irrational number, a real number, and a complex number
2. -6 is an integer, a rational number, a real number, and a complex number
3. 22 is a natural number, a whole number, an integer, a rational number, a real number, and a complex number
4. i is an imaginary number and a complex number
5. $\frac{2}{3}$ is a rational number, a real number, and a complex number
6. 2+3i is a complex number

Problem

Determining whether each statement is true

1. All natural numbers are real numbers.
2. Some integers are whole numbers.
3. Imaginary numbers are not real.
4. No integer is irrational.
5. All rational numbers are integers.

1. True; all natural numbers are real numbers.
2. True; some integers are whole numbers. Not all integers, however, are whole numbers, but all whole numbers are integers.
3. True; imaginary numbers are not real.
4. True; no integer is irrational. Integers are part of the set of rational numbers, and irrational numbers are not rational.
5. False; all rational numbers are NOT integers. All integers are rational, but not all rational numbers are integers.

Problem

In the statements below, * and   represent undefined operations. Name the properties illustrated in each statement and define for which operation(s) * and   each of these statements is true. Also, identify for which sets of numbers these properties are true

1. $a * b = b * a$
2. $a * (b * c) = (a * b) * c$
3. $a * (b\_c) = a * b\_a * c$
4. $a * b = a$

1. $a * b = b * a$ illustrates the commutative property, which is true for any complex numbers a and b when * represents addition or multiplication.

2. $a * (b * c) = (a * b) * c$ illustrates the associative property, which is true for any complex numbers a and b when * represents addition or multiplication.
3. $a * (b\_c) = a * b \_ a * c$ illustrates the distributive property, which is true for any complex numbers a and b when * represents multiplication and _ represents addition or subtraction.
4. $a * b = a$ illustrates an identity, where the quantity a is unchanged by the operation * with the quantity b. This property is true for any complex number a when * represents addition or subtraction and when $b = 0$. This property is true for any complex number a when * represents multiplication or division and $b = 1$.

Note: The operation * can also represent "to the power of" when a is any complex number and $b = 1$ since, by definition, any number raised to the first power is that number.

Problem

Simplify
1. i^{12}
2. $(2i)^8$
3. $(-i)^{25}$

Notice the pattern that emerges when i is raised to consecutive natural number powers:

$$i^1 = i$$
$$i^2 = -1$$
$$i^3 = i^2 i = (-1)(i) = -i$$
$$i^4 = i^2 i^2 = (-1)(-1) = 1$$
$$i^5 = i^4 i = (1)(i) = i$$
$$i^6 = i^4 i^2 = (1)(-1) = -1$$
$$i^7 = i^4 i^3 = (1)(-i) = -i$$
$$i^8 = i^4 i^4 = (-1)(-1) = 1$$

The imaginary number i raised to any whole power$n$ is always $i, -1, -i$, or 1. To find i^n, either continue writing the pattern $i, -1, -i$,1 to find the nth number in the pattern, or, more simply, use properties of exponents to rewrite and simplify i^n.

1. $i^{12} = (i^4)^3 = (1)^3 = 1$
2. $(2i)^8 = (2^8)(i^4)^2 = (2^4)^2(1)^2 = 16^2 = 256$
3. $(-i)^{25} = (-1)^{25}(i^4)^6(i) = (-1)(1)^6(i) = -i$

Problem

Determine the values of a and b for which $\sqrt{a} \cdot \sqrt{b} \neq \sqrt{ab}$.

$\sqrt{a} \cdot \sqrt{b} = \sqrt{ab}$ when either a or b is positive or when both a and b are positive. For example,

$\sqrt{25} \cdot \sqrt{4} = 5 \cdot 2 = 10$ and $\sqrt{25 \cdot 4} = \sqrt{100} = 10$, so $\sqrt{25} \cdot \sqrt{4} = \sqrt{25 \cdot 4}$;

$\sqrt{-25} \cdot \sqrt{4} = 5i \cdot 2 = 10i$ and $\sqrt{-25 \cdot 4} = \sqrt{-100} = 10i$, so $\sqrt{-25} \cdot \sqrt{4} = \sqrt{-25 \cdot 4}$.

However, $\sqrt{a} \cdot \sqrt{b} \neq \sqrt{ab}$ when both a and b are both negative. For example, $\sqrt{-25} \cdot \sqrt{-4} = 5i \cdot 2i = 10i^2 = -10$ but $\sqrt{-25 \cdot -4} = \sqrt{100} = 10$. Since $10 \neq -10, \sqrt{-25} \cdot \sqrt{-4} \neq \sqrt{-25 \cdot -4}$.

Problem

Simplify $\sqrt{-200}$.

$\sqrt{-200} = \sqrt{-1 \cdot 2 \cdot 2 \cdot 2 \cdot 5 \cdot 5} = \sqrt{-1} \cdot \sqrt{2^2} \cdot \sqrt{2} \cdot \sqrt{5^2} = i \cdot 2 \cdot \sqrt{2} \cdot 5 = 10i\sqrt{2}$.

Problem

Simplify the following expressions.

1. $(2 + 3i) + (6 - 2i)$
2. $(2 + 3i) - (6 - 2i)$
3. $(2 + 3i)(6 - 2i)$

The commutative, associative, and distributive properties are true for complex numbers. Complex expressions can be simplified just as real variable expressions are simplified. Keep in mind, however, that i is not a variable but is rather the imaginary number, so be sure to simplify i^2 to -1.

1. $(2 + 3i) + (6 - 2i) = 8 + i$
2. $(2 + 3i) - (6 - 2i) = -4 + 5i$
3. $(2 + 3i)(6 - 2i) = 12 - 4i + 18i - 6i^2 = 12 + 14i + 6 = 18 + 14i$

Problem

Simplify $3i(2 + 4i) - (6 + 2i)^2$.

The commutative, associative, and distributive properties are true for complex numbers. Complex expressions can be simplified just as real, variable expressions are simplified. Keep in mind, however, that i is not a variable but is rather the imaginary number, so be sure to simplify i^2 to -1.

$$3i(2 + 4i) - (6 + 2i)^2$$
$$6i + 12i^2 - (36 + 24i + 4i^2)$$
$$6i + 12i^2 - 36 - 24i - 4i^2$$
$$-18i + 8i^2 - 36$$
$$-18i - 8 - 36$$
$$-44 - 18i$$

Modulus of a complex number

The modulus, or absolute value, of a complex number $z = a + bi$ is the distance from the origin to point z graphed on the complex plane. Since that distance can be represented by the hypotenuse of a right triangle with leg lengths a and b, $|z|=\sqrt{a^2 + b^2}$.

It is **true** that the modulus of a complex number is always a real number and is always positive. Since a and b represent real numbers, their squares are always positive, real numbers. The sum of two positive, real numbers must also be positive and real, so $a^2 + b^2$ is a positive, real quantity. The square root of a positive, real number is also a positive, real number, so $\sqrt{a^2 + b^2}$ must return a number that is both real and positive.

Complex plane

The complex plane is created by the intersection of a real, horizontal axis and an imaginary, vertical axis. For a complex number written in the form $a + bi$, a represents the displacement along the real axis and b along the imaginary axis.

Problem

Graph these numbers on the complex plane.

1. -4
2. $2i$
3. $3 - i$

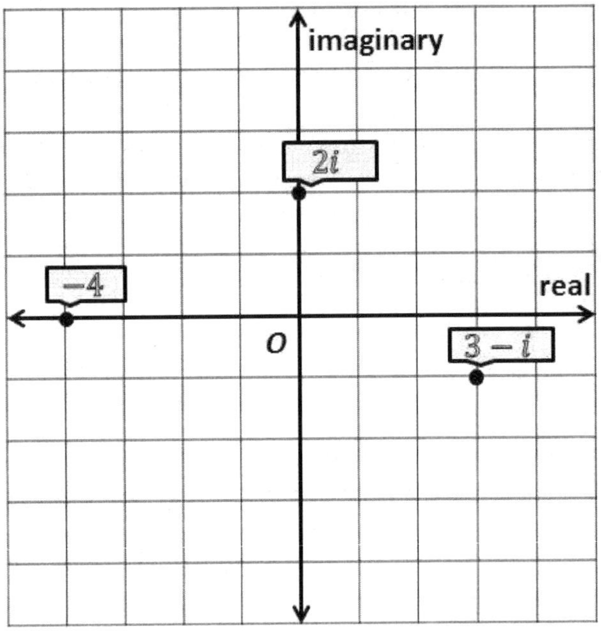

The number -4 is graphed in its appropriate position on the real number line, while $2i$ is graphed on the imaginary axis since its real number component a is 0. The complex number $3 - i$ is represented by a point on the plane which is three units to the right of the origin and one unit down.

Another way to represent each of these points graphically on the complex plane is to draw a vector from the origin to the point (a, b). For example, $3 - i$ is graphed below.

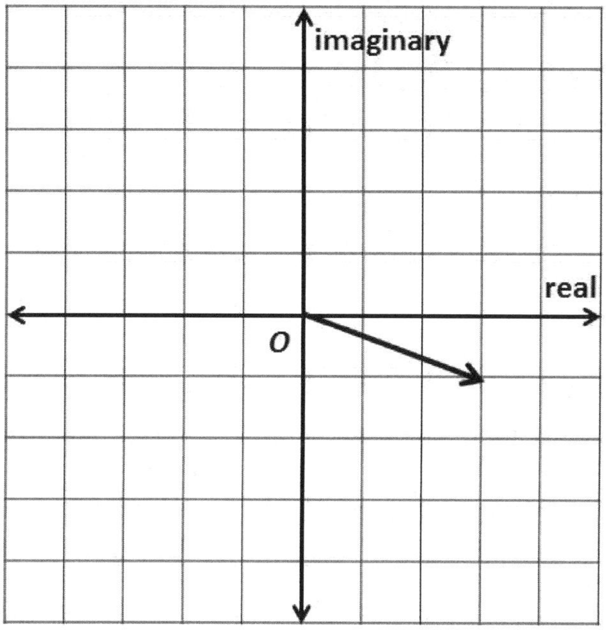

Conjugate of a complex number

The conjugate of a complex number $a + bi$ is $a - bi$. It is **true** that the product of a complex number and its conjugate is always real:

$(a + bi)(a - bi) = a^2 - abi + abi - b^2i^2 = a^2 + b^2$. Since a and b are real, and since squares and sums of real numbers are also real, $a^2 + b^2$ is always real.

Problem

Find the modulus and the conjugate of the complex number $4 + 3i$.

The modulus, or absolute value, of a complex number is the number's distance from the origin when graphed on the complex plane. By graphing $4 + 3i$ on the complex plane, it is easy to see that its distance from the origin is the hypotenuse of a right triangle with leg lengths 4 and 3. Recognize 3-4-5 as a common Pythagorean triple, or evaluate and simply the expression $\sqrt{a^2 + b^2}$, where $a = 4$ and $b = 3$: $\sqrt{4^2 + 3^2} = \sqrt{16 + 9} = \sqrt{25} = 5$. So, the modulus of $4 + 3i$ is 5.

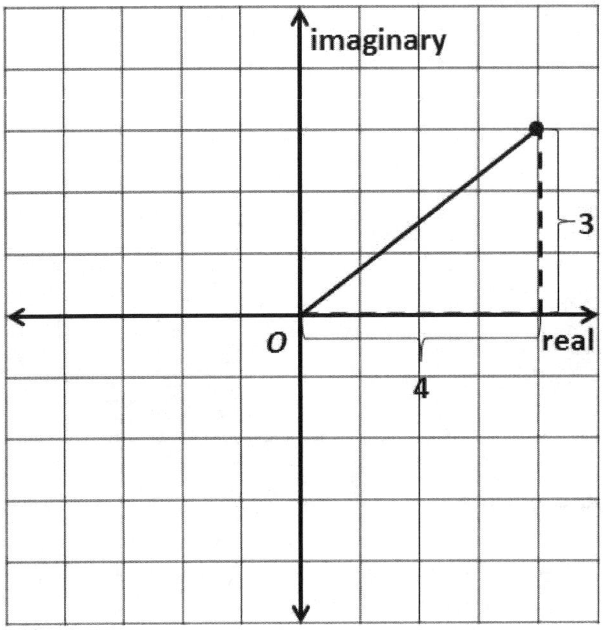

The conjugate of complex number $a + bi$ is defined as $a - bi$, so the conjugate of $4 + 3i$ is $4 - 3i$.

Problem

Write an equation which relates complex number z, its conjugate $\bar{z}$, and its modulus$|z|$.

Let $z = a + bi$. By definition, $\bar{z} = a - bi$, and $|z| = \sqrt{a^2 + b^2}$.
Since $z \cdot \bar{z} = (a + bi)(a - bi) = a^2 - abi + abi - b^2i^2 = a^2 + b^2$, and since $|z|^2 = \left(\sqrt{a^2 + b^2}\right)^2 = a^2 + b^2$,we have the relationship $\mathbf{z} \cdot \bar{\mathbf{z}} = |\mathbf{z}|^2$.

Use the property $z \cdot \bar{z} = |z|^2$, where z is a complex number and $\bar{z}$ and $|z|$are its conjugate and modulus, respectively, to find the modulus of $3 + 4i$.

When $z = 3 + 4i, \bar{z} = 3 - 4i$.

$$|z|^2 = z \cdot \bar{z} = (3 + 4i)(3 - 4i) = 9 - 16i^2 = 25$$
$$|z| = 5$$

The modulus is represents the distance of a complex number from zero on the complex plane and can therefore not be negative. So, the modulus of $3 + 4i$ is 5.

Problem

Simplify $\frac{2-4i}{1+3i}$.

To simplify the quotient of two complex numbers, multiply the numerator and denominator by the complex conjugate of the denominator.

$$\frac{2-4i}{1+3i} = \frac{2-4i}{1+3i} \cdot \frac{1-3i}{1-3i} = \frac{2-6i-4i+12i^2}{1-9i^2} = \frac{2-10i-12}{1+9} = \frac{-10-10i}{10}$$
$$= -1 - i$$

Problem

Simplify $\frac{3-i\sqrt{2}}{3+i\sqrt{2}}$.

To simplify the quotient of two complex numbers, multiply the numerator and denominator by the complex conjugate of the denominator.

$$\frac{3-i\sqrt{2}}{3+i\sqrt{2}} = \frac{3-i\sqrt{2}}{3+i\sqrt{2}} \cdot \frac{3-i\sqrt{2}}{3-i\sqrt{2}} = \frac{9-2i\sqrt{2}+2i^2}{9-2i^2} = \frac{9-2i\sqrt{2}-2}{9+2}$$
$$= \frac{7-2i\sqrt{2}}{11} = \frac{7}{11} - \frac{2\sqrt{2}}{11}i$$

Problem

Use the property $\frac{z_1}{z_2} = \frac{z_1\overline{z_2}}{|z_2|^2}$ to find the quotient of $2 - 4i$ and $1 + 3i$.

$$z_1 = 2 - 4i$$
$$z_2 = 1 + 3i$$
$$\overline{z_2} = 1 - 3i$$
$$|z_2| = \sqrt{1^2 + 3^2} = \sqrt{1+9} = \sqrt{10}$$

So,

$$\frac{2-4i}{1+3i} = \frac{(2-4i)(1-3i)}{\sqrt{10}^2} = \frac{2-6i-4i+12i^2}{10} = \frac{2-10i-12}{10} = \frac{-10-10i}{10}$$
$$= -1 - i$$

Argument of a complex number

A complex number can be represented on the complex plane in both rectangular and polar forms. The polar coordinates (r, θ) can be used to describe the position of a point.

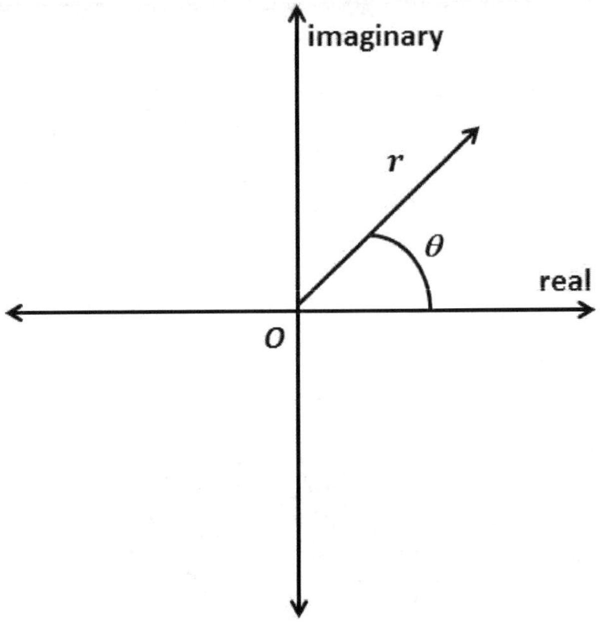

r is the distance from the point to the origin and θ is the angle, in radians, from the positive, real axis to the vector which represents the complex number. This angle θ is called the **argument** of the complex number.

Deriving the polar form of a complex number from its rectangular form

A complex number can be represented on the complex plane in both rectangular and polar forms. The rectangular coordinates (a, b) or the polar coordinates (r, θ) can be used to describe the position of the same point on the plane.

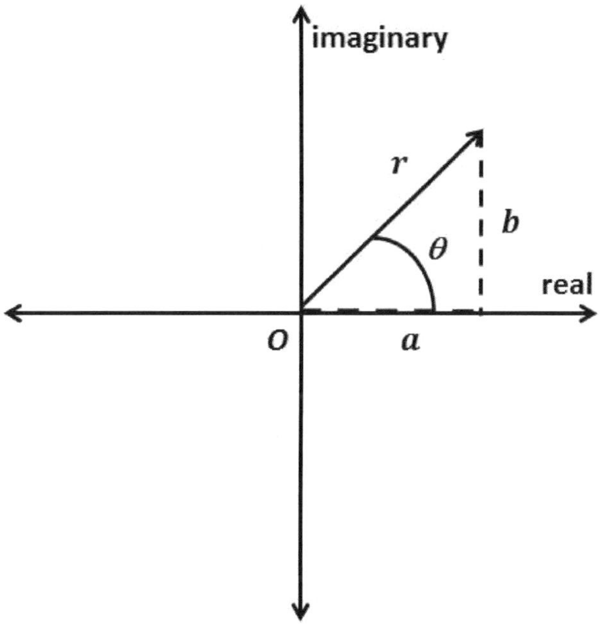

r is the distance from the point to the origin (and for complex z is equivalent to the modulus $|z|$, which equals $\sqrt{a^2 + b^2}$), and θ is the angle, in radians, from the positive, real axis to the vector which represents the complex number. To rewrite a complex number $z = a + bi$ in polar form, find a and b in terms of r and θ. Because $\sin\theta = \frac{b}{r}$ and $\cos\theta = \frac{a}{r}$, we have that $b = r\sin\theta$ and $a = r\cos\theta$. Therefore, $z = r\cos\theta + (r\sin\theta)i$ which is conventionally written $\boldsymbol{z = r(\cos\theta + i\sin\theta)}$.

Graphical relationship between a complex number and its conjugate

When graphed on the complex plane, the conjugate of a complex number is the reflection of the complex number across the real axis.

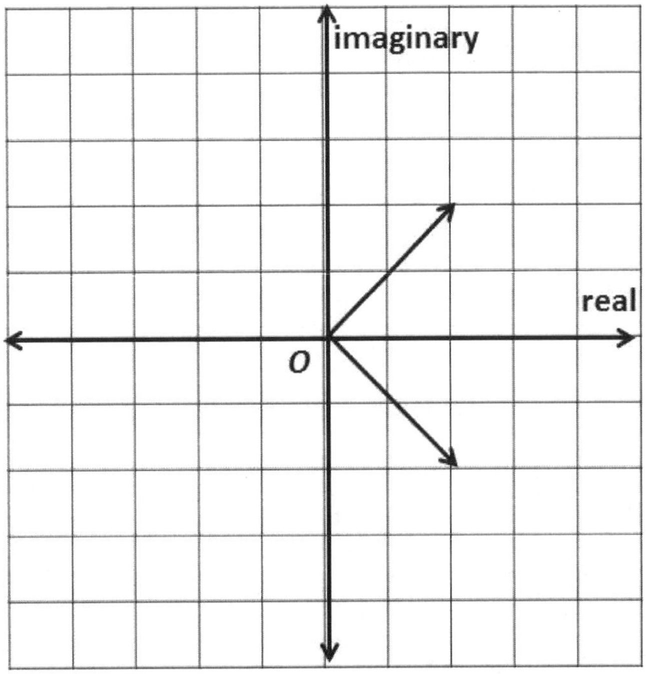

$2 - 2i$ is the reflection across the horizontal axis of $2 + 2i$.

Modulus of a complex number and its conjugate are equivalent

The complex conjugate of $a + bi$ is $a - bi$. The modulus of a complex number is $\sqrt{a^2 + b^2}$. Substituting –b for b gives $\sqrt{a^2 + (-b)^2}$, which equals $\sqrt{a^2 + b^2}$.

Problem

Write the polar form of these complex number.

$$-3$$

The polar form of a complex number is written in the form $z = r(\cos\theta + i\sin\theta)$, where r is the distance from the point to the origin (and for complex z is equivalent to the modulus $|z|$, which equals $\sqrt{a^2 + b^2}$), and θ is the argument, or the angle, measured in radians, from the positive, real axis to the vector which represents the complex number.

For the real number -3, $r = 3$ and $\theta = \pi$. So, the number can be written in polar form as $3(\cos\pi + i\sin\pi)$

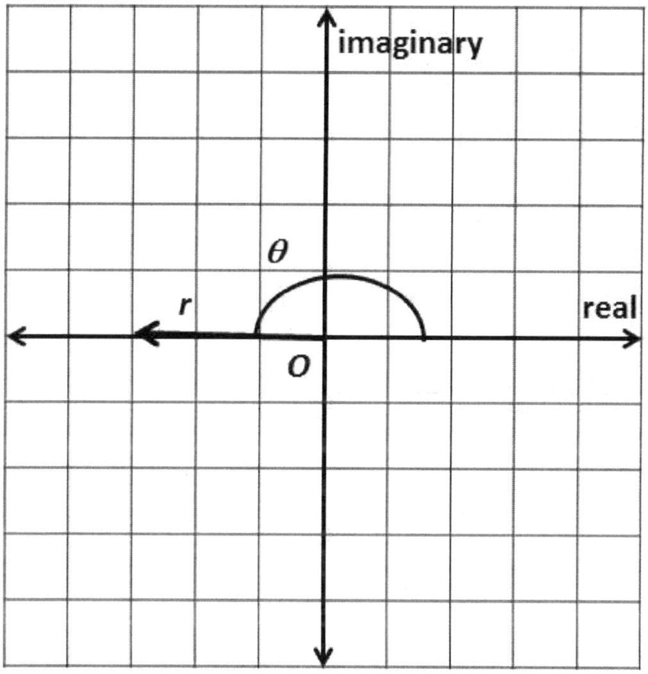

Problem

Write the polar form of these complex number.

$$4i$$

The polar form of a complex number is written in the form $z = r(\cos\theta + i\sin\theta)$, where r is the distance from the point to the origin (and for complex z is equivalent to the modulus $|z|$, which equals $\sqrt{a^2 + b^2}$), and θ is the argument, or the angle, measured in radians, from the positive, real axis to the vector which represents the complex number.

For the imaginary number $4i$, $r = 4$ and $\theta = \frac{\pi}{2}$. So, the number can be written in polar form as $4(\cos\frac{\pi}{2} + i\sin\frac{\pi}{2})$.

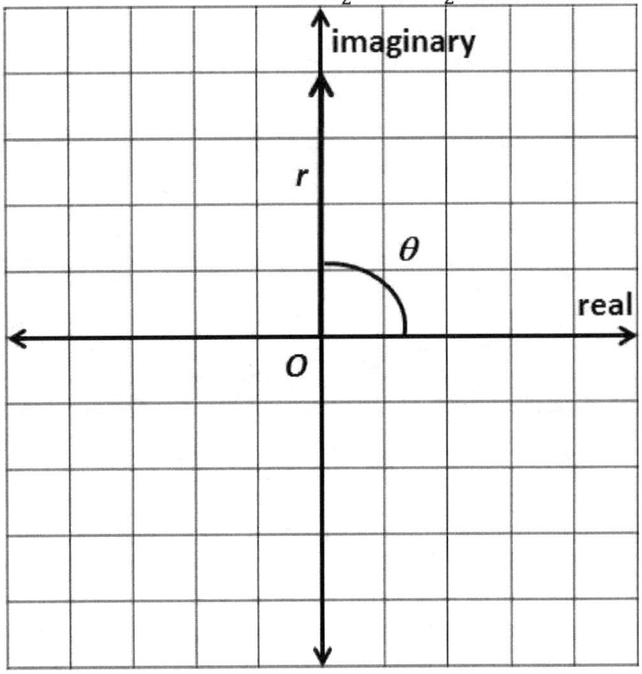

Problem

Write $2 + 2i$ in polar form and graph it on the complex plane.

The polar form of a complex number is written in the form $z = r(\cos\theta + i\sin\theta)$, where r is the distance from the point to the origin (and for complex z is equivalent to the modulus $|z|$, which equals $\sqrt{a^2 + b^2}$), and θ is the argument, or the angle, measured in radians, from the positive, real axis to the vector which represents the complex number.
Calculate r and θ for complex number $2 + 2i$.

$$r = \sqrt{a^2 + b^2} = \sqrt{2^2 + 2^2} = \sqrt{8} = 2\sqrt{2}.$$

$$\theta = \tan\left(\frac{2}{2}\right)$$

$$\theta = \frac{\pi}{4}$$

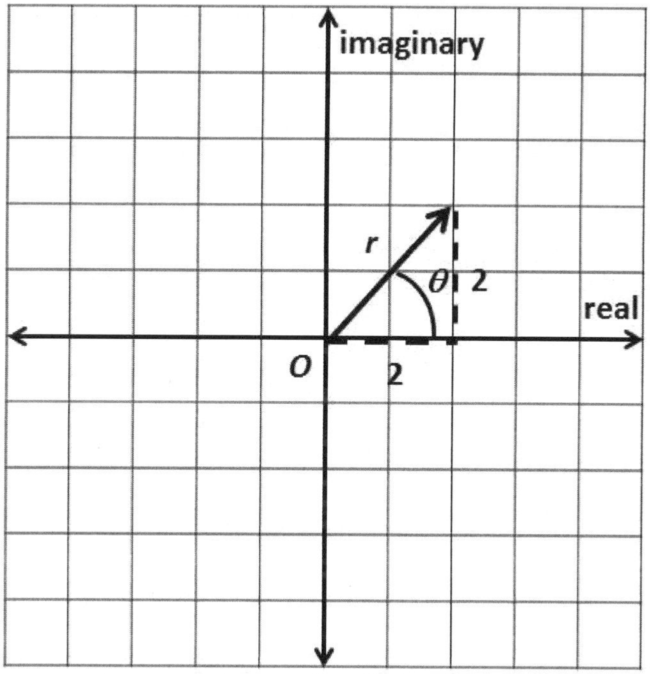

So, the number can be written in polar form as $2\sqrt{2}(\cos\frac{\pi}{4} + i\sin\frac{\pi}{4})$.

Multiplying two complex numbers written in polar form

A complex number z can be written in polar form as $z = r(\cos\theta + i\sin\theta)$, where $r = |z| = \sqrt{a^2 + b^2}$ and θ is the argument of z. Consider the two complex numbers $z_1 = |z_1|(\cos\theta_1 + i\sin\theta_1)$ and $z_2 = |z_2|(\cos\theta_2 + i\sin\theta_2)$.

$$z_1 z_2 = |z_1|(\cos\theta_1 + i\sin\theta_1)\,|z_2|(\cos\theta_2 + i\sin\theta_2)$$

$$= |z_1||z_2|(\cos\theta_1 + i\sin\theta_1)(\cos\theta_2 + i\sin\theta_2)$$

$$= |z_1||z_2|(\cos\theta_1\cos\theta_2 + i\cos\theta_1\sin\theta_2 + i\sin\theta_1\cos\theta_2 + i^2\sin\theta_2\sin\theta_2)$$

$$= |z_1||z_2|(\cos\theta_1\cos\theta_2 + i(\cos\theta_1\sin\theta_2 + \sin\theta_1\cos\theta_2) - \sin\theta_2\sin\theta_2)$$

$$= |z_1||z_2|\left((\cos\theta_1\cos\theta_2 - \sin\theta_2\sin\theta_2) + i(\cos\theta_1\sin\theta_2 + \sin\theta_1\cos\theta_2)\right)$$

Use the trigonometric identities $\cos(A + B) = (\cos A \cos B - \sin A \sin B)$ and $\sin(A + B) = (\cos A \sin B + \sin A \cos B)$ to simplify the expression in parentheses, which gives
$\boldsymbol{z_1 z_2 = |z_1||z_2|((\cos(\theta_1 + \theta_2) + i \sin(\theta_1 + \theta_2))}$.
Notice that the complex number which results from multiplying z_1 and z_2 has a modulus of $|z_1||z_2|$and an argument of $\theta_1 + \theta_2$. So, to multiply two complex numbers, multiply their moduli and add their arguments.

Problem

Rewrite $\sqrt{3} - i$ in polar form. Then, using the properties of multiplication for complex numbers in polar form, calculate $\left(\sqrt{3} - i\right)^3$.

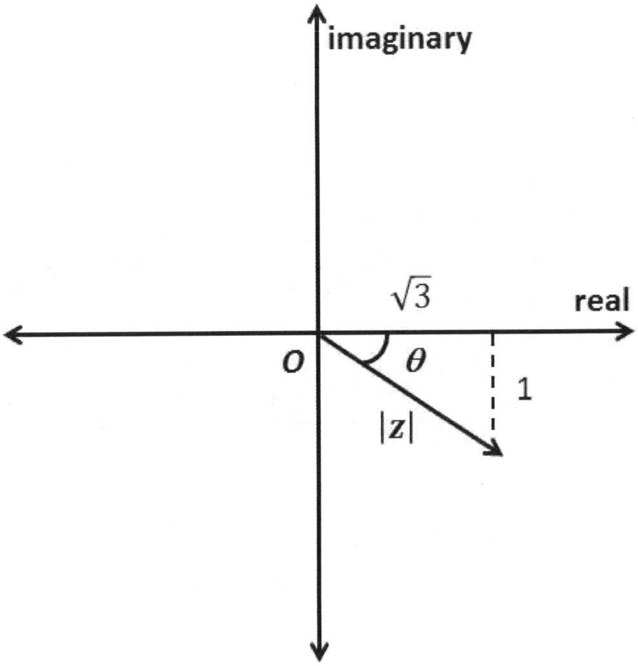

First find the modulus and argument of the complex number $\sqrt{3} - i$. Sketch the graph of $\sqrt{3} - i$.

$|z| = \sqrt{a^2 + b^2} = \sqrt{3 + 1} = 2$.
$\sin\theta = -\frac{1}{2}$ and $\cos\theta = \frac{\sqrt{3}}{2}$, so $\theta = -\frac{\pi}{6}$.
We can rewrite $-\frac{\pi}{6}$ as positive angle $\frac{11\pi}{6}$.
The complex number $\sqrt{3} - i$ can be written in polar form as $z = 2(\cos\frac{11\pi}{6} + i\sin\frac{11\pi}{6})$.

Using the property of multiplication for complex numbers, z^3 has a modulus of $2 \cdot 2 \cdot 2 = 8$ and an argument of $(\frac{11\pi}{6}) + (\frac{11\pi}{6}) + (\frac{11\pi}{6}) = \frac{33\pi}{6}$, which is coterminal with $\frac{3\pi}{2}$ because $\frac{33\pi}{6} - 2\pi - 2\pi = \frac{3\pi}{2}$.

So, $z^3 = 8\left(\cos\left(\frac{3\pi}{2}\right) + i\sin\left(\frac{3\pi}{2}\right)\right) = 8\big(0 + i(-1)\big) = 8(-i) = -8i.$

Problem

Write the complex number $4\sqrt{2}(\cos\frac{5\pi}{4} + i\sin\frac{5\pi}{4})$ in rectangular form.

First, sketch the graph of $4\sqrt{2}(\cos\frac{5\pi}{4} + i\sin\frac{5\pi}{4})$.

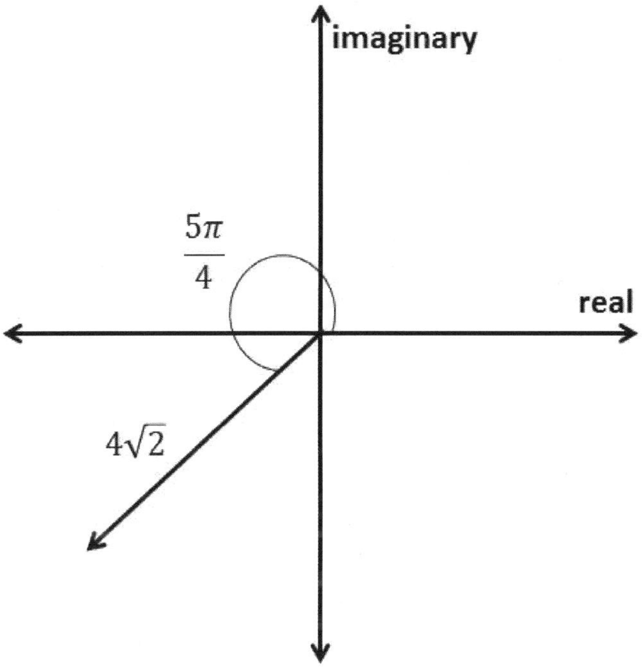

$\frac{b}{4\sqrt{2}} = \sin\frac{5\pi}{4} = \frac{\sqrt{2}}{2}$ simplifies to $b = -4$

$\frac{a}{4\sqrt{2}} = \cos\frac{5\pi}{4} = -\frac{\sqrt{2}}{2}$ simplifies to $a = -4$.

Since the complex number is in the third quadrant, both its real and imaginary components are negative, so its rectangular form is $-4 - 4i$.

Finding the roots of a quadratic polynomial

One way to solve a quadratic equation in the form $ax^2 + bx + c = 0$, where a≠0, is to find the zeros, or x-intercepts, of the related quadratic function's **graph**. Because the roots may be irrational or complex, this method is not the best one to choose when an exact solution is needed.

A second way to solve a quadratic equation in the form $ax^2 + bx + c = 0$, where a≠0 is to **factor**; according to the Zero Product Property, a solution to the equation exists when either factor is equal to zero. This method is especially useful when $c = 0$ or when the factors of the trinomial are easy to determine.

A third way to solve a quadratic equation is to **use the Square Root Property**, completing the square if necessary. (To use this method, the quadratic expression must be a perfect square but need not be set equal to zero.) This method can be used to find both real and complex roots.

A fourth way to solve a quadratic equation in the form $ax^2 + bx + c = 0$ is to **use the Quadratic Formula**, $x = \frac{-b \pm \sqrt{b^2-4ac}}{2a}$. This method can also be used to find real and complex solutions.

<u>Using the discriminant of a quadratic equation to determine the number and types of solutions to the equation</u>
A quadratic equation in the form $ax^2 + bx + c = 0$, where a≠0, has a discriminant of $b^2 - 4ac$. If the discriminant is greater than zero, the equation has two real solutions; more specifically, if the discriminant is a perfect square, those solutions are rational, but if the discriminant is not a perfect square, the solutions are irrational. If the discriminant is equal to zero, the equation has one real, rational root (and is called a double root.). If the discriminant is less than zero, the equation has two complex solutions, which are a conjugate pair.

<u>Problem</u>

Factor $100x^2 + 9$ using complex factors.

Rewrite $100x^2 + 9$ as $100x^2 - 9i^2$. This is a difference of squares, which can be factored as $(10x - 3i)(10x + 3i)$.

<u>Problem</u>

Factor $2x^2 + 8i - 8$ using complex factors.

First, factor out the common factor, which is 2. This gives $2x^2 + 8i - 8 = 2(x^2 + 4i - 4)$. Then, rewrite $x^2 + 4i - 4$ as $x^2 + 4i + 4i^2$, which is a perfect square and can therefore be factored as $(x + 2i)^2$. So, $2x^2 + 8i - 8 = 2(x + 2i)^2$.

Fundamental Theorem of Algebra

The Fundamental Theorem of Algebra states that a single variable polynomial of nth degree with $n > 0$ has *at least* one root. Furthermore, the polynomial has *exactly n* roots if multiplicities, or roots which appear more than once, are counted. In other words, a polynomial of nth degree can always be written as the product of a non-zero constant and n linear factors.

For example, any quadratic polynomial can be written as $k(x - r_1)(x - r_2)$, where r_1r and r_2 are complex roots and k is a non-zero constant. Keep in mind that the set of complex numbers includes real numbers, so the roots may not always be real numbers.

<u>Example</u>

Solve $x^2 + 10x + 25 = 16$ by
1. Graphing
2. Factoring

To solve a quadratic equation by graphing or factoring, rewrite it in the form

$$ax^2 + bx + c = 0.$$

$$x^2 + 10x + 25 = 16$$

$$x^2 + 10x + 25 - \mathbf{16} = 16 - \mathbf{16}$$

$$x^2 + 10x + 9 = 0$$

1. Graph the equation. The graph of a quadratic equation is a parabola. To find the parabola's line of symmetry, use the equation $x = -\frac{b}{2a}$.

$$x = -\frac{10}{2(1)} \rightarrow x = -5$$

The vertex of the parabola lies on the line of symmetry. Find y when $x = -5$.

$y = (-5)^2 + 10(-5) + 9 = 25 - 50 + 9 = -16$

The vertex is $(-5, -16)$.

Graph the vertex and line of symmetry. Find and graph another point on the parabola and reflect it across the line of symmetry.

$y = (0)^2 + 10(0) + 9 = 9$

Another point on the curve is $(0,9)$, which reflects to $(-10,9)$.

The roots of the equation are the x –intercepts -1 and -9.

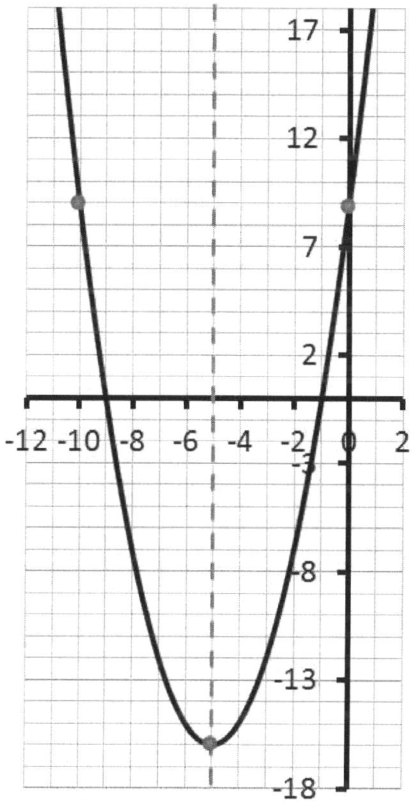

2. Factor and solve using the Zero Product Property

$$(x + 9)(x + 1) = 0$$

$$(x + 9) = 0 \qquad (x + 1) = 0$$

$$x = -9 \qquad x = -1$$

Example

Solve $x^2 + 10x + 25 = 16$ by using

1. The Square Root Property 2. The quadratic formula

1. The trinomial on the left side of the equation is a perfect square. Solve using the Square Root Property.

$$(x+5)^2 = 16$$
$$\sqrt{(x+5)^2} = \pm\sqrt{16}$$
$$x + 5 = \pm 4$$
$$x = -9 \qquad x = -1$$

2. Rewrite the equation in the form $ax^2 + bx + c = 0$ to use the quadratic formula,

$x = \frac{-b \pm \sqrt{b^2 - 4ac}}{2a}$.

$$x^2 + 10x + 25 = 16$$
$$x^2 + 10x + 25 - \mathbf{16} = 16 - \mathbf{16}$$
$$x^2 + 10x + 9 = 0$$
$$x = \frac{-10 \pm \sqrt{10^2 - 4(1)(9)}}{2(1)} = \frac{-10 \pm \sqrt{100 - 36}}{2} = \frac{-10 \pm \sqrt{64}}{2} = \frac{-10 \pm 8}{2}$$
$$x = -\frac{2}{2} = -1 \quad x = -\frac{18}{2} = -9$$

Example

Solve $5x^2 + 120 = 0$

One way to solve this equation is to use the Square Root Property.

$$5x^2 + 120 = 0$$
$$5x^2 = -120$$
$$\frac{5x^2}{5} = \frac{-120}{5}$$
$$x^2 = -24$$
$$\sqrt{x^2} = \pm\sqrt{-24}$$
$$x = \pm 2i\sqrt{6}$$

Example

Solve $3x^2 - 6x = -4$.

Rewrite the equation in the form $ax^2 + bx + c = 0$ and use the quadratic formula, $x = \frac{-b \pm \sqrt{b^2 - 4ac}}{2a}$, to find the roots.

$$3x^2 - 6x + 4 = 0$$

$$x = \frac{-(-6) \pm \sqrt{(-6)^2 - 4(3)(4)}}{2(3)}$$

$$x = \frac{6 \pm \sqrt{36 - 48}}{6}$$

$$x = \frac{6 \pm \sqrt{-12}}{6}$$

$$x = \frac{6 \pm 2i\sqrt{3}}{6}$$

$$x = 1 \pm \frac{i}{3}\sqrt{3}$$

Notice that the quadratic polynomial has two complex roots, which are conjugate pairs.

Example

Sketch the graph of a quadratic function with

1. No real roots
2. One real root
3. Two real roots

The graph of a quadratic function with no real roots does not intersect the x-axis. An example of such a graph is

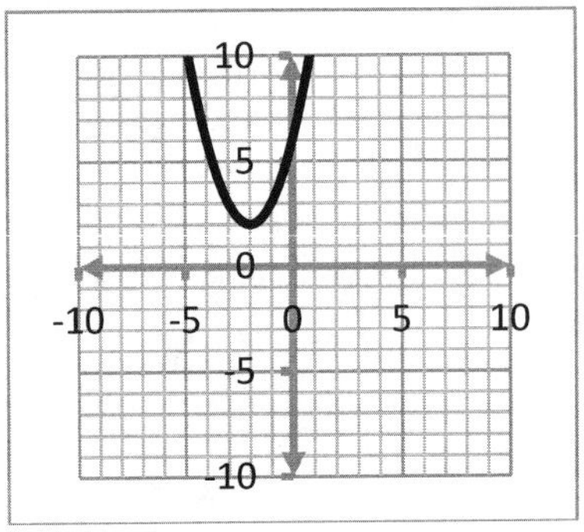

The graph of a quadratic function with one real root intersects the x-axis at one point; in other words, the vertex of the parabolic graph lies on the x-axis. An example of such a graph is

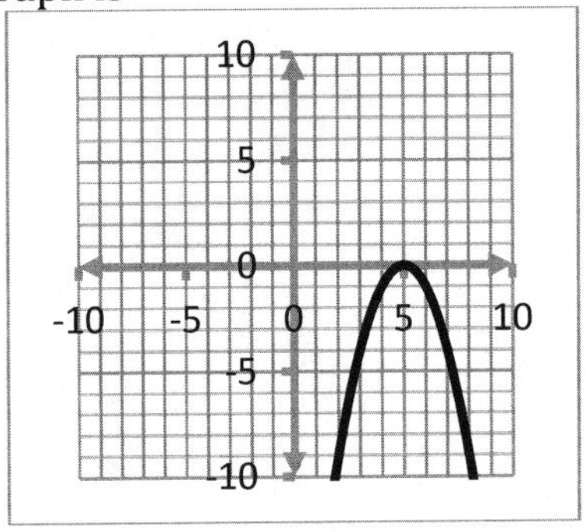

The graph of a quadratic function with two real roots intersects the x-axis at two points. An example of such a graph is

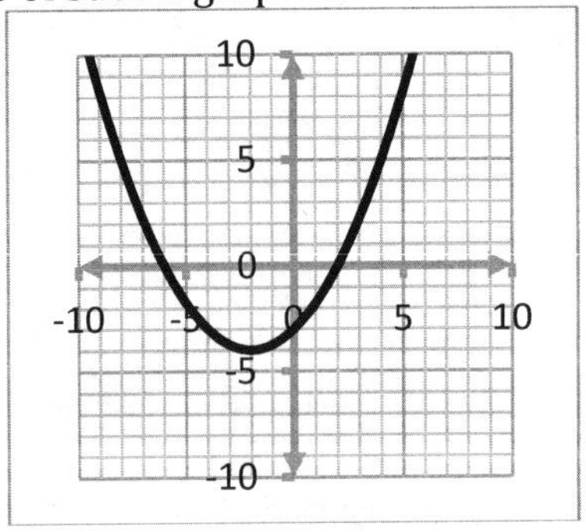

Problem

Determine whether the following statement is always true, sometimes true, or never true: the quadratic equation $ax^2 + bx + c = 0$ has two complex roots when *a, b,* and *c* are real numbers.

According to the Fundamental Theorem of Algebra, $ax^2 + bx + c = 0$ has two roots. These roots are sometimes real, and sometimes they are not. Because the set of real numbers is a subset of the set of complex numbers, the quadratic equation $ax^2 + bx + c = 0$, ALWAYS has two complex roots, regardless of the values of a, b and c.

The Real Number System

Zero exponent and negative exponent properties

The **zero exponent property** states $a^0 = 1$ for all $a \neq 0$. The **negative exponent property** states $a^{-b} = \frac{1}{a^b}$ for all $a \neq 0$.

Consider the series ..., 2, 4, 8, 16, 32, ... Notice that each number is two times the previous number, so the series can be written ... $2, 2 \cdot 2, 2 \cdot 2 \cdot 2, 2 \cdot 2 \cdot 2 \cdot 2, 2 \cdot 2 \cdot 2 \cdot 2 \cdot 2$..., which can be more easily expressed using powers of 2: ..., $2^1, 2^2, 2^3, 2^4, 2^5$, ...

The exponent of each number is one more than the exponent of the previous number. Extend the series a few numbers to the left: ..., $\frac{1}{4}$, $\frac{1}{2}$, 1, 2, 4, 8, 16, 32, ... Also, apply the pattern of exponents to the series written as powers of two: ..., 2^{-2}, 2^{-1}, $2^0, 2^1, 2^2, 2^3, 2^4, 2^5$, ... Compare the relative positions of newly written terms: $2^0 = 1$; $2^{-1} = \frac{1}{2} = \frac{1}{2^1}$; $2^{-2} = \frac{1}{4} = \frac{1}{2^2}$.

Product of powers and quotient of powers properties

The **product of powers** property states that when multiplying two monomials with like bases, add together the powers of that base; for example, $x^7 \cdot x^3 = x^{7+3} = x^{10}$ because $(x \cdot x \cdot x \cdot x \cdot x \cdot x \cdot x) \cdot (x \cdot x \cdot x) = x \cdot x \cdot x \cdot x \cdot x \cdot x \cdot x \cdot x \cdot x \cdot x = x^{10}$. The **quotient of powers** property states that when dividing two monomials with like bases, subtract the powers of that base; for example $\frac{x^7}{x^3} = x^{7-3} = x^4$ because $\frac{x \cdot x \cdot x \cdot x \cdot x \cdot x \cdot x}{x \cdot x \cdot x} = \frac{x}{x} \cdot \frac{x}{x} \cdot \frac{x}{x} \cdot x \cdot x \cdot x \cdot x = 1 \cdot 1 \cdot 1 \cdot x \cdot x \cdot x \cdot x = x^4$.

Power of a product, power of a quotient, and power of a power

The **power of a product** property states that when multiplying together two monomials with the same power but different bases, multiply the bases and keep the power the same; for example, $x^3 \cdot y^3 = (xy)^3$ because $x^3 \cdot y^3 = x \cdot x \cdot x \cdot y \cdot y \cdot y = x \cdot y \cdot x \cdot y \cdot x \cdot y = (x \cdot y) \cdot (x \cdot y) \cdot (x \cdot y) = (xy)^3$. (Notice the use of the commutative and associate properties of multiplication.) Similarly, the **power of a quotient** property states that when diving two monomials with the same power but different bases, divide the bases and keep the power the same; for example, $\frac{x^3}{y^3} = \left(\frac{x}{y}\right)^3$ because , $\frac{x^3}{y^3} = \frac{x \cdot x \cdot x}{y \cdot y \cdot y} = \frac{x}{y} \cdot \frac{x}{y} \cdot \frac{x}{y} = \left(\frac{x}{y}\right)^3$. Lastly, the **power of a power** property states that when raising a monomial to a power, multiply the power of each term in the monomial by the power to which the monomial is raised; for example, $(x^3y^2)^3 = x^{3 \cdot 3}y^{2 \cdot 3} = x^9y^6$ because $(x\hat{}3\ y\hat{}2\ )\hat{}3 = (x \cdot x \cdot x \cdot y \cdot y)\ (x \cdot x \cdot x \cdot y \cdot y)\ (x \cdot x \cdot x \cdot y \cdot y) = x \cdot x \cdot x \cdot x \cdot x \cdot x \cdot x \cdot x \cdot x \cdot y \cdot y \cdot y \cdot y \cdot y \cdot y = x^9y^6$(Again, notice the use of the commutative and associate properties of multiplication.).

Example

Below is an example illustrating $\sqrt[n]{x} = x^{\frac{1}{n}}$.

$\sqrt{3} = 3^{\frac{1}{2}}$	In this example, $x = 3$ and $n = 2$.
$\left(\sqrt{3}\right)^2 = (3^{\frac{1}{2}})^2$	The inverse operation of taking the square root is raising to the second power. Perform the same operation on both sides of the equation.
$3 = 3^{\frac{1}{2} \cdot 2}$	To raise a power to a power, multiply the powers.
$3 = 3^1$	Simplify. $\frac{1}{2} \cdot 2 = 1$.
3=3	Simplify. $3\hat{}1 = 3$.

Problem

Simplifying the expression $\sqrt[6]{9x^4}$

$(9x^4)^{\frac{1}{6}}$	Rewrite the expression using rational exponents
$(3^2x^4)^{\frac{1}{6}}$	Substitute 3^2 for 9.
$3^{\frac{1}{3}}x^{\frac{2}{3}}$	Use the power of a power property of exponents.
$3^{\frac{1}{3}}x^{\frac{1}{3}}x^{\frac{1}{3}}$	Use the product of a power property to rewrite $x^{\frac{2}{3}}$ as the product of $x^{\frac{1}{3}}$ and $x^{\frac{1}{3}}$.
$(3xx)^{\frac{1}{3}}$	Use the product of powers property to rewrite the expression
$\sqrt[3]{3x^2}$	Simplify.

Problem

When two integers are added, subtracted, or multiplied, the resulting sum, difference, or product is also an integer; therefore, the set of integers is closed under these operations. Is the set of rational numbers closed under the same operations?

Given that $a, b, c,$ and d are integers and that b and d do not equal zero,

$$\frac{a}{b}+\frac{c}{d}=\frac{ad+bc}{bd} \text{ and } \frac{a}{b}-\frac{c}{d}=\frac{ad-bc}{bd} \text{ and } \frac{a}{b}\cdot\frac{c}{d}=\frac{ac}{bd}$$

$\frac{a}{b}$ and $\frac{c}{d}$ are rational numbers. The products $ad, bc,$ and bd are integers since the product of two integers is always an integer; likewise, since the sum or difference of two integers is always an integer, $ad + bc$ and $ad - bc$ must also be integers. Therefore, $\frac{ad+bc}{bd}$, $\frac{ad-bc}{bd}$, and $\frac{ac}{bd}$ represent ratios of two integers and are, by definition, rational. So, the set of rational numbers is closed under addition, subtraction, and multiplication.

Problem

Determine if the following statements are true or false. Provide an explanation for the true statement(s) and a counterexample for the false statement(s).

1. The sum of a rational number and an irrational number is always irrational.
2. The sum of two irrational numbers is always irrational

1. It is **true** that the sum of a rational number and an irrational number is always irrational. Consider for a moment that the statement is false; this would require the existence of some irrational number x that when added to rational number a would produce rational number b: $a + x = b$. Solving the equation for x yields $x = b - a$. The difference of b and a must be rational since the set of rational numbers is closed under subtraction. Since $x = b - a$, x must be a rational number; there is no such irrational number x that when added to a rational number yields a rational number. Therefore, the sum of a rational and an irrational number is always irrational.
2. It is false that the sum of two irrational numbers is always irrational. For example, the sum of irrational numbers $\sqrt{3}$ and $-\sqrt{3}$ is zero, which is rational.

Problem

Determine if the following statements are true or false. Provide an explanation for true statements and a counterexample for false statements
1. The product of a nonzero rational number and an irrational number is always irrational.
2. The product of two irrational numbers is always irrational.

1. It is **true** that the product of a nonzero rational number and an irrational number is always irrational. Consider for a moment that the statement is false; this would require the existence of some irrational number x that when multiplied by rational number a would produce rational number b:

$ax = b$. Solving the equation for x yields $x = \frac{b}{a}$; $a \neq 0$. If x is equal to the ratio of two rational numbers, it must also, by definition, be rational. (Note that the ratio of two rational numbers can be rewritten as the ratio of two integers.) So, there is no such irrational number x that when multiplied by a rational number yields a rational number. Therefore, the product of a rational and an irrational number is irrational.
2. It is false that the product of two irrational numbers is always irrational. For example, the product of irrational numbers $\sqrt{3}$ and $-\sqrt{3}$ is -3, which is rational.

Problem

Determine if the following statement is always true, sometimes true, or never true: an integer raised to a non-integer power is an integer.

It is **sometimes true** that an integer raised to a non-integer power is an integer. For example, $4^{\frac{1}{2}} = \sqrt{4} = 2$. However, it is not always true. For example, $3^{\frac{1}{2}} = \sqrt{3}$.

Seeing Structure in Expressions

The expression $6s^2$ gives the surface area of a cube with edge length s. What is the coefficient of this expression?

A term is a product and/or quotient of a real number and one or more variables, each of which may be raised to a nonnegative integer exponent. The real number is the coefficient of the term. A polynomial expression is a term or sum of several terms. The expression $6s^2$ is therefore a single term, and the coefficient is the real number 6. Note that if a term is written, for example, as simply s^2, then the coefficient is 1, because $s^2 = 1s^2$. A coefficient may also be negative, such as in the term $-0.5ab$.

The expression $2W + 2L$ gives the perimeter of a rectangular frame with side lengths W and L. How many terms does this expression have?

A polynomial expression is the sum and/or difference of one or more terms. Each term is a product and/or quotient of one or more variables, each of which may be raised to a nonnegative integer exponent, and a real number. The expression $2W + 2L$ has 2 terms, one of which is $2W$ and the other of which is $2L$. It is important to realize that terms are separated by addition or subtraction. Therefore an expression such as $4xy$ has only 1 term. Also, since an expression such as $2x - 3y$ can be written as $2x + (-3y)$ the second term could be referred to as positive or negative.

What are the factors of the expression $x(5x + 2)(x - 4)$?

The factors of the expression $x(5x + 2)(x - 4)$ are the expressions x, $5x + 2$, and $x - 4$. To identify the factors of an expression, the expression must be written as a product of terms and/or expressions (with any expressions delineated by parentheses). The factors themselves may involve addition or subtraction of multiple terms, but if the expression is not written only as the product of terms or expressions, the expression is not in factored form. For example, the polynomial $x^2 + 2x + 8$ cannot be factored with real numbers, so it is considered to be one factor. The polynomial $x^2 + 6x + 8$ can be factored as $(x + 2)(x + 4)$, and therefore has two factors, $(x + 2)$ and $(x + 4)$.

Interpret the exponent in the expression $5000(1 + \frac{r}{12})^{12t}$. The expression gives the value of an account that earns annual interest rate *r*, after *t* years.

The exponent in the expression is $12t$. Since the variable t represents the number of years, the exponent represents the number of months in t years. For example, if $t = \frac{1}{2}$ or half a year, then $12t = 12 \cdot \frac{1}{2} = 6$ months. Similarly, if $t = 2$, then $12t = 12 \cdot 2 = 24$ months. This means that the exponent $12t$ converts the time since the initial deposit from years to months. Note that this relates to the expression $\frac{r}{12}$, in which 12 represents the number of times annually the interest is compounded (monthly, in this case). For t = 1, the initial amount 5000 is multiplied by the expression $(1 + \frac{r}{12})$ 12 times, corresponding the number of times the interest is compounded by one-twelfth the annual interest rate. [If the interest were compounded quarterly, the expression would read $5000\left(1 + \frac{r}{4}\right)^{4t}$].

In the expression $18,000(1 + r)^{20}$, what is the base of the exponent 20? Evaluate the expression for $r = 0.1$, 0.4, and 0.7 and round to the nearest integer.

In the expression $18{,}000(1 + r)^{20}$, the base of the exponent 20 is $(1 + r)$, not 1 or r. This is because by the order of operations, the sum in parentheses is calculated first, and then this sum is raised to the power of 20. The last step is to then multiply this result by the coefficient 18,000. For $r = 0.1$, 0.4, and 0.7, the expression is equal to the following values (to the nearest integer):

$$8{,}000(1 + r)^{20} = 18{,}000(1.1)^{20} \approx 121{,}095$$

$$18{,}000(1 + r)^{20} = 18{,}000(1.4)^{20} \approx 15{,}060{,}286$$

$$18{,}000(1 + r)^{20} = 18{,}000(1.7)^{20} \approx 731{,}561{,}653$$

Simplify the expression $\frac{2-x}{x-2}$.

To simplify a rational expression, factor both the numerator and denominator, and then simplify by noting that the ratio of identical factors equals 1. In this particular expression, the numerator is the opposite of the denominator. That is, $2 - x = -(-2 + x) = -(x - 2)$. Rewrite the numerator and then simplify:

$$\frac{2 - x}{x - 2} = \frac{-(x - 2)}{x - 2} = -1$$

The expression simplifies to -1. Note that the original expression is equal to -1 for all values of x except $x = 2$. This is because the original expression is not defined for $x = 2$: the denominator would be equal to zero in this case, and division by zero is undefined.

What is the role of the number 2 in the expression $\log_2 \frac{1}{8}$?

The given expression is a logarithm. A logarithm asks the question: "to what exponent does the base need to be raised to equal the argument?" The $\frac{1}{8}$ is the argument, and the 2 is the base of the logarithm. This means that the expression yields the value of the exponent to which 2 must be raised to equal $\frac{1}{8}$. Such an expression can be simplified using the identity $b^{(\log_b x)} = x$ as follows:

$$
\begin{aligned}
&a = \log_2 \frac{1}{8} \\
&2^a = 2^{\left(\log_2 \frac{1}{8}\right)} \\
&2^a = \frac{1}{8} = \frac{1}{2^3} = 2^{-3} \\
&a = -3 \\
&\log_2 \frac{1}{8} = -3
\end{aligned}
$$

Write the leading term of the expanded form of $(3x - 1)^5$.

In order to expand a binomial that is raised to a power apply the binomial theorem. The number of terms will be equal to the exponent, which in this case is 5. The leading term contains the greatest occurring power of x, which will be x^5 in this case. Thus, to obtain the leading term, raise the x-term of the binomial to the 5th power: $(3x)^5 = 243x^5$. Then multiply the result by the first entry (corresponding to the leading term of the expansion) of the 5th row (corresponding to the exponent) of Pascal's triangle. In any row, though, the first entry is 1. Therefore the leading term of the expanded form of $(3x - 1)^5$ is $243x^5$.

How can $9 - (m + 1)^2$ can be rewritten in factored form?

The expression $9 - (m + 1)^2$ can be rewritten by first noting that the expression is a difference of squares. Since $9 = 3^2$, the expression can be written as $(3)^2 - (m + 1)^2$. In general, a difference of squares is factored as $a^2 - b^2 = (a + b)(a - b)$. In this case, $a = 3$ and $b = m + 1$:

$$
\begin{aligned}
&9 - (m + 1)^2 = \\
&3^2 - (m + 1)^2 = \\
&(3 + m + 1)\big(3 - (m + 1)\big) = \\
&(4 + m)(2 - m)
\end{aligned}
$$

How $x^6 - y^6$ is both a difference of squares and a difference of cubes.

A difference of squares can be written as $a^2 - b^2$, and a difference of cubes can be written as $a^3 - b^3$. Both of these are factorable binomials. By using the property of exponents that states
$(a^m)^n = a^{mn}$, the term x^6 can be written as either $(x^2)^3$ or $(x^3)^2$. The term y^6 can be rewritten in a similar way. Therefore $x^6 - y^6 = (x^3)^2 - (y^3)^2$ and, equivalently, $x^6 - y^6 = = (x^2)^3 - (y^2)^3$. Regardless of which method is used, there is only one *completely* factored expression that is equivalent to $x^6 - y^6$. (Since one of the factors of the difference of squares method is $x^3 - y^3$,

which is itself a difference of cubes, the resulting expressions from either method are essentially equivalent).

Rewrite $2x^2 - 6xy - 2x + 6y$ in factored form.

The expression $2x^2 - 6xy - 2x + 6y$ has 4 terms, and therefore may be factorable by grouping. Group terms of like degree: group terms containing the square of a single variable or the product of two variables, for example. The GCF of the first two terms $2x^2$ and $6xy$ is $2x$. The GCF of the last two terms $2x$ and $6y$ is 2. Rewrite the expression as follows:

$$2x^2 - 6xy - 2x + 6y =$$
$$2x(x - 3y) - 2(x - 3y)$$

The factored parts of the expression have a common binomial factor, $(x - 3y)$. Complete the factoring by factoring out $(x - 3y)$:

$$2x(x - 3y) - 2(x - 3y) =$$
$$(x - 3y)(2x - 2)$$

Solve $4^{3x} = 2^{x+10}$.

Two exponential expressions are equal if they have the same base and exponent. To solve for x, rewrite the expressions so they have the same base, and then set the resulting exponents equal to each other. Because $4 = 2^2$, rewrite 4^{3x} with a base of 2:

$$4^{3x} = 2^{x+10}$$
$$(2^2)^{3x} = 2^{x+10}$$
$$2^{6x} = 2^{x+10}$$
$$6x = x + 10$$
$$5x = 10$$
$$x = 2$$

What is the relationship between the linear factors $(x - a)$ and $(x - b)$ of a quadratic expression and the zeros of the related function?

If the linear factors of a quadratic expression are $(x - a)$ and $(x - b)$, then the quadratic function can be written as $y = k(x - a)(x - b)$, where k is a nonzero constant. The zeros of this function are the values of x for which $y = 0$. Direct substitution of a or b for x makes the value of y equal to 0, so $x = a$ and $x = b$ are zeros of the quadratic function. Note that the value of k may affect the shape or direction of the graph of the function, but not the x-intercepts (the zeros of the function).

What are the zeros of the function $y = 4x^2 - 10x$?

The zeros of the function $y = 4x^2 - 10x$ are the values of x for which $y = 0$. To find the zeros, factor the right side of the equation, and set $y = 0$:

$$y = 4x^2 - 10x$$
$$y = 2x(2x - 5)$$
$$0 = 2x(2x - 5)$$

Next, since a product is only equal to zero if at least one of the terms is zero, set the linear factors of the function $2x$ and $(2x - 5)$ equal to 0:

$$2x = 0 \qquad 2x - 5 = 0$$
$$x = 0 \qquad 2x = 5$$
$$x = \frac{5}{2}$$

The zeros of the function $y = 4x^2 - 10x$ are $x = 0$ and $x = \frac{5}{2}$.

Give an example of a quadratic function with zeros $x = 1$ and $x = -3$

If a is a zero of a quadratic function, then $(x - a)$ is a factor of the quadratic expression that defines the function. Therefore $(x - 1)$ and $(x + 3)$ are both factors of the quadratic function. Quadratic functions with these zeros therefore have the form $y = k(x - 1)(x + 3)$. The reason that this is just a form, and not a unique function, is because multiplying the two binomial factors by any nonzero constant results in another quadratic function with the same zeros. For example, the functions $y = -5(x - 1)(x + 3)$ and $y = 7(x - 1)$ $(x + 3)$ have zeros $x = 1$ and $x = -3$.

Find the x-intercepts of $y = 9x^2 - 6x + 1$.

The x-intercepts of $y = 9x^2 - 6x + 1$ are the zeros of the function. These can be determined by first factoring the quadratic expression $9x^2 - 6x + 1$:

$$9x^2 - 6x + 1 = (3x - 1)(3x - 1) = (3x - 1)^2$$

The expression is a perfect square trinomial. Because the two factors are the same, there is only one x-intercept of the function. Set the factor equal to 0:

$$3x - 1 = 0$$
$$3x = 1$$
$$x = \frac{1}{3}$$

The x-intercept of $y = 9x^2 - 6x + 1$ is therefore $x = \frac{1}{3}$.

What is the technique of completing the square?

The quadratic expression $ax^2 + bx + c$ can always be written as the square of a linear binomial, plus some constant. This is useful to solve or graph quadratic equations or functions. The technique is as follows:

$a\left(x^2 + \frac{b}{a}x\right) + c =$ Factor a from the quadratic and linear terms.

$a\left(x^2 + \frac{b}{a}x + \frac{b^2}{4a^2}\right) + c - \frac{b^2}{4a} =$ Add the square of half the coefficient of x within the parentheses; subtract the product of that term and a outside the parentheses.

$a\left(x + \frac{b}{2a}\right)^2 + c - \frac{b^2}{4a} =$ Rewrite the trinomial as a perfect square.

$a\left(x + \frac{b}{2a}\right)^2 + \frac{4ac-b^2}{4a} =$ Simplify.

Complete the square to find the minimum value of $y = x^2 - 4x$.

To complete the square, first factor out the leading coefficient, the coefficient of x^2. This is 1, so no factoring is required. Next, add and subtract the square of half the coefficient of x. This value is
$(\frac{-4}{2})^2 = 4$. Finally, rewrite the first three terms as a square of a linear binomial.

$$y = x^2 - 4x$$
$$y = x^2 - 4x + 4 - 4$$
$$y = (x - 2)^2 - 4$$

The term $(x - 2)^2$ will never be negative; its minimum value is 0 (when $x = 2$). The minimum value of the function $y = (x - 2)^2 - 4$ can be found by substituting the minimum value of the squared binomial: $y_{\min} = 0 - 4 = -4$.

Complete the square to find the maximum value of $y = -2x^2 + 6x$.

In order to determine the maximum value of the function, write the function in standard form by completing the square:

$$y = -2x^2 + 6x$$
$$y = -2(x^2 - 3x)$$
$$y = -2(x^2 - 3x + \frac{9}{4}) + 2 \cdot \frac{9}{4}$$
$$y = -2\left(x - \frac{3}{2}\right)^2 + \frac{9}{2}$$

Since the first term will always be negative unless it is zero (which happens at $x = 3/2$), the vertex of the graph of the function is $(\frac{3}{2}, \frac{9}{2})$. The coefficient of x^2 is negative, so the parabola opens downward. Therefore the maximum value of the function is $\frac{9}{2}$.

The minimum value of $y = x^2 + 4bx$ is -1. Find two possible values of b.

In order to determine the vertex of the function, write the function in standard form by completing the square:

$$y = x^2 + 4bx$$
$$y = x^2 + 4bx + 4b^2 - 4b^2$$
$$y = (x + 2b)^2 - 4b^2$$

The vertex of the graph of the function is therefore $(2b, -4b^2)$. The coefficient of x^2 is positive, so the parabola opens upward. The minimum value is $-4b^2$, which must be equal to -1 in this case. Solving for b gives $b = \pm\frac{1}{2}$. The equation of the function is either $y = x^2 + 2x$ or $y = x^2 - 2x$.

The number of bacteria in a sample doubles approximately every hour. To the nearest million, by what factor does the number of bacteria increase in one day?

The situation is modeled by an exponential function. The bacteria count doubles every hour, so let t represent the number of hours. The equation $b = 2^t$ will give the number of bacteria b present after t hours. For now assume the actual number of bacteria is not important, so at $t = 0$ there is 1 bacterium. There are 24 hours in a day, so if d represents days, $t = 24d$, and the equation becomes $b = 2^t = 2^{24d}$. This equation can be rewritten as $b = (2^{24})^d = 16{,}777{,}216^t$, which means that there are about 17 million times more bacteria each day.

Rewrite the expression 1.3^{2x} so that the only exponent present is $3x$.

In order to write the expression with an exponent of $3x$, use the properties of exponents. First, use the property $a^{mn} = (a^m)^n$ to write $1.3^{2x} = (1.3^2)^x$. The exponent can be changed to $3x$ if the expression is cubed, or raised to the power of 3. To do this without changing the value of the expression, also take the cube root, or raise to the power of $\frac{1}{3}$. This can be written as shown:

$$(1.3^2)^x = [(1.3^2)^{\frac{1}{3}}]^{3x}$$

Using a calculator, $(1.3^2)^{\frac{1}{3}} \approx 1.191$. So, $1.3^{2x} \approx 1.191^{3x}$. To check this, each expression can be evaluated for values of x to see that they are approximately equal.

The table shows the number of decibels for certain power ratios. By what factor does the power ratio increase for an increase of 1 decibel?

Decibels	Power Ratio
10	10
20	100
30	1,000

For each increase of 10 in the number of decibels, the power ratio increases by a factor of 10. Equivalently, the power ratio is equal to 10 raised to a power equal to the number of decibels divided by 10. If P represents the power ratio and d the number of decibels, then $P = 10^{\frac{d}{10}}$. To determine the factor for an increase of 1 decibel, rewrite the equation as $P = 10^{\frac{d}{10}} = (10^{\frac{1}{10}})^d$. Using a calculator, $10^{\frac{1}{10}} \approx 1.259$, so the power ratio increases by a factor of about 1.259 for an increase of 1 decibel.

A cable company has 12,000 current customers. They begin to lose 3% of their current customers each year. On average, about what percent of their customers do they lose each month?

The situation is modeled by an exponential decay function. The number of customers decreases by 3%, or equivalently is multiplied by 0.97 each year. The equation $c = 12{,}000(0.97)^t$ will give the number of customers c present after t years. There are 12 months in a year, so if m represents months, the equation becomes $c = 12{,}000(0.97)^{\frac{m}{12}}$. This equation can be rewritten as $= 12{,}000(0.97^{\frac{1}{12}})^m$ or $c \approx 12{,}000(0.997)^m$, which means that the cable company loses a factor of (1 – 0.997), or about 0.3%, of its current customers each month.

What is the common ratio of a geometric series?

A series is a sum (finite or infinite) of terms of a (finite or infinite) sequence. The series is called *geometric* if the ratio of any term to the preceding term is the same value. This value is called the *common ratio* of the geometric series. For example, in the finite sum 3 + 6 + 12 + 24 + 48, the ratio of any term to the previous term is 2. Therefore, the series is a finite geometric series with a common ratio of 2.

Derive the formula for the sum S of the first $(n+1)$ terms of a finite geometric series given by the equation $S = a + ar + ar^2 + \ldots + ar^n$, where $r \neq 1$.

Write the equation for the sum, and then multiply each side by r:

$S = a + ar + ar^2 + \ldots + ar^n$
$rS = (a + ar + ar^2 + \ldots + ar^n)r$
$rS = ar + ar^2 + ar^3 + \ldots + ar^n + ar^{n+1}$

If the first equation above is subtracted from the third equation, many of the terms will cancel. In fact, the only unique terms are the term a in the first equation and the term ar^{n+1} in the other. Subtract the equations and solve for S to obtain the formula for the sum of the first $(n + 1)$ terms of a finite geometric series:

$rS - S = ar^{n+1} - a$
$S(r - 1) = a(r^{n+1} - 1)$

$$S = \frac{a(r^{n+1} - 1)}{r - 1}$$

Is $8 - 8\left(\frac{1}{2}\right) + 8\left(\frac{1}{2}\right)^2 - 8\left(\frac{1}{2}\right)^3 + \cdots - 8\left(\frac{1}{2}\right)^7$ a finite geometric series?

Yes, the series $8 - 8\left(\frac{1}{2}\right) + 8\left(\frac{1}{2}\right)^2 - 8\left(\frac{1}{2}\right)^3 + \cdots - 8\left(\frac{1}{2}\right)^7$ is a finite geometric series with a common ratio of $-\frac{1}{2}$. When the common ratio of a geometric series is negative, the signs of the terms alternate. This is because even powers of a negative number result in a positive value, and odd powers of a negative number result in a negative value. Also, as required by a geometric series, the ratio of any term and the preceding term will always be $-\frac{1}{2}$, since the ratio has one positive and one negative term. (Any series that has consecutive negative terms must therefore have only negative terms. This occurs when the coefficient of each term is negative, not when the common ration is negative.)

In the formula below, x represents the monthly interest rate and L the loan amount for a 30-year mortgage with a monthly payment P.

$$L = P\left(\frac{1}{1+x} + \frac{1}{(1+x)^2} + \cdots + \frac{1}{(1+x)^{360}}\right)$$

Find the monthly payment for a $250,000 loan with an annual interest rate of 6%.

The part of the equation in parentheses is a geometric series with common ratio $\frac{1}{1+x}$. Use the general formula for the sum of the first n terms of a finite geometric series, $S_n = \frac{a(1-r^n)}{1-r}$, to rewrite the equation, where a is the first term and r is the common ratio. Then solve for P:

$$L = P\left(\frac{1}{1+x} + \frac{1}{(1+x)^2} + \cdots + \frac{1}{(1+x)^{360}}\right)$$

$$= P\left(\frac{\frac{1}{1+x}\left(1-\left(\frac{1}{1+x}\right)^{360}\right)}{1-\frac{1}{1+x}}\right) = P\left(\frac{\frac{1}{1+x}-\left(\frac{1}{1+x}\right)^{361}}{1-\frac{1}{1+x}}\right)$$

$$P = L\left(\frac{1-\frac{1}{1+x}}{\frac{1}{1+x}-\left(\frac{1}{1+x}\right)^{361}}\right)$$

Since x represents the monthly interest rate, $x = \frac{0.06}{12} = 0.005$. Substituting this for x and 250,000 for L gives P = $1498.88, rounded to the nearest cent.

What are the coefficients of the x^2 term, x term, and constant term of the quadratic expression $(2x - 3)(x + 4)$?

To find the coefficients of the x^2 term, x term, and constant term, the quadratic expression must be written in the form $ax^2 + bx + c$. The real numbers a, b, and c are the coefficients. Multiplying the binomials of the factor form gives $2x^2 - 3x + 8x - 12$, and combining like terms $-3x$ and $8x$ yields $2x^2 + 5x - 12$. The coefficient of the x^2 term is 2, the coefficient of the x term is 5, and constant term is −12.

When does the expression $\frac{-b\pm\sqrt{b^2-4ac}}{2a}$ represent a unique number?

The expression $\frac{-b\pm\sqrt{b^2-4ac}}{2a}$ gives the solutions to the quadratic equation $ax^2 + bx + c = 0$. The plus or minus symbol, $\pm$, means that one solution is attained by adding the radical term $\sqrt{b^2-4ac}$ in the numerator and the other solution is attained by subtracting it. For this reason, if the radical term is equal to zero, the entire expression is equal to the (unique) value $\frac{-b}{2a}$. (The radical term is equal to zero if the radicand is equal to zero, that is if $b^2 = 4ac$.)

Factor the expression $x^2 + 2x + 1 - y^2$ by first recognizing a perfect square trinomial.

The first three terms of the expression, $x^2 + 2x + 1$, represent a perfect square trinomial. This means it factors into two identical binomials. The factorization is $x^2 + 2x + 1 = (x + 1)^2$.

Therefore the original expression can be rewritten as $(x + 1)^2 - y^2$, which is a difference of squares. Using the fact $a^2 - b^2 = (a + b)(a - b)$, and setting $a = x + 1$ and $b = y$, the expression $(x + 1)^2 - y^2$ factors as $(x + 1 - y)(x + 1 + y)$.

Find the vertex of the parabola with equation $y = 2x^2 - 4x - 3$.

To find the vertex of the parabola, rewrite the quadratic equation in the form $y = a(x - p)^2 + q$ by completing the square. The point (p, q) is the vertex of the parabola:

$$y = 2x^2 - 4x - 3$$
$$y = 2(x^2 - 2x) - 3$$
$$y = 2(x^2 - 2x + 1) - 3 - 2$$
$$y = 2(x - 1)^2 - 5$$

The vertex of the parabola is (1, –5).

Alternatively, recall the x-coordinate of the vertex is given by $-b/2a$, which in this case is $-(-4)/(2\cdot2) = 1$. Substitute this in for x to obtain $y = 2\cdot1^2 - 4\cdot1 - 3 = -5$. As before, the vertex is at point
(1, –5).

What are the x-intercepts of $y = x^2 - 4x$?

The x-intercepts, or zeros, of the function occur at the values of x that make $y = 0$, that is, when $x^2 - 4x = 0$. A quadratic function can have 0, 1, or 2 x-intercepts. Factor the given expression to get $x(x - 4) = 0$. Since the product of the two factors is equal to zero, either $x = 0$ or $x - 4 = 0$. Therefore the quadratic has two x-intercepts, $x = 0$ and $x = 4$.

Solve for b: $6(4)^b = 3(2)^b$.

The variable b appears in the equation as an exponent. Rewrite the equation so that each side has the same base, then equate the exponent expressions:

$6(4)^b = 3(2)^b$

$3 \cdot 2(4)^b = 3(2)^b$

$2(4)^b = 2^b$

$2^1(2^2)^b = 2^b$

$2^{1 + 2b} = 2^b$

$1 + 2b = b$

$b = -1$

The value of b is –1.

Find the sum $4 + 4(2) + 4\,(2)^2 + 4(2)^3 + \ldots + 4(2)^8$.

The sum represents a finite geometric series. The common ratio r of the series is 2, and the first term a_1 of the series is 4. Note that the first two terms can be written with exponents as $4(2)^0$ and $4(2)^1$. Use the formula for the sum of the first n terms of a finite geometric series $S_n = \frac{a_{1(1-r^n)}}{1-r}$, where n is equal to 1 more than the greatest power of r in the series:

$$S_9 = \frac{a_{1(1-r^9)}}{1-r} = \frac{4(1-(2)^9)}{1-2} = \frac{-2044}{-1} = 2044$$

The sum of the series is 2044.

Give an example of a system of two linear inequalities in two variables that has no solution.

A linear inequality in two variables will have a solution described by a half-plane; that is, by the entire region of the plane that is either above or below the line described by the corresponding linear equation. A system of two inequalities will have a solution region that is the intersection of the two half-planes. Therefore, a system that has no solution can be created by choosing lines that are parallel, and choosing the half-planes on opposite sides of the two lines, so there is no intersection. An example is the system

$$\begin{cases} y < 2x + 1 \\ y > 2x + 4 \end{cases}$$

Arithmetic with Polynomials & Rational Expressions

Polynomials are closed under multiplication.

For a set to have closure under a particular operation, applying the operation to two elements of the set must result in a member of the set. This means that the product of any two polynomials results in another polynomial. This is correct, because every term of a polynomial in x is of the form ax^n, where a is a real number and n is a nonnegative integer. The product of any two such terms would be $ax^m \cdot bx^n = abx^{m+n}$, where ab is a real number and $m + n$ is a nonnegative integer. The last statement relies on the fact that real numbers are closed under multiplication, and nonnegative integers are closed under addition.

Subtract the polynomial $3x^2 - 4x + 1$ from the polynomial $-2x^2 - x + 5$.

To subtract polynomials, subtract like terms. Like terms have the same variable part, such as $3x^2$ and $-2x^2$, which are both are x^2 terms. To find the difference of like terms, find the difference of the coefficients, and retain the same variable part. You can use the distributive property to first distribute the subtraction to each term of the polynomial that is being subtracted.

$$(-2x^2 - x + 5) - (3x^2 - 4x + 1) =$$
$$(-2x^2 - x + 5) - 3x^2 + 4x - 1 =$$
$$(-2x^2 - 3x^2) + (-x + 4x) + (5 - 1) =$$
$$-5x^2 + 3x + 4$$

Is the sum of two cubic polynomials also a cubic polynomial?

The sum of two cubic polynomials is not necessarily a cubic polynomial. However, it is either a cubic polynomial or a polynomial of lesser degree. The sum of two cubic polynomials of the form $ax^3 + bx^2 + cx + d$, where $a \neq 0$, will have the same form, however it is possible that individual like terms are opposites and have a sum of 0. For example, the sum of $-3x^3 + 2x - 3$ and $3x^3 + 5x^2$ is $5x^2 + 2x - 3$, which is a quadratic polynomial. (Notice that coefficients b, c, and d in the cubic polynomial form are each allowed to equal zero; that is, cubic polynomials can be missing any of the terms with degree less than 3.)

Multiply a binomial and a trinomial

To multiply a binomial and a trinomial, use the distributive property. Because a binomial has 2 terms and a trinomial has 3 terms, there will be $2 \cdot 3 = 6$ multiplications when multiplying the polynomials. In the example below, each term of the binomial is multiplied by the entire trinomial. Then, that multiplication is distributed to each term of the trinomial. In the final steps, like terms are combined and the answer is expressed in standard form, with terms written in order of descending degree.
$(x + 2)(x^2 - 3x + 9) = x(x^2 - 3x + 9) + 2(x^2 - 3x + 9) =$
$x^3 - 3x^2 + 9x + 2x^2 - 6x + 18 =$
$x^3 - x^2 + 3x + 18$

What is the Remainder Theorem for polynomials?

The Remainder Theorem for polynomials states that for a polynomial $P(x)$ and a real number a, the remainder when $P(x)$ is divided by $(x - a)$ is $P(a)$, the value of the polynomial evaluated at $x = a$. If there is no remainder, that is if the remainder equals 0, then $P(a) = 0$ and $(x - a)$ is a factor of the polynomial $P(x)$. For example, if $P(x) = (2x - 3)(3x + 1)$, this can be written as $P(x) = 6(x - \frac{3}{2})(x + \frac{1}{3})$. Here $P\left(\frac{3}{2}\right) = 0$ and $P\left(\frac{1}{3}\right) = 0$, so that the remainder is zero when $P(x)$ is divided by $(x - \frac{3}{2})$ and $(x + \frac{1}{3})$; $(x - \frac{3}{2})$ and $(x + \frac{1}{3})$ are therefore factors of $P(x)$.

On the other hand, the Remainder Theorem also can be used to obtain the remainder when the above $P(x)$ is divided by any binomial, such as $(x - 4)$:

$$Rem\left[\frac{P(x)}{x-4}\right] = P(4) = (2(4) - 3)(3(4) + 1)$$
$$= (8 - 3)(12 + 1) = 5 \cdot 13 = 65$$

When a polynomial $P(x)$ is divided by $(x + 2)$, the remainder is –4. What is the value of $P(-2)$?

To solve this question, apply the Remainder Theorem for polynomials. The Remainder Theorem states that for a polynomial $P(x)$ and a real number a, the remainder when $P(x)$ is divided by
$(x - a)$ is $P(a)$. Since $P(x)$ was divided by the factor $(x + 2)$, let $a = -2$ in the theorem. This means that $P(a) = P(-2)$, and this is equal to the remainder. Since the remainder is –4, it must be that
$P(-2) = -4$. Note that it is not required to explicitly know the polynomial $P(x)$ or even its degree to apply the remainder theorem.

Divide the polynomial $x^2 + 2x - 4$ by $(x - 3)$. Verify the Remainder Theorem by evaluating the polynomial at $x = 3$.

Divide the polynomial $x^2 + 2x - 4$ by $(x - 3)$ using synthetic or long division:

$$\begin{array}{r|rrr} 3 & 1 & 2 & -4 \\ & & 3 & 15 \\ \hline & 1 & 5 & 11 \end{array} \qquad \begin{array}{r} x \;\; - 5 \\ x - 3 \,|\, x^2 + 2x - 4 \\ -\underline{x^2 + 3x} \\ 5x - 4 \\ \underline{5x + 15} \\ R\ 11 \end{array}$$

In either case, the remainder is 11. By the Remainder Theorem, for a polynomial $P(x)$ and a real number a, the remainder when $P(x)$ is divided by $(x - a)$ is $P(a)$. In this case, this means the remainder when $x^2 + 2x - 4$ is divided by $(x - 3)$ must be $P(3)$. Verify that $P(3) = 11$ by substituting $x = 3$ into the polynomial: $(3)^2 + 2(3) - 4 = 9 + 6 - 4 = 11$

Let $P(x)$ be a cubic polynomial function such that $P(2) = P(-1) = P(4) = 0$. If the y-intercept of $P(x)$ is 2, what is the equation for $P(x)$?

By the Remainder Theorem, for a polynomial $P(x)$ and a real number a, the remainder when $P(x)$ is divided by $(x - a)$ is $P(a)$. This means that, since their remainders when divided into $P(x)$ are all zero, $(x - 2)$, $(x + 1)$, and $(x - 4)$ are factors of $P(x)$. Because $P(x)$ is a cubic polynomial function, it must then be of the form $P(x) = a(x - 2)(x + 1)(x - 4)$, where a is some real number. To determine a, use the fact that the y-intercept is 2, which means that $P(0) = 2$:

$$P(x) = a(x - 2)(x + 1)(x - 4)$$
$$P(0) = 2 = a(0 - 2)(0 + 1)(0 - 4) = 8a$$
$$2 = 8a$$
$$a = 1/4$$

The equation for $P(x)$, then, is $P(x) = \frac{1}{4}(x - 2)(x + 1)(x - 4)$.

Find the zeros of $y = 2x^2 + 3x - 5$ by factoring.

The zeros of $y = 2x^2 + 3x - 5$ are the values of x for which $y = 0$. These are also the x-intercepts of the graph of the function. Factor $2x^2 + 3x - 5$ and rewrite the equation as $y = (2x + 5)(x - 1)$. In factored form, the zeros are found by setting each linear factor equal to zero:

$$\begin{array}{rcl} 2x - 5 = 0 & \qquad & x - 1 = 0 \\ 2x = 5 & & x = 1 \\ x = \frac{5}{2} & & \end{array}$$

The zeros of $y = 2x^2 + 3x - 5$ are $x = 1$ and $x = \frac{5}{2}$.

Construct a rough graph of $y = x^3 - x^2 - 12x$.

To construct a rough graph of the function, factor the polynomial $x^3 - x^2 - 12x$ to find the zeros of $y = x^3 - x^2 - 12x$. Because $x^3 - x^2 - 12x = x(x^2 - x - 12) = x(x - 4)(x + 3)$, the function has zeros at $x = 0$, $x = 4$, and $x = -3$. The zeroes are x-intercepts of the graph of the function. The coefficient of the leading term x^3 is positive, and x^3 has an odd degree. Therefore the value of y will approach negative infinity as x goes to negative infinity, and approach positive infinity as x goes to positive infinity. Therefore, the value of y increases from $-\infty$ in the range $x = -\infty$ to $x = -3$ where $y = 0$, continues increasing to a local maximum before decreasing through $y = 0$ at $x = 0$ to some local minimum, and finally increases through $y = 0$ at $x = 4$ to $+\infty$ as x goes to $+\infty$. A rough sketch is shown.

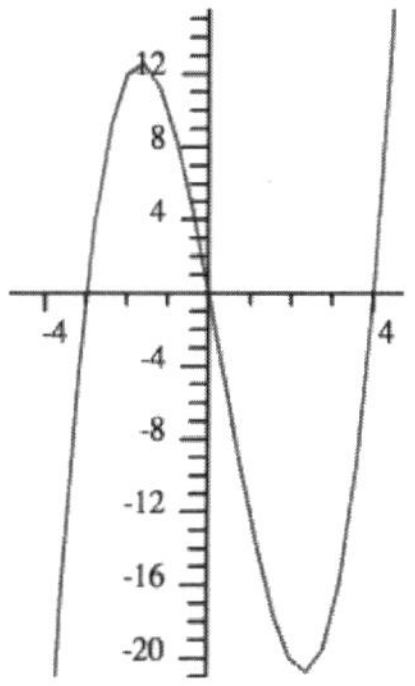

Sketch a cubic function with zeros at $x = -1$ and $x = 3$ that does not pass through the 4th quadrant. Explain your reasoning.

The cubic function has zeros at $x = -1$ and $x = 3$, so these will be x-intercepts of the function. The function does not pass through the 4th quadrant, which must mean that the curve is tangent to the x-axis at (3, 0), and does not pass through the x-axis at this point. For this same reason, the value of y will approach negative infinity as x goes to negative infinity, and approach positive infinity as x goes to positive infinity. A possible sketch is shown.

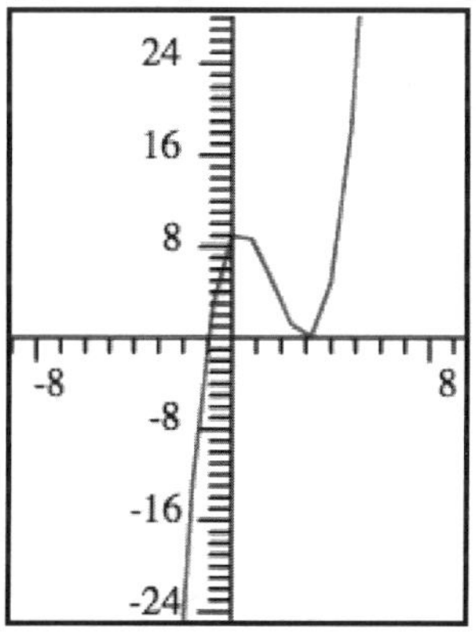

Write the equation for the parabola shown.

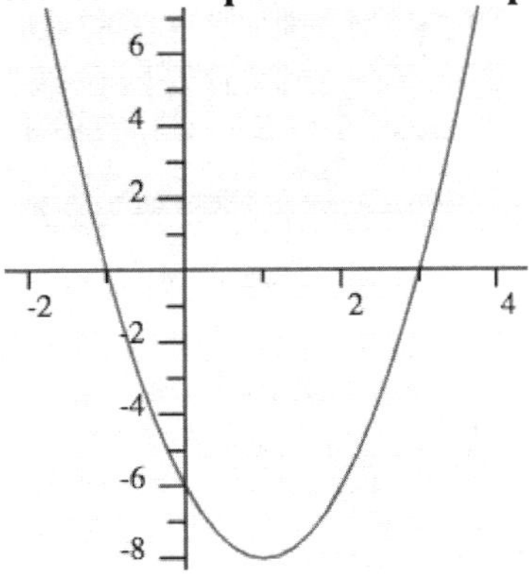

To determine the equation for the parabola, identify the zeros from the graph. The zeros are $x = -1$ and $x = 3$, which means that $(x + 1)$ and $(x - 3)$ are factors of the polynomial that represents the function. Since the parabola is the graph of a quadratic equation, write $y = a(x + 1)(x - 3)$. To determine the value of a, use the fact that the graph passes through the point $(0, -6)$:

$y = a(x + 1)(x - 3)$
$-6 = a(0 + 1)(0 - 3)$
$-6 = -3a$
$a = 2$

Therefore, the equation for the parabola is $y = 2(x + 1)(x - 3)$.

Tony has 4 sections of fence that are *m* feet long, and 4 sections of fence that are *n* feet long. He encloses two square areas with the fencing, one of side *m* and one of side *n*. How much more area can he enclose by making one large square area instead?

Sketch a diagram of what Tony did:

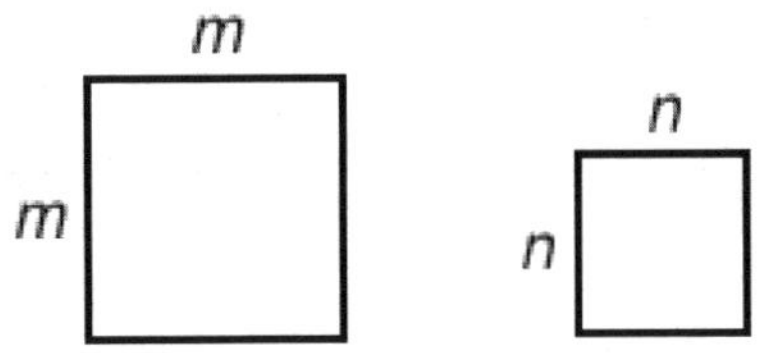

The total area of the enclosures is $m^2 + n^2$. Now sketch a diagram of how Tony could make one large enclosure:

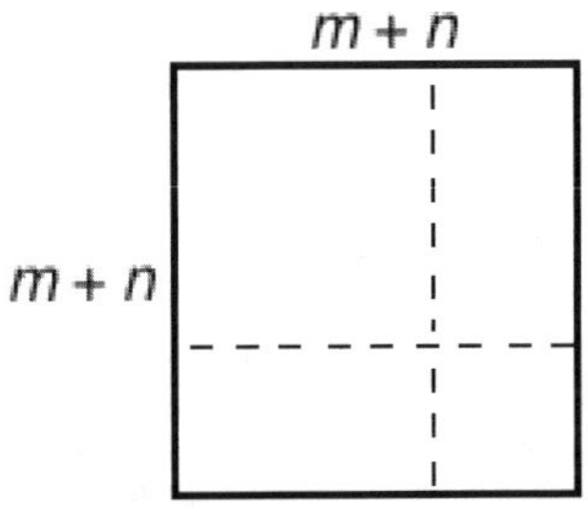

The total area of this enclosure is $(m + n)^2 = m^2 + 2mn + n^2$. Therefore one large fenced area encloses $2mn$ more square feet.

Determine how the expressions m, $\frac{m^2-1}{2}$, and $\frac{m^2+1}{2}$ can be used to generate Pythagorean triples for certain values of m.

A Pythagorean triple is a set of three positive integers that satisfy the Pythagorean Theorem, $a^2 + b^2 = c^2$. For example, the set of numbers {3, 4, 5} is a Pythagorean triple since $3^2 + 4^2 = 5^2$. To show how the given expressions can be used, show that the sum of the squares of two of the expressions equals the square of the remaining term:

$$m^2 + \left(\frac{m^2-1}{2}\right)^2 = m^2 + \left(\frac{m^2-1}{2}\right)\left(\frac{m^2-1}{2}\right)$$
$$= m^2 + \frac{1}{4}(m^4 - 2m^2 + 1)$$
$$= \frac{1}{4}(4m^2 + m^4 - 2m^2 + 1) = \frac{1}{4}(m^4 + 2m^2 + 1)$$
$$= \frac{1}{4}(m^2+1)^2 = \left(\frac{m^2+1}{2}\right)^2$$

Clearly, the divisions by 2 require the numerators of those expressions to be even (in order to produce integer results). This occurs for odd m. For $m = 1$, though, one of the terms becomes 0, which is, of course, not allowable. Since negative m produce identical values, for odd m such that $|m| \geq 3$, the expressions generate Pythagorean triples

Meaning of a polynomial identity.

A polynomial identity refers to two polynomials that can be shown equivalent by factoring, multiplying, or simplifying. For any value or values of the variables in the two polynomials, the values of the expressions will be identical. For example, the difference of squares formula $a^2 - b^2 = (a + b)(a - b)$ is a polynomial identity. The left side can be factored to obtain the right side, and/or the right side can be multiplied to obtain the left side. For any real numbers a and b, $a^2 - b^2$ yields the same result as $(a + b)(a - b)$.

Show that the sum of the squares of three consecutive integers a, b, and c, is given by the expression $3b^2 + 2$, where b is the middle integer.

Examples of three consecutive integers are 4, 5, and 6, or 21, 22, and 23. If x represents the middle of 3 consecutive integers, then the other two integers are given by the expressions $x + 1$ and $x - 1$. The squares of these expressions are x^2, $(x + 1)^2$, and $(x - 1)^2$. Now show that $x^2 + (x + 1)^2 + (x - 1)^2 = 3x^2 + 2$:

$$x^2 + (x+1)^2 + (x-1)^2 =$$
$$x^2 + x^2 + 2x + 1 + x^2 - 2x + 1 =$$
$$3x^2 + 2$$

What is the Binomial Theorem for expanding the power of a binomial?

The Binomial Theorem gives the expansion of the expression $(x + y)^n$, where x and y are real numbers and n is a positive integer. In other words, it gives a way to write each of the terms of the polynomial that results when $(x + y)$ is written as a multiplicative factor n times. The theorem can be written as follows:
$(x+y)^n = a_0x^ny^0 + a_1x^{n-1}y^1 + a_2x^{n-2}y^2 + \cdots + a_{n-1}x^1y^{n-1} + a_nx^0y^n$where the coefficients $a_0, a_1, \ldots, a_n$, are given by the $(n + 1)^{\text{th}}$ row of Pascal's Triangle. Pascal's Triangle is shown below up to $n = 4$, and the pattern continues such that each entry is the sum of the two entries diagonally above it.

1
1 1
1 2 1
1 3 3 1

Expand the expression $(b - 2)^4$ using the Binomial Theorem.

The Binomial Theorem is shown below.

$$(x+y)^n = a_0x^ny^0 + a_1x^{n-1}y^1 + a_2x^{n-2}y^2 + \cdots + a_{n-1}x^1y^{n-1} + a_nx^0y^n$$

where the coefficients $a_0, a_1, \ldots, a_n$ are given by the $(n + 1)^{\text{th}}$ row of Pascal's Triangle. Applying the formula with $x = b$ and $y = -2$ gives:

$$(b-2)^4 = a_0b^4(-2)^0 + a_1b^3(-2)^1 + a_2b^2(-2)^2 + a_3b^1(-2)^3 + a_4b^0(-2)^4$$
$$= a_0b^4 - 2a_1b^3 + 4a_2b^2 - 8a_3b + 16a_4$$

The coefficients $a_0, a_1, \ldots, a_n$ are given by the 5th row of Pascal's Triangle, which is 1, 4, 6, 4, 1. So the expansion becomes
$b^4 - 8b^3 + 24b^2 - 32b + 16$.

Write the 6th row of. Show what you did.

Pascal's Triangle is a pattern of numbers that give the coefficients of the terms in a binomial expansion. The numbers in row $(n + 1)$ of the triangle represent the coefficients for the terms of the expansion $(x + y)^n$. The first 4 rows of the triangle are shown below:

1
1 1
1 2 1
1 3 3 1

The pattern continues indefinitely, where each entry is the sum of the two entries diagonally above it.. The first and last entries of every row are 1. Therefore, the next row of the triangle will be 1, 4, 6, 4, 1. The 6th row of Pascal's Triangle is 1, (1 + 4), (4 + 6), (6 + 4), (4 + 1), 1 = 1, 5, 10, 10, 5, 1.

What is the coefficient of the x^5 term in the expansion of $(2x - 1)^5$?

The Binomial Theorem gives the expansion of the expression
$(x + y)^n$, where x and y are real numbers and n is a positive integer. The theorem can be written as follows:

$$(x+y)^n=a_0x^ny^0+a_1x^{n-1}y^1+a_2x^{n-2}y^2+\ldots+a_{n-1}x^1y^{n-1}+a_nx^0y^n$$

where the coefficients $a_0, a_1, \ldots, a_n$ are given by the $(n + 1)^{\text{th}}$ row of Pascal's Triangle. Since n = 5, use the 6th row of the Triangle, which has the values 1, 5, 10, 10, 5, and 1. The x^5 term is the first term; $a_0 = 1$. The x^5 term is therefore $1(2x)^5(-1)^0 = 32x^5$. The coefficient of the x^5 term is 32.

Long division for polynomials.

Long division for polynomials is similar to long division of integers. For example, when dividing 385 by 12, you first determine how many times 12 goes into 38 (and write 3 as the corresponding digit of the quotient). Then you subtract 36 from 38, giving 2, and the 5 is brought down to form 25, and so on. With polynomial division, the first term written for the quotient is equal to the first term of the dividend divided by the first term of the divisor. For example, if $5x^2 + 10x + 3$ is being divided by $x - 2$, the first term for the quotient is $\frac{5x^2}{x} = 5x$. $5x$ times $x - 2$ is $5x^2 - 10x$, and then $5x^2 - 10x$ is subtracted from $5x^2 + 10x$, yielding $20x$; the 3 is then brought down to form $20x + 3$. This process continues until the remainder is determined.

Find the remainder when $2b^2 + 3b + 2$ is divided by $2b + 1$.

The remainder when $2b^2 + 3b + 2$ is divided by $2b + 1$ can be found by long division. To divide polynomials using long division, find the first term of the quotient by dividing $2b^2$ by $2b$, which gives b. Multiply this by the divisor to get $2b^2 + b$, and then subtract this result from the first two terms of the dividend to obtain $2b$. Then bring down the +2 to form $2b + 2$, and continue in this way. The complete division is shown below.

When the degree of the result after a subtraction is less than that of the divisor, the result is the remainder. So, the remainder is 1, and $2b^2 + 3b + 2$ divided by $2b + 1$ is equal to $b + 1 + \frac{1}{2b+1}$.
(Note: synthetic division cannot be used in this case, since the divisor is not a linear factor.)

Rewrite the rational expression $\frac{3x^3+2x^2}{x}$ by inspection.

The rational expression has a monomial for a denominator. This means that when each term of the numerator is divided by the denominator, the result of each division can be found by applying properties of exponents. In particular, the property $\frac{x^n}{x^m} = x^{n-m}$ can be used to rewrite each term as shown:

$$\frac{3x^3 + 2x^2}{x} = \frac{3x^3}{x} + \frac{2x^2}{x} = 3x^2 + 2x$$

The polynomial $3x^2 + 2x$ is equivalent to the original rational expression. Note that the only exception is the value $x = 0$, because the original rational expression is undefined for $x = 0$.

Add the expressions $\frac{1}{x+1} + \frac{x}{x+1}$ and simplify the result.

To add rational expressions, first obtain a common denominator. Then add the numerators, and keep the same denominator. Since the denominator of each expression is $x + 1$, the expressions can be added directly:

$$\frac{1}{x+1} + \frac{x}{x+1} = \frac{1+x}{x+1}$$

The expressions $1 + x$ and $x + 1$ are equivalent. By dividing the numerator and denominator by $x + 1$, the expression can be further simplified:

$$\frac{1+x}{x+1} = \frac{x+1}{x+1} = 1$$

The sum of the rational expressions is equal to 1. This is true for all values of x except $x = -1$, since the original expressions are undefined for $x = -1$.

What is the least common denominator of $\frac{3x}{x^2-x-6}$ and $\frac{2x}{x^2-6x+9}$?

To determine the least common denominator, or LCD, of two rational expressions, factor the denominators completely. The LCD is equal to the product of the greatest occurring power of each unique factor.

$x^2 - x - 6 = (x - 3)(x + 2)$
$x^2 - 6x + 9 = (x - 3)^2$

The unique factors are $(x + 2)$ and $(x - 3)$. The greatest occurring power of $(x - 3)$ is 2. Therefore the LCD of the two expressions is
$(x + 2)(x - 3)^2$.

Multiply the expressions $\frac{1-x}{x^2+2x+1}$ and $\frac{5}{x^2-1}$. Simplify the result.

To multiply two rational expressions, multiply the numerators to obtain the new numerator, and multiply the denominators to obtain the new denominator:

$$\frac{1-x}{x^2+2x+1} \cdot \frac{5}{x^2-1} = \frac{5(1-x)}{(x^2+2x+1)(x^2-1)}$$

To simplify the result, factor the numerator and denominator completely. The factor $1 - x$ in the numerator can be rewritten as $-(x - 1)$, and the common factor $(x - 1)$ in the numerator and denominator can be cancelled:

$$\frac{5(1-x)}{(x^2+2x+1)(x^2-1)} = \frac{-5(x-1)}{(x+1)(x+1)(x+1)(x-1)} = \frac{-5}{(x+1)^3}$$

Note that this expression is equivalent to the original product for all x except $x = \pm 1$, since the original expressions are undefined for these values.

Rational expressions are closed under subtraction using closure properties of polynomials.

Rational expressions are closed under subtraction if the difference of any two rational expressions results in a rational expression. Consider two rational expressions $\frac{a(x)}{b(x)}$ and $\frac{c(x)}{d(x)}$, where $a(x)$, $b(x)$, $c(x)$, and $d(x)$ are polynomials. Their difference can be written as follows:

$$\frac{a(x)}{b(x)} - \frac{c(x)}{d(x)} = \frac{a(x) \cdot d(x) - b(x) \cdot c(x)}{b(x) \cdot d(x)}$$

Since polynomials are closed under multiplication, the products in the right side of the equation (including the denominator) are all polynomials. Since polynomials are closed under subtraction, the numerator is also a polynomial. So, the expression is a ratio of polynomials and is therefore a rational expression.

Prove that polynomials are not closed under division.

Polynomials are additions, subtractions and/or multiplication (but not division by variables) of variable expressions containing only non-negative integer exponents. To prove that polynomials are not closed under division, use a counterexample. Assume that polynomials are closed under division. This means the quotient $(x + 1) \div x = \frac{x+1}{x} = 1 + \frac{1}{x} = 1 + x^{-1}$ would have to be a polynomial. This expression, however, is not a polynomial, because the term x^{-1} contains a negative exponent (or would have to be written as the division by x). All terms of a polynomial must be of the form ax^n, where a is a real number and n is a non-negative integer. Although there are *some* quotients of polynomials that are polynomials, closure requires this to be true for *all* polynomials.

If $p(x)$ is a polynomial and $\frac{p(x)}{x-3}$ leaves a reminder of –6, what is $p(3)$?

By the Remainder Theorem, for a polynomial $p(x)$ and a real number a, the remainder when $p(x)$ is divided by $(x - a)$ is $p(a)$. In the given equation, $p(x)$ is divided by the binomial $x - 3$, and leaves a reminder of –6. This means that the value of $p(3)$ is –6. Note that the theorem can be applied without needing to know the actual terms of the polynomial $p(x)$.

What are the zeros of the polynomial $(2x - 1)(x^2 - 9)$?

The zeros of the polynomial can be determined by factoring. The expression $x^2 - 9$ is a difference of squares, and factors as $(x - 3)(x + 3)$. The factored form of the full polynomial is therefore $(2x - 1)(x - 3)(x + 3)$. Set each of the linear factors equal to zero and solve for x:

$2x - 1 = 0$	$x - 3 = 0$	$x + 3 = 0$	
$2x = 1$	$x = 3$	$x = -3$	$x = \frac{1}{2}$

The zeros of the polynomial are $\frac{1}{2}$, 3, and –3.

Prove that the product of two consecutive even or odd integers is equal to 1 less than the square of their mean.

Let n represent the first of two consecutive even or odd integers. Then the following consecutive integer is given by the expression $n + 2$. The mean of the two numbers is $n + 1$, since $\frac{n+n+2}{2} = \frac{2n+2}{2} = n + 1$. One less than the square of this expression is written as $(n + 1)^2 - 1$. Show that this expression is equal to the product of the two consecutive even or odd integers by factoring the expression as a difference of squares:

$(n + 1)^2 - 1 = (n + 1 - 1)(n + 1 + 1) = (n + 0)(n + 2) = n(n + 2)$

What is the constant term in the expansion of $(-2 - 4m)^5$?

The Binomial Theorem gives the expansion of the expression $(x + y)^n$, where x and y are real numbers and n is a positive integer. The theorem can be written as follows:

$$(x+y)^n = a_0x^ny^0 + a_1x^{n-1}y^1 + a_2x^{n-2}y^2 + \ldots + a_{n-1}x^1y^{n-1} + a_nx^0y^n$$

where the coefficients $a_0, a_1, \ldots, a_n$ are given by the $(n + 1)$th row of Pascal's Triangle. For the expression $(-2 - 4m)^5$, let $x = -2$ and $y = 4m$ in the equation above. The first term, $a_0x^ny^0$, must represent the constant term in this case, since the variable y is raised to the power of zero. Also, the first term in each row of Pascal's Triangle is one, so a_0 is 1. The constant term is therefore $1(-2)^5 = -32$.

Simplify the rational expression $\frac{x-1}{1-x^2}$.

To simplify a rational expression, factor the numerator and denominator completely. Factors that are the same and appear in the numerator and denominator have a ratio of 1. The denominator, $1 - x^2$, is a difference of squares. It can be factored as $(1 - x)(1 + x)$. The factor $1 - x$ and the numerator $x - 1$ are opposites, and have a ratio of -1. Rewrite the numerator as $-1(1 - x)$. So, the rational expression can be simplified as follows:

$$\frac{x-1}{1-x^2} = \frac{-1(1-x)}{(1-x)(1+x)} = \frac{-1}{1+x}$$

(Note that since the original expression is defined for $x \neq \{-1, 1\}$, the simplified expression has the same restrictions.)

Alison knows that rational expressions are closed under division, assuming a nonzero divisor. She then claims that since all polynomials are rational expressions, polynomials are also closed under division, assuming a nonzero divisor. Find her error.

Alison is correct that rational expressions are closed under division, assuming a nonzero divisor. She is also correct in saying that all polynomials are rational expressions, since the polynomial could be written with a denominator of 1, such as $3x^2 + 4 = \frac{3x^2+4}{1}$. However, closure of rational expressions only guarantees that dividing one rational expression by another results in a rational expression. Polynomials are a subset of the rational expressions, but the ratio of two polynomials is only a polynomial if the divisor is a nonzero constant. Since there are divisors of polynomials that do not yield polynomial quotients, polynomials are not closed under division.

Simplify the quotient: $\frac{x-2}{3x} \div \frac{x^2-4}{6x^2}$.

To simplify the quotient, first rewrite it as a product by taking the reciprocal of the divisor. Then completely factor the numerators and denominators, and simplify by recognizing identical factors in the numerator and the denominator have a ratio of 1:

$$\frac{x-2}{3x} \div \frac{x^2-4}{6x^2} =$$
$$\frac{x-2}{3x} \cdot \frac{6x^2}{x^2-4} =$$
$$\frac{x-2}{3x} \cdot \frac{2x(3x)}{(x-2)(x+2)} =$$
$$\frac{2x}{x+2}$$

Reasoning with Equations & Inequalities

Solve $3x - 2 = -5$ by first assuming the solution exists. Explicitly justify each step.

Assume that the solution exists, and that each side of the equation represents the same real number. In this case, that real number is –5, since the right side of the equation is –5. Adding 2 to each side results in two more equal numbers. So, the equation can be transformed as follows:

$3x - 2 = -5$
$3x - 2 + 2 = -5 + 2$
$3x = -3$

The same approach can be taken with the new equation. Since each side of the equation represents the same real number, divide each side by 3:

$$3x = -3$$
$$\frac{3x}{3} = \frac{-3}{3}$$
$$x = -1$$

The solution of the equation is $x = -1$.

Tom says the equation $3x = 5x$ has no solution. Find his error.

Tom made an error, because the correct (and only) solution is $x = 0$. Tom may have incorrectly thought that 3 times a number can't possibly equal 5 times the same number, or perhaps he divided each side by the variable x. A correct method of solving the equation would be to assume there is a solution, so that each side equals the same real number. Subtract $3x$ from each side, yielding $0 = 2x$, each side of which equals some real number as well, since $3x$ was a real number. Dividing each side by 2 yields $x = 0$, which is the correct solution.

Find the solution of the equation $x^2 = 36$. Justify your solution method.

One method of solution is to assume there is a solution, so that x^2 and 36 each represent the same real number. Subtract 36 from each side, so that $x^2 - 36 = 0$. The expression on the left side can be factored, and the equation rewritten as $(x + 6)(x - 6) = 0$. If a product of two numbers is equal to zero, then one (or the other) of the numbers must be zero. This leads to the two equations $x + 6 = 0$ and $x - 6 = 0$. Assuming these equations have solutions, add (or subtract) 6 from each side to arrive at the two solutions, $x = -6$ or $x = 6$.

Solve $\frac{6}{x} = \frac{9}{10}$. Determine how each step follows from the equality of numbers.

Assume that the solution exists, and that $\frac{6}{x}$ and $\frac{9}{10}$ equal the same real number. Since $\frac{9}{10}$ is positive, and a positive number divided by a positive number is positive, the value of x must be positive. Multiply each side of the equation by x to get $6 = \frac{9x}{10}$, where each side again represents the same real number. Then multiply each side by $\frac{10}{9}$, to arrive at the solution $\frac{60}{9} = x$.

What is an extraneous solution is, and why they may arise when solving a rational or radical equation.

An extraneous solution is the solution of an equation that arises during the process of solving an equation, which is <u>not</u> a solution of the original equation. When solving a rational equation, each side is often multiplied by x or an expression containing x. Since the value of x is unknown, this may mean multiplying by zero, which will make any equation the true statement $0 = 0$. Similarly, when solving a radical expression, each side of the equation is often squared, or raised to some power. This can also change the sign of unknown expressions. For example, the equation $3 = -3$ is false, but squaring each side gives $9 = 9$, which is true.

Solve the rational equation $\frac{2}{x} - 2 = x - 1$.

To solve the rational equation, multiply each side of the equation by the LCD, which is x. This will transform the rational equation into a quadratic equation that can be solved by factoring:

$$\frac{2}{x} - 2 = x - 1$$
$$x\left(\frac{2}{x} - 2\right) = x(x - 1)$$
$$2 - 2x = x^2 - x$$
$$x^2 + x - 2 = 0$$
$$(x + 2)(x - 1) = 0$$
$$x = -2, x = 1$$

Both $x = -2$ and $x = 1$ check out in the original equation. The solution is $x = \{-2, 1\}$.

Solve the radical equation $\sqrt{x-1}+3=x$.

To solve the radical equation, isolate the radical $\sqrt{x-1}$ on one side of the equation. Then square both sides and solve the resulting quadratic equation:

$$\begin{aligned}
&\sqrt{x-1}+3=x\\
&\sqrt{x-1}=x-3\\
&\left(\sqrt{x-1}\right)^2=(x-3)^2\\
&x-1=x^2-6x+9\\
&x^2-7x+10=0\\
&(x-5)(x-2)=0\\
&x=2,x=5
\end{aligned}$$

Only x = 5 checks out in the original equation; $\sqrt{2-1}+3 \overset{?}{\Leftrightarrow} 2 \xrightarrow{yields} \sqrt{1}+3=4\neq 2!$

The solution, then, is just x = {5}.

Solve $x+1=\sqrt{x+1}$. Check for extraneous solutions.

To solve the radical equation, square both sides and solve the resulting quadratic equation by factoring:

$$\begin{aligned}
&x+1=\sqrt{x+1}\\
&(x+1)^2=\left(\sqrt{x+1}\right)^2\\
&x^2+2x+1=x+1\\
&x^2+x=0\\
&x(x+1)=0\\
&x=-1,x=0
\end{aligned}$$

To check whether either solution is extraneous, substitute into the original equation:

$x+1=\sqrt{x+1}$	$x+1=\sqrt{x+1}$
$-1+1=\sqrt{-1+1}$	$0+1=\sqrt{0+1}$
$0=0$	$0=0$

Both solutions are valid. The solution is x = {-1, 0}.

Find the solution of the inequality
$-4x+2\leq-10$.

To solve the inequality, isolate the variable x on one side. When multiplying or dividing by negative numbers, change the inequality symbol from ≤ to ≥, or vice versa:

$-4x+2\leq-10$
$-4x+2-2\leq-10-2$
$-4x\leq-12$

$$\frac{-4x}{-4}\geq\frac{-12}{-4}$$
$$x\geq3$$

The solution of the inequality is $x \geq 3$. (Note that when $x = 3$, both sides of the inequality equal -10. Also, when $x = 4$, the inequality is $-14 \leq -10$, which is true. Therefore the solution is correct.)

A softball player's average is the number of hits divided by the number of at-bats. Gene currently has 20 hits in 75 at-bats. If he can get 30 more at-bats, how many hits must he get to have an average of 0.300 or better?

Let h represent the number of additional hits Gene gets in the 30 at-bats. His total number of hits will be $20 + h$, and his total number of at-bats will be $75 + 30 = 105$. The quotient of these two expressions represents Gene's average. Write a greater-than-or-equal-to inequality for this situation:

$$\frac{20 + h}{105} \geq 0.300$$
$$20 + h \geq 31.5$$
$$h \geq 11.5$$

Since there is no such thing as half a hit, Gene needs 12 or more hits in the next 30 at-bats to have an average of 0.300 or better.

A cab company charges \$8 to enter the cab, and then \$.42 per mile. If the ride cost \$19.76, how long was the trip, in miles?

Let m represent the number of miles for a ride in the cab. The total cost is the \$8 to enter the cab, plus \$.42 per mile. If c represents the total cost for a ride of m miles, an equation for the total cost is
$c = 8 + 0.42m$. Substitute 19.76 for c in the equation and solve for$m$:

$8 + 0.42m = 19.76$
$0.42m = 11.76$

$$\frac{0.42m}{0.42} = \frac{11.76}{0.42}$$
$$m = 28$$

A ride that cost \$19.76 was 28 miles long.

Solve the linear equation $ax + b = c$, where a, b, and c are real numbers. State any restrictions on the values of a, b, and c.

The equation can be solved the same way as if the parameters a, b, and c were real numbers. Isolate x on one side of the equation:

$$ax + b = c$$
$$ax = c - b$$
$$\frac{ax}{a} = \frac{c - b}{a}$$
$$x = \frac{c - b}{a}$$

The solution is $x = \frac{c-b}{a}$. Since division by zero is undefined, the value of a must be nonzero. However, if the value of a were zero, the original equation would not be a one-variable equation, but would simply read $b = c$.

Rewrite $x^2 + 4x = 2$ in the form $(x - p)^2 = q$.

To rewrite $x^2 + 4x = 2$ in the form $(x - p)^2 = q$, complete the square. Begin by adding the square of one half the coefficient of x to each side. In this case, the coefficient is 4, so add $(\frac{1}{2} \cdot 4)^2 = 4$ to both sides, and rewrite the trinomial as a squared binomial:

$$
\begin{aligned}
&x^2 + 4x = 2 \\
&x^2 + 4x + 4 = 2 + 4 \\
&x^2 + 4x + 4 = 6 \\
&(x + 2)^2 = 6
\end{aligned}
$$

This equation is in the form $(x - p)^2 = q$, with $p = -2$ and $q = 6$.

Complete the square in the equation
$3x^2 - 5x = 2$.

To complete the square, first divide by 3 so that the leading coefficient (the coefficient of x^2) is 1. Then add the square of one half the coefficient of x to each side of the equation, and rewrite the trinomial as a squared binomial:

$$
\begin{aligned}
&3x^2 - 5x = 2 \\
&x^2 - \frac{5}{3}x = \frac{2}{3} \\
&x^2 - \frac{5}{3}x + \left(\frac{5}{6}\right)^2 = 2 + \left(\frac{5}{6}\right)^2 \\
&x^2 - \frac{5}{3}x + \frac{25}{36} = \frac{72}{36} + \frac{25}{36} = \frac{97}{36} \\
&\left(x + \frac{5}{6}\right)^2 = \frac{97}{36}
\end{aligned}
$$

Derive the quadratic formula by completing the square in the general quadratic equation $ax^2 + bx + c = 0$.

The quadratic formula gives the solutions to the equation $ax^2 + bx + c = 0$ in terms of the parameters a, b, and c. To derive the formula by completing the square:

$a\left(x^2 + \frac{b}{a}x\right) = c$ Subtract c from each side, and factor out a.

$a\left(x^2 + \frac{b}{a}x + \frac{b^2}{4a^2}\right) = \frac{b^2}{4a} - c$ Complete the square and add $\left(\frac{1}{2}\cdot\frac{b}{a}\right)^2 = \frac{b^2}{4a}$ to both.

$\left(x + \frac{b}{2a}\right)^2 = \frac{b^2}{4a^2} - \frac{c}{a}$ Rewrite the trinomial as a perfect square and divide both sides by a.

$x + \frac{b}{2a} = \pm\frac{\sqrt{(b^2-4ac)}}{2a}$ Take the square root of each side, simplifying the denominator.

$x = \frac{-b\pm\sqrt{b^2-4ac}}{2a}$ Solve for x and simplify.

Compare the quadratic forms $a(x - m)(x - n) = 0$ and $(x - p)^2 = q$. What are the solutions of each equation?

The quadratic equation $a(x - m)(x - n) = 0$ is in factored form. Since the right side of the equation is zero, the factors make it easy to find the solutions: the two equations $x - m = 0$ and $x - n = 0$ give the solutions $x = m$ and $x = n$. The equation $(x - p)^2 = q$ has the form of a quadratic after completing the square, which means the left side is a squared binomial. Taking the square root of each side and then adding p to each side of the equation gives the solutions $x = p \pm \sqrt{q}$.

What is the general form of a complex number?

The general form of a complex number is $a + bi$, where a and b are real numbers. The imaginary number i is equal to the square root of -1: $i = \sqrt{-1}$. Therefore the number i itself is a complex number, with $a = 0$ and $b = 1$. Other examples of complex numbers include $-12i$ and $\sqrt{3} + 4i$. Note that all real numbers are also complex numbers: if b = 0, then $a + bi = a + 0i = a$, which is a real number.

Solve $4x^2 = 100$ by inspection.

To solve an equation by inspection means to solve using fairly obvious mental math, without performing calculations on paper or with a calculator. Dividing each side of the equation by 4 gives $x^2 = 25$. The two square roots of 25 are -5 and 5, so the solution of the equation is $x = -5$ or $x = 5$. A check of each solution (by substituting into the original equation) can seem self-evident:

$4x^2 = 100$	$4x^2 = 100$
$4(-5)^2 = 100$	$4(5)^2 = 100$
$4(25) = 100$	$4(25) = 100$
$100 = 100$	$100 = 100$

Write the quadratic formula. Apply it to solve the equation $2x^2 = 5x - 1$.

The quadratic formula is $x = \frac{-b \pm \sqrt{b^2 - 4ac}}{2a}$. It gives the solution of the quadratic equation $ax^2 + bx + c = 0$. The equation $2x^2 = 5x - 1$ can be written in this form as $2x^2 - 5x + 1 = 0$. Substitute into the quadratic formula with $a = 2$, $b = -5$, and $c = 1$:

$$x = \frac{-b \pm \sqrt{b^2 - 4ac}}{2a}$$

$$x = \frac{-(-5) \pm \sqrt{(-5)^2 - 4(2)(1)}}{2(2)}$$

$$x = \frac{5 \pm \sqrt{17}}{4}$$

The solutions of the equation are $x = \frac{5+\sqrt{17}}{4}$ and $x = \frac{5-\sqrt{17}}{4}$.

Bethany claims the solutions of $(x - 2)(x + 3) = -4$ are $x = -3$ and $x = 2$. Correct her error.

Bethany applied the zero product property to an equation that does not equal zero. Although her values of x make the left side of the equation zero, the right side is -4. To correct her error, she should first multiply the binomials, and then write the equation so that the right side is zero:

$(x - 2)(x + 3) = -4$
$x^2 - 2x + 3x - 6 = -4$
$x^2 + x - 6 = -4$
$x^2 + x - 2 = 0$
$(x + 2)(x - 1) = 0$
$x = -2$ or $x = 1$
The solution is $x = \{-2, 1\}$.

Solve the system $\begin{cases} \frac{x}{2} + \frac{y}{3} = -1 \\ \frac{x}{5} - \frac{y}{3} = 1 \end{cases}$. Describe your solution method.

To solve the system, multiply each equation by the least common denominator, or LCD. This will eliminate the fractions, and transform the system into one with integer coefficients.

$$\begin{cases} \left(\frac{x}{2} + \frac{y}{3} = -1\right)6 \\ \left(\frac{x}{5} - \frac{y}{3} = 1\right)15 \end{cases}$$

$$\begin{cases} 3x + 2y = -6 \\ 3x - 5y = 15 \end{cases}$$

Subtracting the equations results in the equation $7y = -21$, so $y = -3$. Substitute -3 for y into $3x + 2y = -6$ to get $3x = 0$, so $x = 0$. The solution of the system is $(0, -3)$.

Without solving either system, explain why the systems below have the same solution. Then verify this fact.

$$\begin{cases} x + y = 4 \\ 2x - y = -1 \end{cases} \qquad \begin{cases} x + y = 4 \\ 3x = 3 \end{cases}$$

When comparing the two systems, it is clear that the first equation of each system is the same. If an equation of one system is a linear combination of the equations of the other system, then the systems are equivalent and therefore have the same solution. A linear combination is the sum of two equations, with either equation possibly multiplied by a real number. Adding the two equations of the first system results in the equation $3x = 3$. This is the 2nd equation of the other system, so the systems are equivalent and have the same solution. The solution is $(x, y) = (1, 3)$ and satisfies both systems.

Show that if (a, b) is the solution to the system on the left below, then it is also the solution to the system on the right. In the system on the right, one equation was replaced with the sum of that equation and a multiple of the first equation.

$$\begin{cases} 3x+8y=2 \\ 2x-5y=-7 \end{cases} \qquad \begin{cases} 3x+8y=2 \\ 3x+8y+k(2x-5y)=2-7k \end{cases}$$

The solution of the original system is (a, b). Substituting these values for x and y in the equations gives the following true statements:

$$3a + 8b = 2$$
$$2a - 5b = -7$$

To show that (a, b) is the solution of the system on the right, show that (a, b) makes both equations true. The first equation $3x + 8y = 2$ is true, because it is the same equation as the other system and $3a + 8b = 2$. Substituting a and b for x and y in the second equation gives $3a + 8b + k(2a - 5b) = 2 - 7k$. Using the two true equations above, substitute 2 for $3a + 8b$ and -7 for $2a - 5b$ gives $2 + k(-7) = 2 - 7k$, which is an identity and true for any value of k.

Solve the system $\begin{cases} x - 4y = 3 \\ 2x + y = -3 \end{cases}$

The first equation of the system is $x - 4y = 3$. This equation can easily be solved for x, resulting in the equation $x = 4y + 3$. Substitute this expression for x into the other equation and solve for y:

$2x + y = -3$

$2(4y + 3) + y = -3$

$8y + 6 + y = -3$

$9y = -9$

$y = -1$

Substitute -1 for y in the equation $2x + y = -3$ gives $2x = -2$, and $x = -1$. The solution of the system is therefore $(-1, -1)$.

Use a graph to approximate the solution of the system $\begin{cases} -x + y = 9 \\ 2x + y = 5 \end{cases}$ to the nearest integer values of x and y.

The solution to a linear system is the intersection of the graphs of the system. The equations can be sketched by using the x- and y- intercepts of each line. For example, for $-x + y = 9$, the x- and y- intercepts are $(-9, 0)$ and $(0, 9)$, respectively. The intercepts for the other equation are determined similarly.

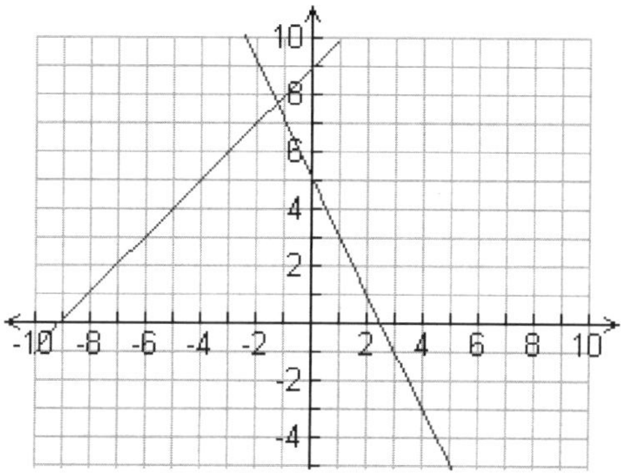

The intersection point is in the second quadrant. To the nearest integer values of x and y, the solution is $(-1, 8)$.

Describe the graph of a linear system with no solution.

If a linear system has no solution, there is no value of x and y that satisfies both equations of the system. Graphically, this means that the lines that represent each equation of the system will never intersect. Lines that never intersect are by definition parallel. Parallel lines have the same slope, so it can often be determined that a system has no solution without graphing or solving algebraically. For example, if the equations of the system are $y = -2x + 3$ and $y = -2x - 5$, the system has no solution. The equations represent distinct parallel lines.

At what point or points does the line $y = -x + 2$ intersect a circle with radius 2 and center at the origin?

The equation of a circle centered at the origin with radius r is $x^2 + y^2 = r^2$. For a radius of 2, this becomes $x^2 + y^2 = 4$. Substitute the expression $-x + 2$ for y in the equation of the circle, and solve for x:

$x^2 + y^2 = 4$
$x^2 + (-x + 2)^2 = 4$
$x^2 + x^2 - 4x + 4 = 4$
$2x^2 - 4x = 0$
$2x(x - 2) = 0$
$x = 0, x = 2$

If $x = 0$, then $y = -(0) + 2 = 2$. If $x = 2$, the $y = -(2) + 2 = 0$. The points of intersection, then, are $(0, 2)$ and $(2, 0)$.

Solve the system $\begin{cases} 3x - y = 6 \\ y = 4 - x^2 \end{cases}$, and find any intersection points.

The first equation of the system can be rewritten as $y = 3x - 6$. Substitute the expression $3x - 6$ for y in the quadratic equation:

$y = 4 - x^2$
$3x - 6 = 4 - x^2$
$x^2 + 3x - 10 = 0$
$(x + 5)(x - 2) = 0$
$x = -5, x = 2$

If $x = -5$, then $y = 3(-5) - 6 = -21$. If $x = 2$, then $y = 3(2) - 6 = 0$. The points of intersection are $(-5, -21)$ and $(2, 0)$.

A system consists of a linear equation and a quadratic equation. How many solutions are possible? Compare with a linear system.

For a system that consists of a linear equation and a quadratic equation, it is possible to have 0, 1, or 2 solutions. This is different than a linear system, which has 0 solutions, 1 solutions, or infinitely many solutions. When a linear solution has infinitely many solutions, the two equations in the system are equivalent. A line may never intersect a parabola (0 solutions), or may be tangent to the parabola (1 solution), or may intersect the parabola in two points (2 solutions). Since solving a linear/quadratic system leads to a quadratic equation, it is not possible to have more than 2 solutions; that is, no line can intersect a parabola at more than 2 points.

Solve the system $\begin{cases} y = 4 - x^2 \\ y - 3 = 0 \end{cases}$ by graphing.

The equation $y = 4 - x^2$, which can be written as $y = -x^2 + 4$, represents a parabola that opens downward with vertex at $(0, 4)$. The equation $y - 3 = 0$ can be written as $y = 3$, the equation of a horizontal line passing through the point $(0, 3)$. The graph of the equations is shown below.

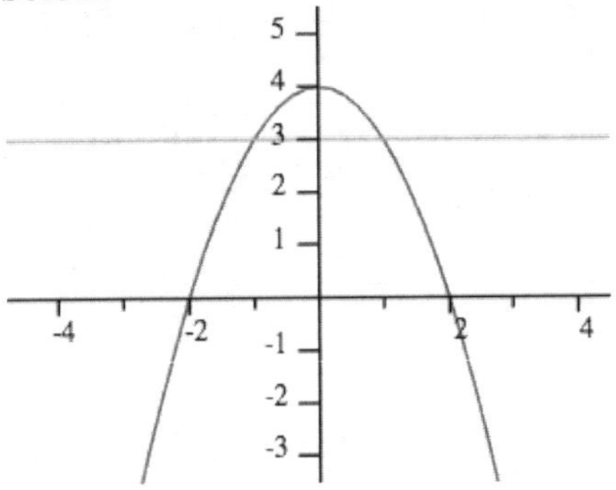

There are two points of intersection of the graphs, $(-1, 3)$ and $(1, 3)$. These are the solutions to the system; both points check out algebraically.

What is a matrix? How can a matrix represent several variables as a vector?

A matrix is a rectangular array of real numbers. These numbers can represent coefficients of a linear system. For example, consider the system $\begin{cases} x + 3y = 1 \\ x - y = 2 \end{cases}$. The coefficients can be represented using the matrix $\begin{bmatrix} 1 & 3 \\ 1 & -1 \end{bmatrix}$. Similarly, a matrix can represent a vector variable, which can represent several non-vector variables. Using the same example, the matrix $\begin{bmatrix} x \\ y \end{bmatrix}$ represents the vector variable $\langle x, y \rangle$, which represents x and y in the linear system.

Represent the system $\begin{cases} 2x - 3y = 11 \\ 6x - y = 20 \end{cases}$ using a matrix equation.

To write the system with a matrix equation, first define matrices for the coefficients of the variables, the variables, and the constants.

Coefficient matrix: $\begin{bmatrix} 2 & -3 \\ 6 & -1 \end{bmatrix}$

Variable matrix: $\begin{bmatrix} x \\ y \end{bmatrix}$

Constant matrix: $\begin{bmatrix} 11 \\ 20 \end{bmatrix}$

The product of the coefficient matrix and the variable matrix equals the constant matrix. This can be written as a matrix equation as follows:

$$\begin{bmatrix} 2 & -3 \\ 6 & -1 \end{bmatrix} \begin{bmatrix} x \\ y \end{bmatrix} = \begin{bmatrix} 11 \\ 20 \end{bmatrix}$$

Write the linear system represented by the matrix equation.

$$\begin{bmatrix} 3 & -7 \\ 1 & 5 \end{bmatrix} \begin{bmatrix} x \\ y \end{bmatrix} = \begin{bmatrix} 10 \\ -2 \end{bmatrix}$$

By multiplying the matrices on the left, a 2 by 1 matrix is formed. Each entry of this matrix is equal to the corresponding entry in the matrix $\begin{bmatrix} 10 \\ -2 \end{bmatrix}$. Multiplying the first row of $\begin{bmatrix} 3 & -7 \\ 1 & 5 \end{bmatrix}$ by the column of the matrix $\begin{bmatrix} x \\ y \end{bmatrix}$ gives the expression $3x - 7y$. Multiplying the second row of $\begin{bmatrix} 3 & -7 \\ 1 & 5 \end{bmatrix}$ by the column of the matrix $\begin{bmatrix} x \\ y \end{bmatrix}$ gives the expression $x + 5y$. These two equations are equal to 10 and –2, respectively. The linear system is therefore $\begin{cases} 3x - 7y = 10 \\ x + 5y = -2 \end{cases}$

Represent the system $\begin{cases} 2x - 3z = -1 \\ 6x - y = 2 \\ 2y + z = 4 \end{cases}$ using a matrix equation.

The equations describe a three-variable linear system. Since each equation only has two variable terms, the coefficient of the missing term is 0 in each equation. So, for the first row of the coefficient matrix, the entries are 2, 0, and –3, since there is no y-term in the first equation. That is, the first equation could be written as $2x + 0y - 3z = -1$. A matrix equation for the system is shown below:

$$\begin{bmatrix} 2 & 0 & -3 \\ 6 & -1 & 0 \\ 0 & 2 & 1 \end{bmatrix} \begin{bmatrix} x \\ y \\ z \end{bmatrix} = \begin{bmatrix} -1 \\ 2 \\ 4 \end{bmatrix}$$

What is the inverse of a matrix? Which matrices have an inverse?

An inverse of a matrix A is the matrix A^{-1} such that $A(A^{-1}) = I$. The matrix I is the identity matrix, which has the value 1 on the main diagonal, and 0 elsewhere. Only square matrices (same number of rows as columns) have an inverse. Additionally, the determinant of the square matrix must not be zero for the matrix to have an inverse. As example, the inverse of the matrix $\begin{bmatrix} 3 & 1 \\ 5 & 2 \end{bmatrix}$ is $\begin{bmatrix} 2 & -1 \\ -5 & 3 \end{bmatrix}$ as illustrated below:

$$\begin{bmatrix} 3 & 1 \\ 5 & 2 \end{bmatrix} \begin{bmatrix} 2 & -1 \\ -5 & 3 \end{bmatrix} = \begin{bmatrix} 6\text{-}5 & -3+3 \\ 10\text{-}(-10) & -5+6 \end{bmatrix} = \begin{bmatrix} 1 & 0 \\ 0 & 1 \end{bmatrix}$$

What is the inverse of the matrix $\begin{bmatrix} 5 & 7 \\ 3 & 4 \end{bmatrix}$?

The inverse of a 2 by 2 matrix $A = \begin{bmatrix} a & b \\ c & d \end{bmatrix}$ is given by the following matrix:

$$\frac{1}{\det A} \begin{bmatrix} d & -b \\ -c & a \end{bmatrix}$$

The notation $\det A$ represents the determinant of the matrix A. For the 2 by 2 matrix $A = \begin{bmatrix} a & b \\ c & d \end{bmatrix}$, $\det A = ad - bc$. Note that since the inverse involves the reciprocal of the determinant, if the determinant is 0, the inverse does not exist. The determinant of $\begin{bmatrix} 5 & 7 \\ 3 & 4 \end{bmatrix}$ is $5(4) - 3(7) = 20 - 21 = -1$, and the inverse is therefore $\frac{1}{-1}\begin{bmatrix} 4 & -7 \\ -3 & 5 \end{bmatrix} = \begin{bmatrix} -4 & 7 \\ 3 & -5 \end{bmatrix}$.

Use a graphing calculator to find the inverse of $\begin{bmatrix} -1 & 2 & 3 \\ 2 & 1 & 1 \\ 3 & 0 & -2 \end{bmatrix}$**.**

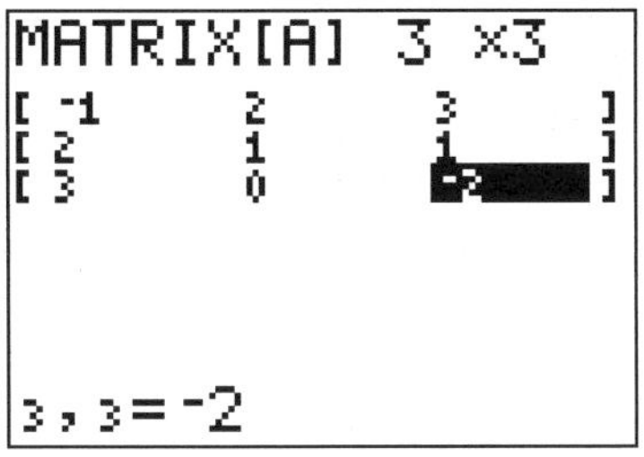

To find the inverse of the matrix, select to edit a 3 by 3 matrix on the calculator. You may have to enter the dimensions first. Then, enter each value for each row of the matrix. Check that the matrix is entered correctly:

The matrix shown is named A. Next, calculate the inverse, A^{-1}. In the second screen shot on the right, the entries are displayed as fractions.

Solve the system $\begin{cases} 2x - 3y = -2 \\ x + 4y = 10 \end{cases}$ **by using an inverse matrix.**

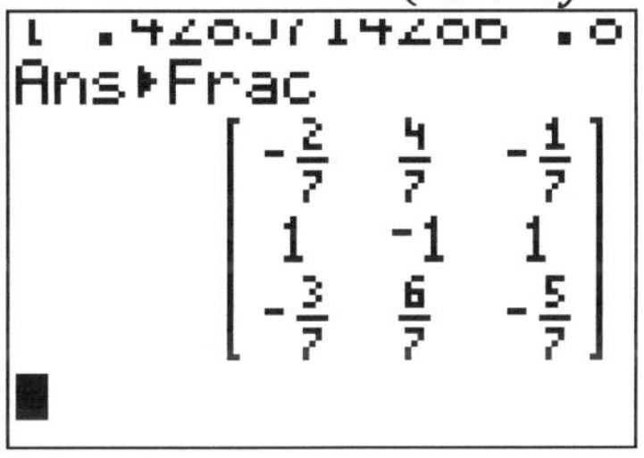

To solve the system using an inverse matrix, first write the corresponding matrix equation for the system.

$$\begin{bmatrix} 2 & -3 \\ 1 & 4 \end{bmatrix} \begin{bmatrix} x \\ y \end{bmatrix} = \begin{bmatrix} -2 \\ 10 \end{bmatrix}$$

Multiply each side of the matrix equation from the left by the inverse of the matrix $\begin{bmatrix} 2 & -3 \\ 1 & 4 \end{bmatrix}$, which is $\frac{1}{11}\begin{bmatrix} 4 & 3 \\ -1 & 2 \end{bmatrix} = \begin{bmatrix} \frac{4}{11} & \frac{3}{11} \\ -\frac{1}{11} & \frac{2}{11} \end{bmatrix}$. The result is shown below.

$$\begin{bmatrix} 1 & 0 \\ 0 & 1 \end{bmatrix} \begin{bmatrix} x \\ y \end{bmatrix} = \begin{bmatrix} \frac{4}{11} & \frac{3}{11} \\ -\frac{1}{11} & \frac{2}{11} \end{bmatrix} \begin{bmatrix} -2 \\ 10 \end{bmatrix}$$

$$\begin{bmatrix} x \\ y \end{bmatrix} = \begin{bmatrix} 2 \\ 2 \end{bmatrix}$$

The solution of the system is (2, 2).

How can you show the solutions of the equation $x + y = 10$ graphically?

The solutions of a two-variable equation are all the ordered pairs that make the equation true. For the equation $x + y = 10$, all of the points (x, y) that satisfy the equation can be shown in the coordinate plane. For example, (3, 7) is a solution of the equation, as is (–2, 12). All of the solutions will fall on a straight line that passes through these two points, given by the equation $y = 10 - x$. The ordered pair (–856, 866) is also a solution, although it may not be visible on the graph of the equation. There are infinitely many solutions, and the line extends in both directions without end.

Must a graph in the coordinate plane have an equation with two variables in it? If not, give an example.

A graph in the coordinate plane is used to show the relationship between two variables. For example, the graph of the equation $y = 2x$ shows all the points such that the y-value is twice the x-value. The equation does not, however, have to have two variables in it. For example, the equation $y = 2$ is a horizontal line that passes through the point (0, 2). For any x-value, the value of y is 2. There is still a relationship, but the value of y does not depend on the value of x.

Describe how to graphically determine the solution of $3x + 4 = x^2$.

A one-variable equation can be solved graphically by considering each side of the equation as the expression for a function of y. By graphing the two equations in the coordinate plane, the x-value of the intersection point(s), if there are any, represent the solution(s) of the equation. The graphs of $y = 3x + 4$ and $y = x^2$ are shown below, and intersect at (–1, 1) and (4, 16). Therefore the solution to the equation is $x = \{-2, 4\}$.

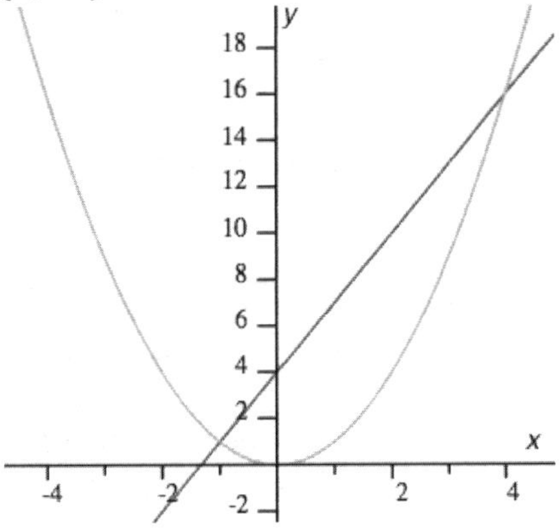

Use a table to determine if $f(x) = 3x^2$ and $g(x) = 8x + 3$ intersect. Use integer values of x from −1 to 5.

Set up a table that shows x, $f(x)$, and $g(x)$. The values for x in the table range from −1 to 5, and the values of $f(x)$ and $g(x)$ are the functions evaluated at the particular value of x.

x	$f(x)$	$g(x)$
−1	3	-5
0	0	3
1	3	11
2	12	19
3	27	27
4	48	35
5	75	43

The table reveals that $f(3) = g(3) = 27$. This means that the functions intersect at the point (3, 27). Also, in the interval from $x = -1$ to $x = 0$, $f(x)$ changes from being greater than $g(x)$ to less than $g(x)$. This means that the functions intersect at another x-value between −1 and 0, although the table does not show this value.

Find an approximate solution to $3^x = -(x + 2)$. Use a graphing calculator.

The equation $3^x = -(x + 2)$ cannot be solved for x. An approximate solution can be found by graphing the equations $y = 3^x$ and $y = -(x + 2)$ on a graphing calculator. The intersection points, if there are any, will have an x-coordinate that is a solution to the equation. The graphs intersect at approximately (−2.0996, 0.0996). This is the only intersection point, since the linear function is decreasing and the exponential function is increasing. The approximate solution, then, of the equation is $x = -2.0996$. Another solution is to graph the equation $y = 3^x + x + 2$ and determine where it crosses the x-axis.

What is the process of successive approximations for finding the solution of the equation $f(x) = g(x)$? Use $\ln x = -x^2$ as an example.

The process of successive approximations involves making a guess, or an approximation, for a solution to an equation. Then make another guess that is close to the original guess, and determine whether the result makes each side of the equation closer to being equal. For example, a reasonable first guess for the solution to $\ln x = -x^2$ is $x = 0.5$. This gives −0.6931 and −0.25, and the guess $x = -0.6$ yields −0.5108 and −0.36. Since $x = -0.6$ is better, next guess $x = -0.7$, which yields −0.3567 and−0.49, only a slight improvement. Perhaps guess $x = -0.65$ next, which yields −0.4308 and −0.4225 which are equal to the tenths place. Therefore, $x = -0.65$ is an approximate solution accurate to the tenths place. Further guesses might yield even better approximations.

Sketch the graph of $y \geq -2x + 4$ in the coordinate plane.

To sketch the graph of $y \geq -2x + 4$, begin by graphing the corresponding linear equation $y = -2x + 4$. Draw the line as a solid line, since the greater-than-or-equal-to sign indicates that the line itself is part of the solution. The test point (0, 0), when substituted into the inequality, gives $0 \geq 4$, which is FALSE. Therefore, the half-plane that represents the solution region is the side of the line that does not contain (0, 0). Shade this region, which is above the line, as shown below.

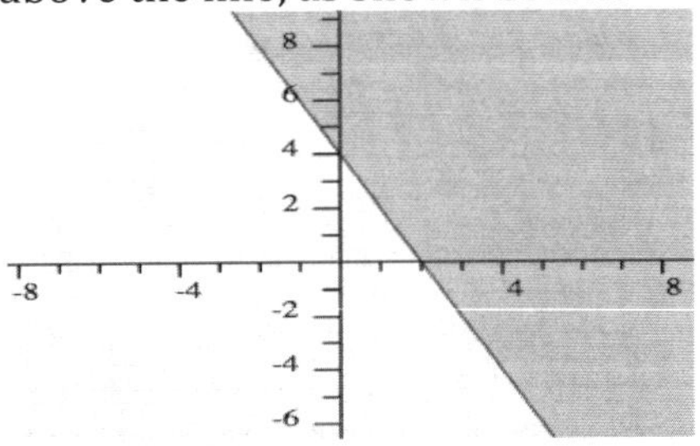

Graph the solution of the system $\begin{cases} x \leq y - 1 \\ 2x \geq y \end{cases}$.

To sketch the graph of the system, graph the equations $y = x + 1$ and $y = 2x$. The lines for $y = 2x$ and $y = x + 1$ should be solid, since the inequality symbols include equality. Shade the half-plane that represents the solution for each inequality. The shaded areas intersect in a triangular region in the first quadrant, as shown in the graph. This represents the solution of the system. Note that the boundary of the solution region is included in the solution.

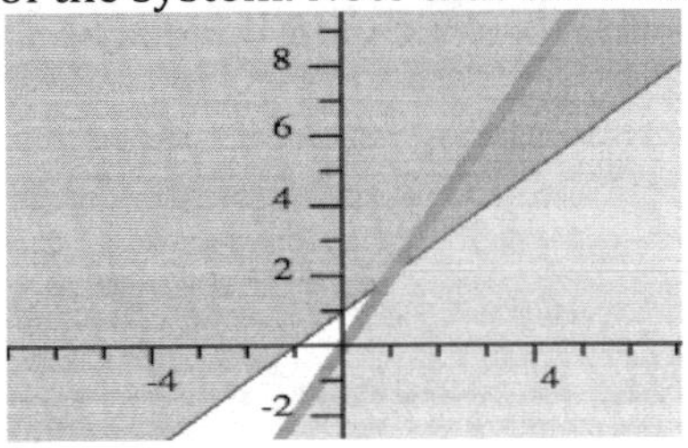

What system of inequalities describes the points in the 3rd quadrant of the coordinate plane?

The coordinate plane is divided into 4 quadrants. The points in each quadrant can be described the signs of the coordinates of the points:
1st quadrant: both coordinates positive
2nd quadrant: y-coordinates positive, x-coordinates negative
3rd quadrant: both coordinates negative
4th quadrant: x-coordinate positive, y-coordinate negative
The x-coordinates are negative, so $x < 0$. Similarly, the y-coordinates are negative, so $y < 0$. A system of inequalities that describes the points is $\begin{cases} x < 0 \\ y < 0 \end{cases}$.

When is the boundary line of the graph of a linear inequality in two variables part of the solution?

The boundary line of a linear inequality in two variables is the line that represents the corresponding equation of the inequality. For example, in both inequalities $y < 3x + 5$ and $y \geq 3x + 5$, the boundary line is given by the equation $y = 3x + 5$. When the inequality has the symbol < or >, the boundary line is not part of the solution. This is indicated by drawing a dashed line for the equation. When the inequality has the symbol $\leq$ or $\geq$, the boundary line is part of the solution. This is indicated by drawing a solid line for the equation.

Construct a viable argument to show the solution to the equation $|1 - x| = |x - 1|$ is all real numbers.

Assuming there is a solution to the equation, there are two possibilities. Either $1 - x = x - 1$, or $1 - x = -(x - 1)$. In other words, the expressions inside absolute value signs are either equal or opposite in value. Assume that $1 - x = x - 1$ has a solution, and that the expressions equal the same real number. Then adding $x + 1$ to each side will give two expressions equal to a new same real number. Doing this results in the equation $2 = 2x$, and dividing by 2 gives $1 = x$. Assume also that $1 - x = -(x - 1)$ has a solution, or equivalently $1 - x = -x + 1$. Adding x to each side gives $1 = 1$, which is always true. Therefore x can equal any real number.

The reciprocal of a number is 0.45 more than the number. Find the number.

Let n represent the unknown number. Then the reciprocal of this number, assuming the number is not zero, is given by the expression $\frac{1}{n}$. This number is 0.45 more than the original number, or $\frac{1}{n} = 0.45 + n$.

$$\frac{1}{n} = 0.45 + n$$
$$n\left(\frac{1}{n}\right) = n(0.45 + n)$$
$$1 = 0.45n + n^2$$

This equation could be solved using the quadratic formula, but also through factoring:

$$100n^2 + 45n - 100 = 0$$
$$20n^2 + 9n - 20 = 0$$
$$(4n + 5)(5n - 4) = 0$$
$$n = -\frac{5}{4} \text{ or } n = \frac{4}{5}$$

There are two possible values of n, $-\frac{5}{4}$ and $\frac{4}{5}$.

Solve the equation $2(3 - (4 - x) - 3x) = 4$.

To solve the equation, use the Distributive Property. First, distribute the subtraction that is inside the parentheses:

$2(3 - (4 - x) - 3x) = 4$

$2(3 - 4 + x - 3x) = 4$

Next, simplify the expression inside the parentheses by combining like terms:

$$2(3 - 4 + x - 3x) = 4$$
$$2(-1 - 2x) = 4$$

Distribute one more time, and then isolate x:

$$2(-1 - 2x) = 4$$
$$-2 - 4x = 4$$
$$-4x = 6$$
$$x = -\frac{3}{2}$$

Ron completes the square of the expression $3x^2 - 10x$ by writing the equivalent expression $3(x - 5)^2 - \frac{25}{3}$. Is Ron correct?

Ron is not correct. This is evident by noting that while the original expression does not have a constant term, Ron's answer will have the constants 75 and $\frac{25}{3}$ in it, which are not opposites so their sum is not zero. This breaks the equality the method of completing the square preserves. Ron should have proceeded as follows:

$$3x^2 - 10x =$$
$$3\left(x^2 - \frac{10}{3}x\right) =$$
$$3\left(x^2 - \frac{10}{3}x + \left(\frac{1}{2}\cdot\frac{10}{3}\right)^2\right) - 3\left(\frac{1}{2}\cdot\frac{10}{3}\right)^2 =$$
$$33\left(x^2 - \frac{10}{3}x + \left(\frac{10}{6}\right)^2\right) - 3\left(\frac{10}{6}\right)^2 = 3\left(x^2 - \frac{10}{3}x + \frac{25}{9}\right) - \frac{25}{3} =$$
$$3\left(x - \frac{5}{3}\right)^2 - \frac{25}{3}$$

Show that the quadratic formula and factoring give the same solution set for the equation $x^2 - 3x + 2 = 0$.

To factor the equation, find two numbers with a product of 2 and a sum of −3. The numbers are −1 and −2, so $x^2 - 3x + 2 = (x - 1)(x - 2)$, and the equation becomes $(x - 1)(x - 2) = 0$, and the solutions are {1, 2}. The quadratic formula, with $a = 1$, $b = -3$, and $c = 2$, gives:

$$x = \frac{-b \pm \sqrt{b^2 - 4ac}}{2a} =$$
$$\frac{3 \pm \sqrt{(-3)^2 - 4(1)(2)}}{2(1)} =$$
$$\frac{3 \pm \sqrt{1}}{2}$$
$$\therefore x = \frac{3+1}{2}, \frac{3-1}{2}$$

The two expressions are equal to 2 and 1, so the solution is the same.

Solve the linear system $\begin{cases} x - y = -3 \\ 2x + 6 = 2y \end{cases}$

The second equation can be simplified by dividing by 2. This gives the equation $x + 3 = y$. The first equation can be rewritten as $x + 3 = y$. Since these are the same equation, there are infinitely many solutions. To verify this, substitute $x + 3$ for y in the first equation to create an equation with only x as a variable:

$$\begin{aligned} &x - y = -3 \\ &x - (x + 3) = -3 \\ &x - x - 3 = -3 \\ &-3 = -3 \end{aligned}$$

The equation that results is always true. This means that the two equations that make up the system are the same equation. There are therefore infinitely many solutions, and the solution can be written $\{(x, y) \mid x - y = -3\}$. (Graphically, this solution describes a line.)

Solve the system $\begin{cases} x - y^2 = 2 \\ x + y = 4 \end{cases}$

Solve the first equation for x. This gives $x = y^2 + 2$, and the expression $y^2 + 2$ can be substituted into the second equation, which can then be solved for y:

$x + y = 4$
$y^2 + 2 + y = 4$
$y^2 + y - 2 = 0$
$(y + 2)(y - 1) = 0$
$y = -2$ or $y = 1$

If $y = -2$, then $x = 6$. If $y = 1$, then $x = 3$. There are two solutions of the system, $(6, -2)$ and $(3, 1)$. Each solution makes both equations of the system true.

Write the linear system represented by the matrix equation.

$$\begin{bmatrix} 1 & 0 & -1 \\ 0 & 4 & 2 \\ -1 & 3 & 3 \end{bmatrix} \begin{bmatrix} x \\ y \\ z \end{bmatrix} = \begin{bmatrix} 1 \\ -2 \\ 5 \end{bmatrix}$$

By multiplying the matrices on the left, a 3 by 1 matrix is formed. Each entry of this matrix is equal to the corresponding entry in the matrix $\begin{bmatrix} 1 \\ -2 \\ 5 \end{bmatrix}$. Multiplying the first row of $\begin{bmatrix} 1 & 0 & -1 \\ 0 & 4 & 2 \\ -1 & 3 & 3 \end{bmatrix}$ by the column matrix $\begin{bmatrix} x \\ y \\ z \end{bmatrix}$ gives the expression $x - z$. Multiplying the second row of $\begin{bmatrix} 1 & 0 & -1 \\ 0 & 4 & 2 \\ -1 & 3 & 3 \end{bmatrix}$ by the column matrix $\begin{bmatrix} x \\ y \\ z \end{bmatrix}$ gives the expression $4y + 2z$. Multiplying the third row of $\begin{bmatrix} 1 & 0 & -1 \\ 0 & 4 & 2 \\ -1 & 3 & 3 \end{bmatrix}$ by the column matrix $\begin{bmatrix} x \\ y \\ z \end{bmatrix}$ gives the expression $-x + 3y + 3z$. These three equations are equal to 1, -2, and 5, respectively. The linear system is therefore

$$\begin{cases} x - z = 1 \\ 4y + 2z = -2 \\ -x + 3y + 3z = 5 \end{cases}$$

The inverse of the matrix $\begin{bmatrix} a & -4 \\ 7 & -2 \end{bmatrix}$ does not exist. What is the value of a?

In order for the inverse of the matrix $\begin{bmatrix} a & -4 \\ 7 & -2 \end{bmatrix}$ to not exist, its determinant must be zero. The determinant of a 2 by 2 matrix $\begin{bmatrix} a & b \\ c & d \end{bmatrix}$ is given by the expression $ad - bc$. Write an equation that represents this situation:

$-2(a) - 7(-4) = 0$
$-2a = -28$
$a = 14$

The value of a is 14. For any other value of a, the matrix would have an inverse.

Find two exact solutions of $\frac{1}{x^2+1} = 2^x$ using a graphing calculator. Verify the solutions are true.

The solutions can be found by graphing the equations $y = \frac{1}{x^2+1}$ and $y = 2^x$ on a graphing calculator. The intersection points, if there are any, will have x-coordinates that are solutions to the equation. The graphs appear to intersect at the points (0, 2) and (−1, 0.5). Therefore the two solutions of the equation are $x = 0$ and $x = -1$. Substitute to verify the solutions:

$$\frac{1}{x^2+1} = 2^x \qquad \frac{1}{(-1)^2+1} = 2^{-1}$$

$$\frac{1}{0^2+1} = 2^0 \qquad \frac{1}{1+1} = \frac{1}{2}$$

$$1 = 1 \qquad \frac{1}{2} = \frac{1}{2}$$

Interpreting Functions

A function is a relation between two sets, the *domain* and the *range*, such that each element of the domain is associated with exactly one element of the range.

There are other ways this definition can be phrased. A less technical wording is that a function is a relation that associates each possible value of one variable, x, with a unique value of a second variable, y.

Note that it is *not* necessarily the case that each element of the *range* is associated with exactly one element of the *domain* (or, under the other definition, that each value of y is associated with a unique value of x). However, a relation for which this condition does hold is *invertible*—in this case, interchanging the domain and the range of the function gives rise to another function (the original function's *inverse*).

Linear, quadratic, polynomial, and rational functions

A *linear* function is a function the graph of which is a straight line. The expression for a linear function includes x (possibly multiplied by some constant coefficient, and possibly added to some other constant), but does not include x^2 or any higher powers of x. The following, for example, are all linear functions: $f(x) = x$, $f(x) = 1 - 2x$, $f(x) = \frac{3}{4}x + 3$.

The expression for a *quadratic* function includes a term containing x^2 (again possibly multiplied by some constant coefficient), but no term contains x^3 or any higher powers of x. The following, for example, are all quadratic functions: $f(x) = x^2 + x + 1$, $f(x) = 3x^2 - 2$, $f(x) = -\frac{1}{2}x^2$.

The expression for a *polynomial* function is a sum of one or more powers of x, possibly multiplied by constant coefficients. (Note that $1 = x^0$ is a power of x.) All linear and quadratic functions are polynomials; so are the following: $f(x) = 3x^7$, $f(x) = 2x^3 - 2x^2 + 5x - 6$, $f(x) = x^{2000} - x^{169}$.

A *rational function* is a ratio of polynomials. Examples include $\frac{x^2-1}{x}$, $\frac{1}{3x^3+2x^2+x}$, and $\frac{x^4+3}{x^2-2}$.

Determine how you can tell from looking at a graph whether the graph represents a function

The simplest way to tell by visual inspection whether a graph represents a function is a procedure sometimes known as the "vertical line test". Imagine a vertical line scanning across the graph. If, at any point, the line intersects more than one point on the graph, the graph does *not* represent a function. Otherwise, it does.

For example, consider the following graphs.

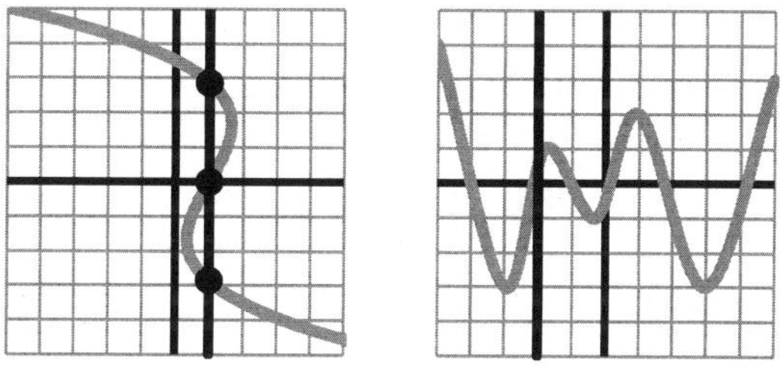

The vertical line in the image on the left intersects the graph in three points. Therefore, the graph on the left does *not* represent a function. On the right, however, no matter where we place the vertical line, it will never intersect more than one point. Therefore, the graph on the right represents a function.

Finding the domain of the function

The *domain* of a function $f(x)$ is the set of all possible input values of the function—that is, of every possible value of x for which the function is defined.

Example

Given a function expressed in a table like the one below, determine how you can find the domain of the function.

x	0	3	2	1	8	10	6	7
$f(x)$	2	8	6	8	2	3	4	5

For a function expressed in a table like the one in this example, it's simple to find the domain, because every point in the function—that is, every input-output pair—is given explicitly. To find the domain, we just list all the x values: in this case, that would be {0, 3, 2, 1, 8, 10, 6, 7}, or, putting them in ascending order, {0, 1, 2, 3, 6, 7, 8, 10}. (Putting the values in ascending order isn't strictly necessary, but generally makes the set easier to read.)

Note that we don't have to worry about the possibility of an input value being repeated: by definition of a function, no input value can be matched to more than one output value.

Example

Given a function expressed in analytic form such as

$$f(x) = sin\, x$$
$$g(x) = \sqrt{x+1}$$
$$h(x) = \frac{x}{x^2-1}$$

explain how you can find the domain of the function.

Some functions, such as $f(x) = \sin x$, are defined for any real value of x; in this case, the domain of $f(x)$ is $(-\infty, \infty)$, that is, it includes all real numbers. There are functions, however, for which that isn't true. For instance, consider $g(x) = \sqrt{x+1}$. The square root of a negative number is not defined (at least as a real number), so in order for $g(x)$ to be defined we must have $x + 1 \geq 0$, so $x \geq -1$. The domain of $g(x)$ is thus $[-1, \infty)$. Similarly, $h(x) = \frac{x}{x^2-1}$ is not defined when the denominator is zero, which is true when $x = \pm 1$. The domain therefore includes all real numbers *except* 1 and –1, which we can write as
$(-\infty, -1) \cup (-1,1) \cup (1, \infty)$.

Finding the range of a function

The *range* of a function $f(x)$ is the set of all possible output values of the function—that is, of every possible value of $f(x)$, for any value of x in the function's domain.

Example

Given a function expressed in a table like the one below, determine how you can find the range of the function.

x	-1	4	2	1	0	3	8	6
$f(x)$	3	0	3	−1	−1	2	4	6

For a function expressed in a table like the one in this example, it's simple to find the range, because every point in the function—that is, every input-output pair—is given explicitly. To find the range, we just list all the values of $f(x)$; in this case, that would be {3, 0, 3, −1, −1, 2, 4, 6}. Note that some of these values appear more than once. This is entirely permissible for a function; while each value of x must be matched to a unique value of $f(x)$, the converse is not true. We don't need to list each value more than once, so eliminating duplicates, the range is {3, 0, −1, 2, 4, 6}, or, putting them in ascending order, {-1, 0, 2, 3, 4, 6}. (Putting the values in ascending order isn't strictly necessary, but generally makes the set easier to read.)

Example

Given a function expressed in analytic form such as

$$f(x) = x^3$$
$$g(x) = x^2 - 2x + 4$$
$$h(x) = \frac{1}{x}$$

explain how you can find the range of the function.

For a continuous function, we can find the range by just finding the maximum and minimum values of the function; the range comprises all the points in between. Some functions have no maximum or minimum; this is the case, for instance, with $f(x) = x^3$. At the left, the function decreases indefinitely, and on the right, it increases indefinitely. The range therefore includes all real numbers, $(-\infty, \infty)$. Other functions may have a maximum, but no minimum, or vice versa. The quadratic function $g(x) = x^2 - 2x + 4$ has a minimum at (1,3), but no maximum, so its range is $[3, \infty)$.

For a discontinuous function, we must examine each part separately. $h(x) = 1/x$ has a discontinuity at $x = 0$. On the left side, the function has no minimum, but has an asymptotic maximum of 0 (asymptotic because it approaches 0 but never actually reaches it); the range of this side is $(-\infty, 0)$. Similarly, the right side has a range of $(0, \infty)$. The total range of the function is the union of these two ranges, hence $(-\infty, 0) \cup (0, \infty)$.

Example

Suppose $f(x) = x^2 + 1$ and $g(x) = x - 1$. How would you find each of the following

$f(3)$ $g(3)$ $f(y^2)$ $g(z + 1)$

In function notation, "$f(3)$" can be thought of as a shorthand for "$f(x)$ when $x = 3$". To evaluate the function at this point, just replace the x in the expression for the function with the number. If $f(x) = x^2 + 1$, then to find $f(3)$ we just replace each x in "$x^2 + 1$" with 3. So $f(3) = 3^2 + 1$, which we can simplify to 10. Similarly, $g(3) = 3 - 1 = 2$.

The same principle holds when instead of a number, there is a variable or an expression within the parentheses. To find $f(y^2)$, where $f(x) = x^2 + 1$, we replace each x in "$x^2 + 1$" with "y^2" (or "(y^2)"—including parentheses may make it easier to keep track of the substitution). This yields $f(y^2) = (y^2)^2 + 1 = y^4 + 1$. Similarly, $g(z + 1) = (z + 1) - 1 = z$.

Example

Describe in words what a statement such as $f(x) = x^2 + 1$ means

This kind of statement defines a particular function; it tells how to match up each point in the domain with a point in the range. The possible values of x comprise the domain—this can usually be assumed to include all real numbers unless specified otherwise, or unless there are some points for which the expression on the right side of the equation is undefined. Each value of x is then matched with a (not necessarily unique) value of $f(x)$ (or y); all the values of $f(x)$ that are matched to values of x comprise the range.

In the case of the statement $f(x) = x^2 + 1$, this defines a function in which each real number x is matched to the number $x^2 + 1$. For instance, $x = 0$ corresponds to $f(0) = 0^2 + 1 = 1$, when $x = 1$ $f(1) = 1^2 + 1 = 2$, and so forth. Note that $f(x)$ in this case can never be less than 1, so the range of this function is $[1, \infty)$.

Real-world situations that can be modeled by statements that use function notation

A statement using function notation can model any situation in which one quantity depends uniquely on one or more other quantities. For example, the area of a rectangle can be expressed as a function of its width and height. The maximum vertical distance a projectile travels can be expressed as a function of its initial vertical speed. An object's position, the amount of money in a bank account, or any other quantity that changes over time can be expressed as a function of time.

A relationship *cannot* be modeled with a function, however, if it involves two quantities neither of which is uniquely determined by the other—that is, if each quantity may have multiple values corresponding to the same value of the other. For example, we could *not* write a function to represent the relationship between peoples' height in inches and their weight in pounds. There are people of the same height with different weights, and people of the same weight but different heights.

Defining a function recursively

To define a function recursively is to give the value of the function for a given input value in terms of the function's values for other input values—for example, to define $f(x)$ in terms of $f(x-1)$. A function cannot be defined *purely* recursively; it's necessary to define the function absolutely for at least one point to give a starting point for the recursion.

For example, the factorial function, $f(n) = n! = n(n-1)(n-2) \dots (2)(1)$, can be defined recursively as follows: $f(1) = 1$, otherwise $f(n) = n \cdot f(n-1)$. The domain of this function is the positive integers. (Technically, the factorial function is also defined at $n = 0$, where $0! = 1$, but that's not important for this example.) Then, for example, $f(3) = 3 \cdot f(2) = 3 \cdot 2 \cdot f(1) = 3 \cdot 2 \cdot 1$.

Sequence

A sequence is a function in which the domain is confined to the integers, or some subset of the integers. Very often, the subset in question is the positive integers, in which case the sequence can be thought of as an ordered list of the elements of the range, with $f(n)$ identified directly with the nth element of the sequence. Such sequences are often written in list form; the sequence $f(n) = \frac{n^2+n}{2}$, where $f(1) = 1, f(2) = 3, f(3) = 6$, and so on, can simply be written as $1, 3, 6, 10, 15, \dots$

Sequences are often defined recursively, with the first few elements of the sequence defined explicitly and with $f(n)$ otherwise defined in terms of $f(n-1)$ or in general of function values for smaller versions of n. Many functions can be equivalently defined explicitly or recursively. For instance, the sequence above, $f(n) = \frac{n^2+n}{2}$, can also be defined as $f(1) = 1$ and $f(n) = f(n-1) + n$.

Fibonacci sequence

The Fibonacci sequence is a sequence in which the first two terms are 1 and each succeeding term is the sum of the preceding two terms: 1, 1, 2, 3, 5, 8, 13, 21... Written algebraically, $f(1) = f(2) = 1$, and thereafter $f(n) = f(n-1) + f(n-2)$. (There are some variations in its definition; sometimes the domain starts at 0 instead of 1, for instance, or the first term may be defined as 0 instead of 1.)

The Fibonacci sequence is the most common and perhaps the simplest sequence that is recursively defined in terms of more than one earlier term in the sequence (rather than each term being only defined in terms of the immediately preceding term). It also arises in many real-world phenomena.

Example

Given a function definition such as $(x) = x^2 - 9$, determine how you would find the function's x and y intercepts

To find the y intercept, simply find $f(0)$. The y intercept is by definition the point where the function crosses the y-axis, which means it's the function's value when $x = 0$. For the example function definition, $f(x) = x^2 - 9$, $f(0) = 0^2 - 9 = -9$. So the y intercept is (0, -9). Since no function can have multiple y values associated with a single value of x, a function cannot have more than one y intercept.

To find the x intercepts, we need to find where the function crosses the x-axis, so we have to find the value(s) of x, if any, for which $f(x) = 0$. There may be more than one such value. In the case of the example function, $f(x) = x^2 - 9$, this means $0 = x^2 - 9$. Solving for x, we get $x^2 = 9$, so $x = \pm 3$. So this function has two x intercepts, (-3, 0) and (3, 0).

All functions do not necessarily have x and y intercepts

No, not all functions necessarily have x and y intercepts. To have a y intercept, a function must be defined at $x = 0$. This is not true of all functions: $f(x) = \sqrt{x-1}$, for instance, does not have a y intercept, because $f(0) = \sqrt{-1}$ is not defined in the real numbers. For a function $f(x)$ to have an x intercept, there must be one or more values of x such that $f(x) = 0$. This, again, is not true of all functions. For instance, for $f(x) = x^2 + 1$, there is no value of x for which $f(x) = 0$, since we cannot find a real value of x that satisfies the equation $x^2 + 1 = 0$. This function has no x intercept.

It is possible for a function to have neither an x nor a y intercept. One simple example is $f(x) = {}^1/_x$. Since ${}^1/_0$ is undefined, this function does not have a y intercept. Since there is no finite value of x satisfying ${}^1/_x = 0$, this function does not have an x intercept.

Relative maximum and relative minimum of a function

A "relative maximum" of a function is a point at which the function has a higher value than any other point in its immediate vicinity. More technically, a relative maximum is a point (x, y) such that if we choose a sufficiently small interval around x, $f(x) > f(x')$ for any other point x' within the interval.

A relative minimum is just the opposite: a point at which the function has a *lower* value than any other point in its immediate vicinity, or, more technically, a point (x, y) such that if we choose a sufficiently small interval around x, $f(x) < f(x')$ for any other point x' within the interval.

A function may have multiple relative maxima and relative minima, or it may have none. A linear function such as $y = x$, for instance, has no relative maxima or minima, while $y = \sin(x)$ has infinitely many of each.

Finding a relative maximum or minimum from a graph

At a relative maximum, the graph goes from increasing to decreasing, forming a "peak" on the graph which is generally easy to spot visually. Similarly, at a relative minimum, the graph goes from decreasing to increasing, forming a "trough". On the graph below, for instance, points A and C are relative maxima, and point B is a relative minimum.

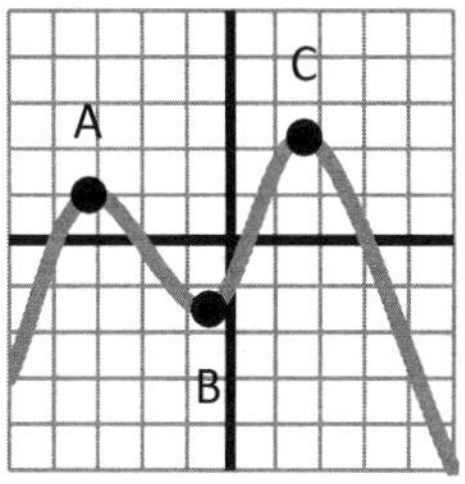

Note that point A is a relative maximum, but not an absolute maximum; the function has a higher value at point C. Similarly, point B is a relative minimum, but not an absolute minimum; the function has a lower value at the left and right ends of the graph than it does at point B. Point C, however, is both a relative and an absolute maximum; nowhere on the graph does the function have a higher value than at point C.

Determining how you can tell over what intervals a function is increasing or decreasing

If the function is presented in graph form, it's easy to tell by inspection where it's increasing and where it's decreasing. Where the slope of the graph is positive—where the graph goes from lower left to upper right—the function is increasing. Where the slope is negative—where the graph goes from upper left to lower right—the function is decreasing. In the graph below, for example, the graph is increasing over the intervals $(-\infty, -3)$ and $(0, 3)$, and decreasing over the intervals $(-3, 0)$ and $(3, \infty)$.

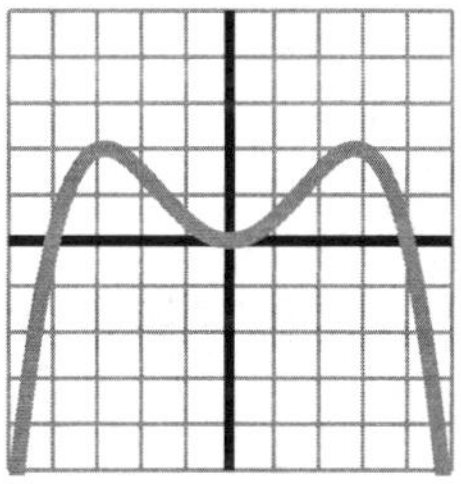

If the function is presented explicitly, such as $f(x) = x^2 - x^4$, we can graph the function and then find the appropriate intervals as above, but we can also, for instance, find the relative maxima and minima; an interval with a minimum on the left and a maximum on the right is increasing, and one with a maximum on the left and minimum on the right is decreasing.

Features that may be useful in sketching its graph

Sketching a graph without the aid of technology is facilitated by first determining some key properties of the function. If the function has horizontal asymptotes, we can use these as guidelines for the function's end behavior. If it doesn't have horizontal asymptotes, we can often determine the end behavior by other means. A function's vertical asymptotes likewise indicate its behavior near the corresponding values of x.

Also useful in determining the shape of a function are the relative maxima and minima, and the intervals over which the function is increasing or decreasing. The x and y intercepts provide a few points we know the function passes through. If the function has any symmetries or periodicity, these are also helpful in plotting it. Of course, if all else fails, we can also just pick a few x values at random, solve for $f(x)$ at those points, and plot those points to get a feel for the function's shape.

Periodic functions

A function is *periodic* if it comprises successive repetitions of an identical shape. That is, a periodic function is unchanged if displaced by some constant P. This constant—the length of the repeating portion—is called the function's *period*. Periodicity can be defined in a more precise, mathematical form: a function $f(x)$ is periodic if $f(x+P) = f(x)$ for all x. (If this is true for P, it's also true for all multiples of P, but the function's period is defined as the smallest possible value of P for which the relation holds.)

For instance, the function $f(x) = \sin(x)$ is periodic with a period of 2π, since $\sin(x+2\pi) = \sin(x)$ for all x. (It's also true that, for instance, $\sin(x+4\pi) = \sin(x)$, and $\sin(x+6\pi) = \sin(x)$, but there is no positive value of P *smaller* than 2π satisfying $\sin(x+P) = \sin(x)$.

Symmetrical functions

A function is symmetrical if it remains unchanged under certain kinds of transformations. While there are many kinds of transformations and many kinds of symmetries, for functions the type of transformation most often considered is reflection. Particularly important are reflections through the y-axis and reflections through the origin.

A function is symmetrical under a reflection through the y-axis if it stays the same when "flipped over" around the y-axis into its mirror image—mathematically, $f(x) = f(-x)$. Such a function is by definition *even*. A function is symmetrical under a reflection through the origin if it stays the same when each point is reflected to the opposite side of the origin—mathematically, $f(x) = -f(-x)$. Such a function is by definition *odd*.

A periodic function is also symmetrical, not necessarily under reflection, but under an appropriate *translation*. The function is unchanged when translated (moved) horizontally by a distance equal to the function's period.

Function's end behavior

A function's *end behavior* refers to its tendency at the extreme right and left sides of the graph—that is, what happens to the function as x tends toward $\pm\infty$. There are essentially three possibilities: either $f(x)$ increases without limit ($f(x)$ goes to ∞), $f(x)$ decreases without limit ($f(x)$ goes to $-\infty$), or $f(x)$ tends toward some finite value (a horizontal asymptote). The behavior may be different at the two sides: while $f(x) = x^2$ goes to ∞ on both sides, $g(x) = x^3$ goes to ∞ on the right side and to $-\infty$ on the left, and $h(x) = e^{-x}$ goes to ∞ on the left and tends toward the horizontal asymptote $y = 0$ on the right.

Determining the function's domain

Sometimes the domain is given explicitly; if given the earnings of a company between 1980 and 2000, then if you write this as a function of the company's earnings over time in years, the domain would run from 1980 to 2000.

When not given explicitly, the domain must be deduced by considering logically within what limits the function applies. Often this involves noting that the function and/or its argument must be non-negative. For instance, suppose a word problem says that a builder wishes to use 100 feet of fence to enclose three sides of a rectangle, and asks for the rectangle's length as a function of its width. Such a function could be written as $f(x) = 100 - 2x$, where x is the width and $f(x)$ the length. Clearly, the width cannot be negative, so we must have $x \geq 0$. Nor can the length be negative, so we must have $f(x) \geq 0$, i.e. $100 - 2x \geq 0$, so $x \leq 50$. Therefore, the domain is $0 \leq x \leq 50$.

<u>Determining the domain of a function from its graph</u>
The *domain* of a function is the set of x values for which the function is defined. This can be seen from the graph by observing for what values of x the function is drawn. Essentially, if a vertical line drawn through the graph at a particular value of x intercepts the graph of the function, then the function is defined at that point. If a vertical line intercepts the function no matter where it is drawn, then the domain contains all real numbers.

If this is not the case, then special considerations apply at the endpoints of intervals over which the function is defined. A function is never defined at a vertical asymptote. If $f(x)$ is finite at the endpoint of the interval, however, then the endpoint is drawn either as a filled circle to indicate that it is included in the function, or a hollow circle if not. Of the two graphs below, for instance, the left has a domain of $[-2, \infty)$, and the right of $(-2, \infty)$.

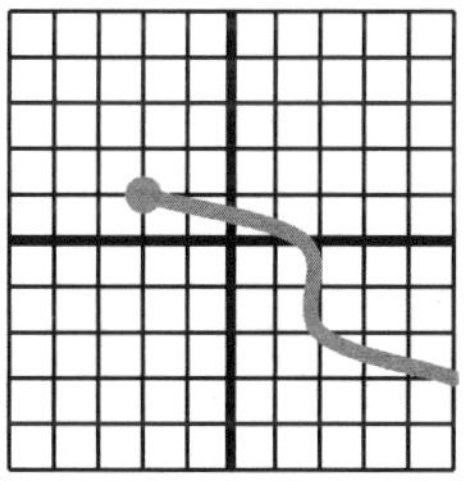
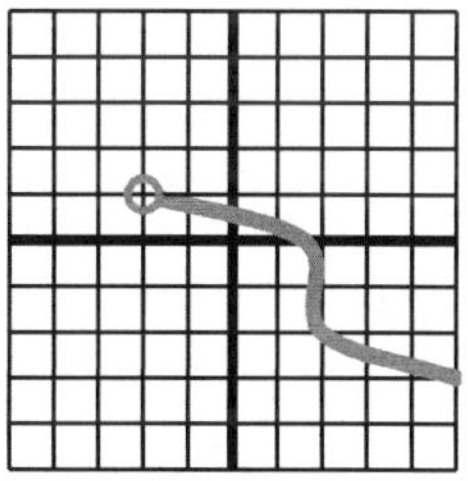

Example

Determine the domains of each of the functions shown below

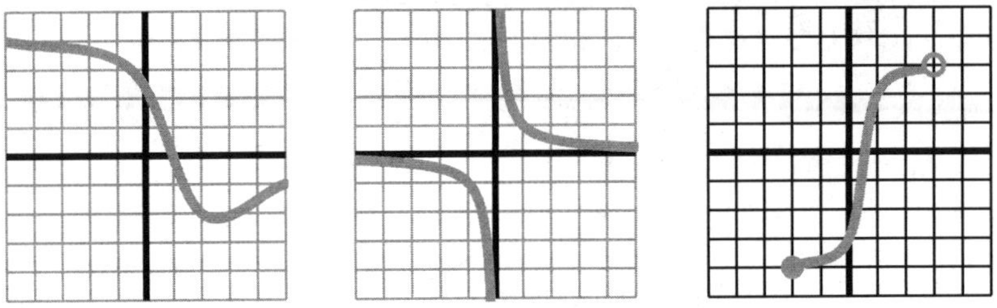

The domain of a function can be seen from its graph by observing what values along the x-axis have part of the function directly above or below them. Often the domain comprises all real numbers, $(-\infty, \infty)$. This is the case for the sample function shown on the left: the function extends unbroken from the left edge of the graph to its right edge; there is no x value for which it is not defined. For a function with a vertical asymptote, the x value corresponding to that asymptote is not part of the domain. The middle example function has a vertical asymptote at $x = 0$, so its domain is $(-\infty, 0) \cup (0, \infty)$.

Other functions are only defined over particular intervals. In this case, a solid circle at the end of the interval means that end point is included in the function's domain, and a hollow circle means it isn't. The example function on the right, then, is defined at $x = -2$ but not at $x = 3$; its domain is $[-2,3)$.

Example

Calculating a function's average rate of change over a specific interval when the function is given as a table

x	0	2	4	6	8	10	12	14	16
$f(x)$	-100	-54	-26	-10	0	10	26	54	100

The function's average rate of change over the interval $[x_1, x_2]$ can be calculated as $\frac{f(x_2)-f(x_1)}{x_2-x_1}$. For the sample table, for instance, if we want to determine the function's rate of change during the entire interval represented in the table, then $x_1 = 0$ and $x_2 = 16$. By reference to the table, $f(x_1) = f(0) = -100$, and $f(x_2) = f(16) = 100$. Thus, the function's rate of change is equal to $\frac{100-(-100)}{16-0} = \frac{200}{16} = 12.5$. If on the other hand we only want to find the rate of change between 0 and 4, then $x_1 = 0$, $x_2 = 4$, $f(x_1) = f(0) = -100$, and $f(x_2) = f(4) = -26$. The rate of change is then $\frac{-26-(-100)}{4-0} = \frac{74}{4} = 18.5$. If we are asked for the rate of change in the interval $[6, 10]$, then $x_1 = 6$, $x_2 = 10$, $f(x_1) = f(6) = -10$, and $f(x_2) = f(10) = 10$. The rate of change is then $\frac{10-(-10)}{10-6} = \frac{20}{4} = 5$.

Example

Calculating a function's average rate of change over a specific interval when the function is given algebraically, such as $f(x) = x^2 + 1$

The function's average rate of change over the interval $[x_1, x_2]$ can be calculated as $\frac{f(x_2)-f(x_1)}{x_2-x_1}$. For the sample function, for instance, suppose we're asked to find the function's average rate of change between 0 and 10. Then $x_1 = 0$ and $x_2 = 10$. To find $f(x_1)$ and $f(x_2)$, we simply evaluate the function at these two points: $f(x_1) = f(0) = 0^2 + 1 = 1$, and $f(x_2) = f(10) = 10^2 + 1 = 101$. The function's average rate of change in this interval is therefore $\frac{101-1}{10-0} = \frac{100}{10} = 10$.

If we're asked to find the function's average rate of change over the interval [-4, 2], then $x_1 = -4$, $x_2 = 2$, $f(x_1) = f(-4) = (-4)^2 + 1 = 17$, and $f(x_2) = f(2) = 2^2 + 1 = 5$. The average rate of change is therefore $\frac{5-17}{2-(-4)} = \frac{-12}{6} = -2$. If we're asked to find the average rate of change over the interval [-5, 5], then $x_1 = -5$, $x_2 = 5$, $f(x_1) = f(-5) = (-5)^2 + 1 = 26$, and $f(x_2) = f(5) = 5^2 + 1 = 26$. The average rate of change is therefore $\frac{26-26}{5-(-5)} = \frac{0}{10} = 0$.

Estimating a function's average rate of change over a specific interval

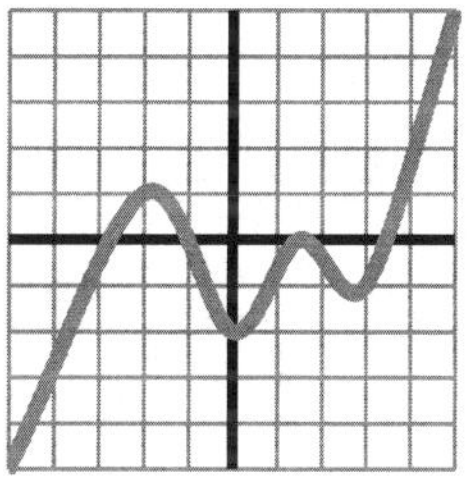

A function's average rate of change over an interval $[a, b]$ contained in the function's domain is the change in the value of $f(x)$ in that interval relative to the change in x. In other words, mathematically, it can be expressed as $\frac{f(b)-f(a)}{b-a}$. To estimate the average rate of change over an interval for a function given graphically, then, we have to estimate the coordinates of the endpoints of the desired interval and then put the appropriate values into that expression and carry out the calculation. For example, consider the sample function over the entire interval shown on the graph, [−5,5]. At the left end is passes through the point $(-5, -5)$, and at the right end (5,5); the average rate of change is therefore $\frac{f(5)-f(-5)}{5-(-5)} = \frac{5-(-5)}{10} = \frac{10}{10} = 1$. If we instead consider the interval [−2,0], the left endpoint is about $(-2,1)$ and the right about $(0, -2)$; the average rate of change over the interval $[-2, 0]$ is then $\frac{f(0)-f(-2)}{0-(-2)} = \frac{-2-1}{2} = \frac{-3}{2} = -\frac{3}{2}$. The average rate of change over the interval $[-5, 0]$ is $\frac{f(0)-f(-5)}{0-(-5)} = \frac{-2-(-5)}{5} = \frac{3}{5}$.

Graphing a linear function

Graphing a linear function given in slope-intercept form

There are several ways to graph a linear function. For a function given in slope-intercept form, like this example, it's usually easiest to use the slope and the y intercept. The slope-intercept form of a linear function takes the form $y = mx + b$, where m is the slope and b the y intercept. (If the x has no coefficient, the slope is 1.) For the sample function $f(x) = 3x + 1$ (i.e. $y = 3x + 1$), the slope is 3 and the y-intercept is 1. Therefore, we can plot the point (0,1), and then draw a line through that point with the appropriate slope: for every 1 unit to the right, the line goes 3 units up. If the slope is negative, then instead of up and to the right, it goes down and to the right (or, equivalently, up and to the left). A graph of the sample function therefore looks as follows:

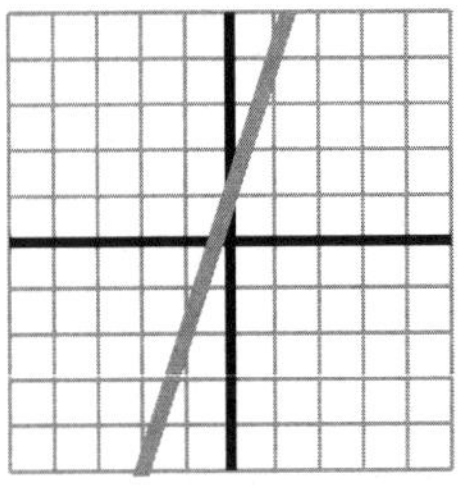

Graphing a linear function given in standard form

There are several ways to graph a linear function. If the function is given in standard form, $Ax + By = C$, like this example, then it's usually easiest to use the x and y intercepts. Consider the example equation, $2x - 3y = 12$. When $x = 0$, we get $-3y = 12$, so $y = -4$; this is the y intercept. When $y = 0$, we get $2x = 12$, so $x = 6$; this is the x intercept. We now know the points $(0, -4)$ and $(6, 0)$ are on the graph, so we can plot these two points and draw a straight line through them. A graph of the sample function therefore looks as follows:

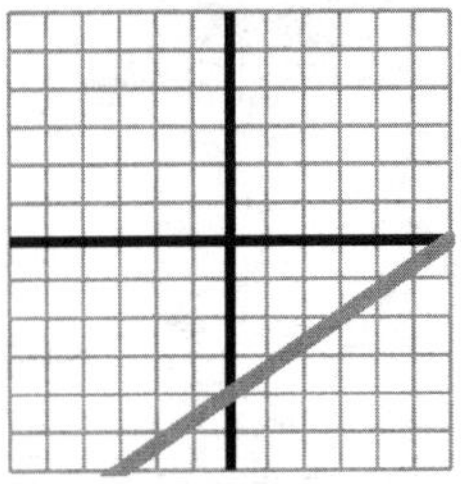

Graphing a quadratic function

If a quadratic function is in *vertex form*, $a(x - h)^2 + k$, we can see at a glance the coordinates of the vertex: they are simply (h, k). In this case, $h = 4$ and $k = 3$, so the vertex is at (4,3). We can use the coefficient a to see the direction of the opening: if $a > 0$, the graph opens upward, while if $a < 0$ it opens downward. Here $a = 2 > 0$, so this graph opens upward. After that, the only remaining feature to distinguish the quadratic function is its width. We can get a feel for this by simply plotting a few other points. The x intercepts are good choices, but some quadratic functions have no x intercepts, like this one: the equation $0 = 2(x - 4)^2 + 3$ has no real solutions.

However, we can still choose other values to plot: $f(3) = 2(3-4)^2 + 3 = 5$ and $f(5) = 2(5-4)^2 + 3 = 5$, so we can plot the points (3,5) and (5,5). Our final graph in this case looks like this:

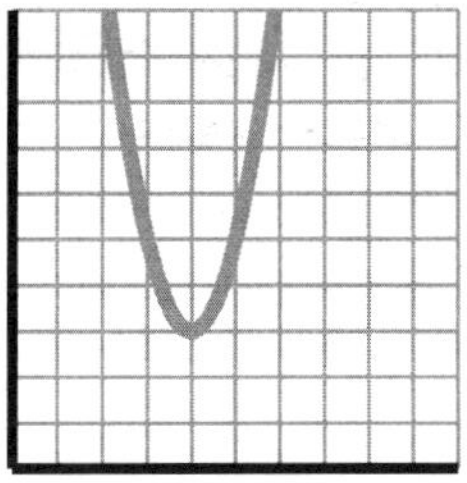

Piecewise-defined function

A *piecewise-defined function* is a function that has different definitions on two or more different intervals. The following, for instance, is one example of a piecewise-defined function:

$$f(x) = \begin{cases} x^2, & x < 0 \\ x, & 0 \le x \le 2 \\ (x-2)^2, & x > 2 \end{cases}$$

To graph this function, we'd simply graph each part separately in the appropriate domain. Our final graph would look like this:

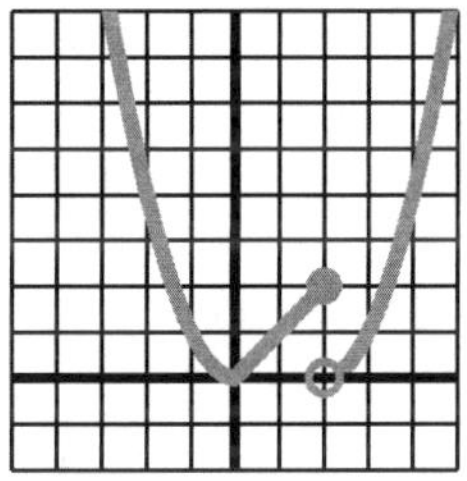

Note the filled and hollow dots at the discontinuity at $x = 2$. This is important to show which side of the graph that point corresponds to. Because $f(x) = x$ on the closed interval $0 \le x \le 2$, $f(2) = 2$. The point (2,2) is therefore marked with a filled circle, and the point (2,0), which is the endpoint of the rightmost $(x-2)^2$ part of the graph but *not actually part of the function*, is marked with a hollow dot to indicate this.

Graphing a square root function

All square root functions have a characteristic shape (essentially, the shape of half a quadratic function rotated ninety degrees). They vary, however, in their dimensions and displacement. If we rewrite the given function as $f(x) = -2\sqrt{4(x+1)}$, we can see by inspection how it differs from the "plain" square root function $f(x) = \sqrt{x}$: it is shifted one unit to the left (because of the $x + 1$), flipped over vertically (because of the sign of the coefficient -2), stretched vertically by a factor of 2, and squashed horizontally by a factor of 4.

Alternately, we can just plot a few points to get a feel for the graph's shape: for instance, $f(-1) = -2\sqrt{-4+4} = 0$, $f(0) = -2\sqrt{0+4} = -4$, and $f(1) = -2\sqrt{4+4} = -4\sqrt{2} \approx -5.66$. Our final graph looks like this:

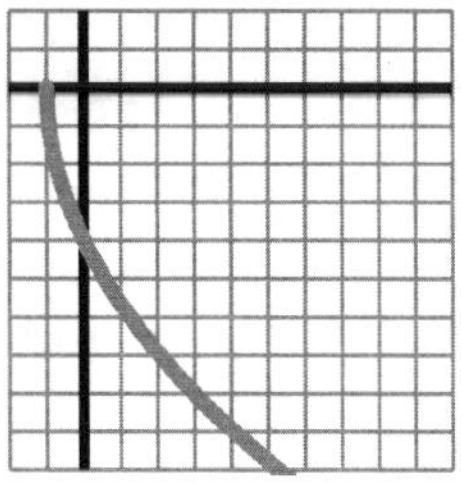

Graphing a cube root function

All cube root functions have a characteristic shape (somewhat like a stretched-out S—note that unlike that of the square root, the domain of the cube root function encompasses all real numbers). They vary, however, in their dimensions and displacement. In the case of the given function, $3\sqrt[3]{x} - 2$, we can see by inspection how it differs from the "plain" cube root function $f(x) = \sqrt[3]{x}$: it is stretched vertically by a factor of 3 (because of the coefficient 3), and shifted two units downward (because of the -2). We can just draw a cube root function modified accordingly. Alternately, we can just plot a few points to get a feel for the graph's shape: for instance, $f(0) = 3\sqrt[3]{0} - 2 = -2$, $f(1) = 3\sqrt[3]{1} - 2 = 1$, $f(8) = 3\sqrt[3]{8} - 2 = 4$, and so on. Our final graph looks like this:

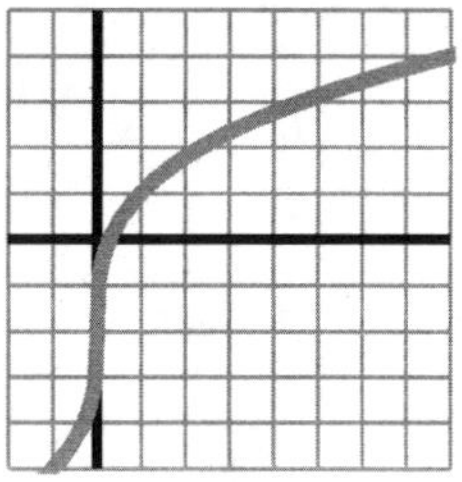

Graphing an absolute value function

The key to graphing an absolute value function is to recognize that its behavior depends on whether the expression within the absolute value sign is positive or negative, and to graph these parts separately. In the case of the function $f(x) = 2|x+1| - 3$, the point at which the behavior changes is when $x + 1 = 0$, i.e. when $x = -1$. When $x \geq -1$, $|x+1| = x+1$, and the function reduces to the linear function $f_+(x) = 2(x+1) - 3 = 2x - 1$. When $x \leq -1$, $|x+1| = -(x+1)$, and the function reduces to $f_-(x) = 2\big(-(x+1)\big) - 3 = -2x - 5$.

So we can graph $y = -2x - 5$ to the left of $x = -1$ and $y = 2x - 1$ to the right, yielding the following graph:

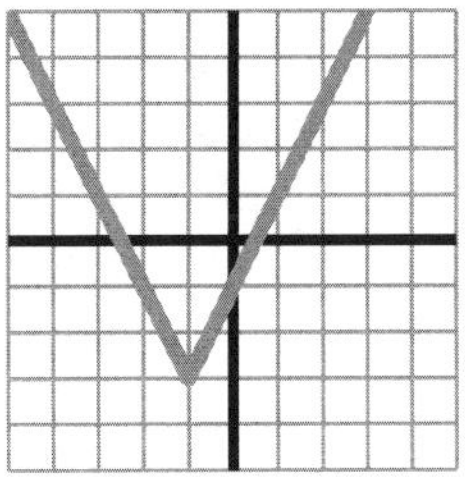

Graphing a step function

The double brackets indicate a step function. For a step function, all values inside the double brackets are rounded down to the nearest integer. The graph of the function $f_0(x) = [\![x]\!]$ appears as shown on the graph on the left below. In this case, we can see by inspection how the given $f(x) = 2\left[\!\left[\frac{1}{3}(x-1)\right]\!\right]$ differs from $f_0(x)$. The coefficient of 2 shows that it's stretched vertically by a factor of 2 (so there's a vertical distance of 2 units between successive "steps"). The coefficient of $\frac{1}{3}$ in front of the x shows that it's stretched horizontally by a factor of 3 (so each "step" is three units long), and the $x - 1$ shows that it's displaced one unit to the right. The final graph, then, is on the right below.

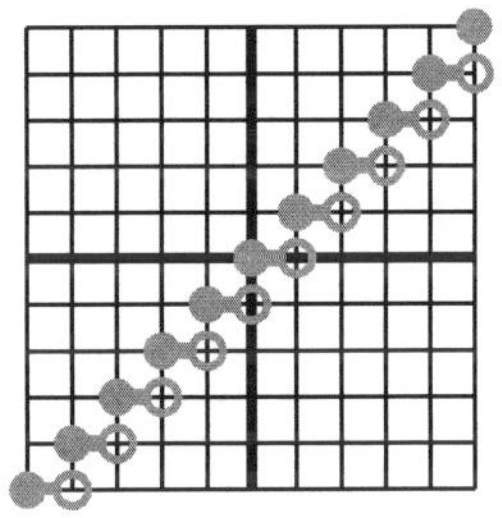 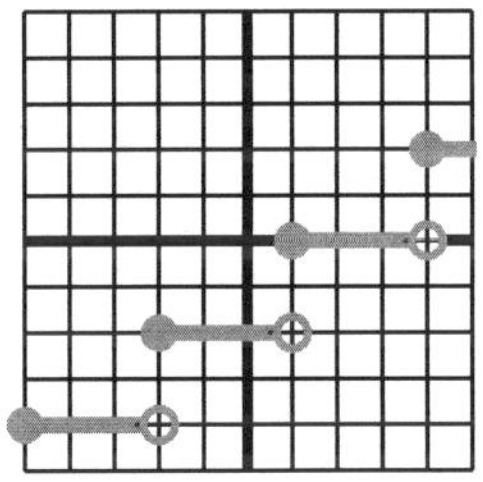

Determining the end behavior of a polynomial function

The "end behavior" of a function is what happens to the function when $|x|$ is very large. For a polynomial function, there are only two possibilities: either the function continues increasing indefinitely (it "goes to infinity"), or the function continues *de*creasing indefinitely (it "goes to negative infinity").

To see which is true, we need only look at the largest-order term of the polynomial, that is, the term with the largest exponent. To find the behavior of the function as $x \to \infty$ (at the right end), we just look at the coefficient of that term: if it's positive, the function goes to infinity; if it's negative, the function goes to negative infinity. The behavior of the function as $x \to -\infty$ (at the left end) is only slightly more complicated. If the exponent is even, the same rule holds as for the right end. If the exponent is odd, they're reversed: if the coefficient is positive, the function goes to negative infinity, and if it's negative, the function goes to positive infinity.

Graphing a polynomial

To graph a polynomial, like most other functions, there are a few key characteristics we can observe. First, we can observe the end behavior, which depends only on the largest order term. To find the y intercept, we evaluate the function at $x = 0$. To find the x intercepts, the points where the polynomial equals zero, is a little harder, but often we can factor the function and set each factor equal to zero. Depending on the polynomial, there may be other characteristics we can find, such as the local maxima and minima.

Example

Graphing a polynomial such as $\frac{1}{4}x^4 - \frac{9}{4}x^2$

For the given example, since the highest order term has an even order and a positive coefficient, the polynomial goes to positive infinity at both ends. The y intercept is at $\frac{1}{4}(0^4) - \frac{9}{4}(0^2) = 0$. We can factor the polynomial as $\frac{1}{4}x^4 - \frac{9}{4}x^2 = \frac{1}{4}x^2(x^2 - 9) = \frac{1}{4}x^2(x + 3)(x - 3)$, so it has x intercepts at $x = 0, 3$, and -3. Its graph looks like this:

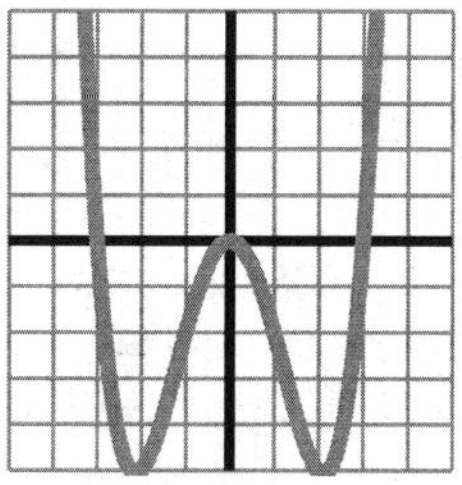

Example

Identifying the zeroes of a polynomial such as $x^3 - 3x^2 - 4x$ or $x^3 + 2x^2 - 2x - 4$

We can find the zeroes of a polynomial by factoring it. Cubics and higher polynomials can be difficult to factor, but there are special cases that can be readily factored. In the first sample polynomial here, for instance, $x^3 - 3x^2 - 4x$, it's clear that every term of the polynomial is divisible by x. We can therefore factor out the x to get $x(x^2 - 3x - 4)$. This now leaves a quadratic factor, which can be further factored to yield $x(x + 1)(x - 4)$. The zeroes of the polynomial are therefore 0, –1, and 4.

In the second polynomial, $x^3 + 2x^2 - 2x - 4$, there's no such divisor that goes into every term. If we compare the first two terms with the last two, however, we note that both *pairs* of terms are divisible by $x + 2$. We can then write the polynomial as $x^2(x + 2) - 2(x + 2)$, or $(x^2 - 2)(x + 2)$, and further factoring the first term, $(x + \sqrt{2})(x - \sqrt{2})(x + 2)$. The zeroes of this polynomial are –2 and $\pm\sqrt{2}$.

Finding the horizontal asymptote of a rational function

A rational function is a ratio of polynomials, and the horizontal asymptote is a horizontal line that the rational function tends toward as x approaches $\pm\infty$. To find the horizontal asymptote, first compare the orders of the numerator and the denominator—that is, the largest exponents appearing in them. If the numerator has a larger order than the denominator (as in $\frac{x^2-1}{x}$ or $\frac{x^4+x+2}{x^2-x}$), then the function has no horizontal asymptote. If the numerator has a smaller order the denominator (as in $\frac{x}{x^2-1}$ or $\frac{x^2+x+1}{x^5}$), then the function has a horizontal asymptote at $y = 0$.

If the orders of the numerator and denominator are equal (as in $\frac{2x^2+2}{x^2+2x+1}$ or $\frac{3x-4}{4x-3}$), then the horizontal asymptote is $y = y_0$, where y_0 is the ratio of the coefficients of the highest-order terms. For instance, the rational function $\frac{2x^2+2}{x^2+2x+1}$ has a horizontal asymptote at $y = \frac{2}{1} = 2$; $\frac{3x-4}{4x-3}$ has a horizontal asymptote at $y = \frac{3}{4}$.

Determining whether a rational function has a horizontal asymptote, a slant asymptote, or neither

To determine the end behavior of a rational function, it is only necessary to compare the orders of the numerator and the denominator—that is, the largest exponents appearing in them. If the order of the numerator is less than or equal to the order of the denominator, then the function has a horizontal asymptote. If the order of the numerator is one more than the order of the denominator, then the function has a slant asymptote. If the order of the numerator exceeds the order of the denominator by two or more, then the function has neither a horizontal nor a slant asymptote.

For instance, consider the rational function $\frac{3x^3+4x^2-2}{5x^7-5}$. The order of the numerator is 3; the order of the denominator is 7. Since $3 \leq 7$, this function has a horizontal asymptote (at $y = 0$). In the rational function $\frac{2x^4-x^2+3}{x^3-x}$, the order of the numerator is 4 and the order of the denominator is 3. Since $4 = 3 + 1$, this function has a slant asymptote.

Finding the vertical asymptotes of a rational function

Generally, a rational function has a vertical asymptote where the denominator is equal to zero, making the function undefined at that point (since the result of dividing by zero is undefined). For instance, consider the function $\frac{x^2+4x+4}{x^3-1}$. $1^3 - 1 = 0$, so this function has a vertical asymptote at $x = 1$.

There is one important exception to the above rule, however. If there is a common term to the numerator and denominator of the rational function, then it has vertical asymptotes only where the denominator is zero *after canceling common terms*. For instance, the function $f(x) = \frac{x^2-2x+1}{x^2+x-2}$ is undefined at $x = 1$, since $1^2 + 1 - 2 = 0$. However, $\frac{x^2-2x+1}{x^2+x-2} = \frac{(x-1)(x-1)}{(x-1)(x+2)}$; canceling the common term yields $\frac{x-1}{x+2}$. So $f(x)$ has a vertical asymptote at $x = -2$, but *not* at $x = 1$. (This doesn't change the fact that $f(x)$ is *undefined* at $x = 1$, but it can be undefined there without having a vertical asymptote.)

Determining the end behavior of a rational function

To determine the end behavior of a rational function, it's only necessary to consider the leading terms of the numerator and denominator—the terms with the largest exponents. If the leading term of the denominator has a larger exponent, then $f(x)$ goes to zero as x goes to $\pm\infty$. We can then take the ratio of these leading terms, which will result in a single term of which the end behavior should be clear.

Example

Determine the end behavior of a $f(x) = \frac{3x^2+2x-3}{6x^3-2x^2+1}$ *or* $g(x) = \frac{-7x^7+1}{2x^2-x+3}$

For example, consider the first example, $f(x) = \frac{3x^2+2x-3}{6x^3-2x^2+1}$. The leading term of the numerator is $3x^2$, and the leading term of the denominator is $6x^3$. The latter has a larger exponent, so this function goes to zero as x goes to $\pm\infty$. In the second function, $g(x) = \frac{-7x^7+1}{2x^2-x+3}$, the leading term of the numerator is $-7x^7$, and the leading term of the numerator is $2x^2$. The ratio is $\frac{-7x^7}{2x^2} = -\frac{7}{2}x^5$, which goes to ∞ as x goes to $-\infty$ and $-\infty$ as x goes to ∞.

Finding the zeroes of a rational function

A rational function $R(x)$ is a ratio of two polynomials, which we can write as $\frac{P(x)}{Q(x)}$. The rational function has a zero at any point $x = x_0$ for which the numerator $P(x_0)$ is equal to zero and the denominator $Q(x_0)$ is *not* equal to zero. If $Q(x_0) = 0$, then $R(x_0)$ is undefined.

Example

Find the zeroes of $f(x) = \frac{x^2+3x+2}{x^3+x+1}$ *or* $g(x) = \frac{x^4-x^2}{x^3-2x^2+1}$.

In the first sample function, $f(x) = \frac{x^2+3x+2}{x^3+x+1}$, the numerator $P(x) = x^2 + 3x + 2$ has zeroes at $x = -1$ and $x = -2$. Neither of these is a zero of the denominator $Q(x) = x^3 + x + 1$: $Q(-1) = -1$, and $Q(-2) = -9$. So both of these are zeroes of $f(x)$.

In the second sample function, $g(x) = \frac{x^4-x^2}{x^3-2x^2+1}$, the numerator $P(x) = x^4 - x^2 = x^2(x^2 - 1)$ has zeroes at $x = 0$ and $x = \pm 1$. Before concluding that these are zeroes of $g(x)$, though, we have to check whether they're zeroes of the denominator $Q(x) = x^3 - 2x^2 + 1$. $Q(-1) = -2$, $Q(0) = 1$, and $Q(1) = 0$. This means $x = 1$ is *not* a zero of $g(x)$, so the zeroes of$g(x)$ are $x = -1$ and $x = 0$.

Example

Given a trigonometric function of the form $f(x) = A\sin(Bx + C) + D$ (such as $f(x) = 2 + \frac{3}{2}\sin\left(\pi x + \frac{\pi}{2}\right)$), determine how you would find the function's period, amplitude, and midline and use them to graph the function

In the function $f(x) = A\sin(Bx + C) + D$, the amplitude is simply equal to A, and the midline is $y = D$. The period is only a little more complicated; the period is equal to $2\pi/_B$. For instance, consider the example function $f(x) = 2 + \frac{3}{2}\sin\left(\pi x + \frac{\pi}{2}\right)$. Here $A = \frac{3}{2}$, $B = \pi$, $C = \frac{\pi}{2}$, and $D = 2$, so the midline is at $y = 2$, the amplitude is $\frac{3}{2}$, and the period is $2\pi/_\pi = 2$.

To graph this equation, we center the sine wave on the midline and extend it to a height above and below the midline equal to the amplitude—so this graph would have a minimum value of $2 - \frac{3}{2} = \frac{1}{2}$ and a maximum of $2 + \frac{3}{2} = \frac{7}{2}$. The period (here equal to 2) is the distance between successive peaks or troughs. As for the last value, C, this is related to the *phase shift*, which is equal to $-\frac{C}{B}$ (in this case $-\frac{1}{2}$) and can be thought of as a starting point where $f(x) = D$ (the midline) and increasing. So the function above would be graphed as follows:

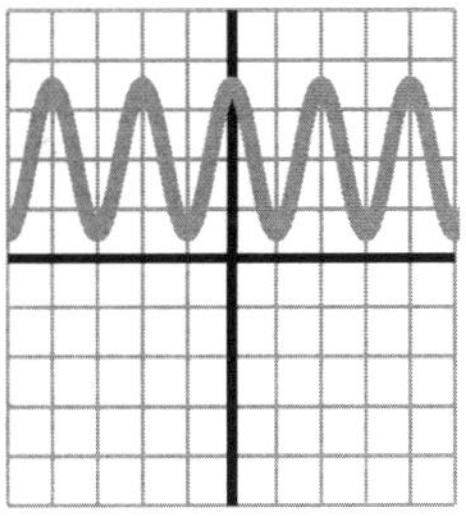

<u>Example</u>

Find the x and y intercepts, if any, of an exponential function of the form $f(x) = Ae^{bx} + C$

To find the y intercept, we just evaluate the function at $x = 0$. This gives $f(0) = Ae^{b\cdot 0} + C = Ae^0 + C = A(1) + C = A + C$. For instance, if $f(x) = \frac{1}{2}e^{3x} - 4$, $f(0) = \frac{1}{2}e^{3\cdot 0} - 4 = \frac{1}{2}(1) - 4 = -\frac{7}{2}$. This function has a y intercept at $(0, -\frac{7}{2})$.

To find the x intercept, we have to find a value of x for which $f(x) = 0$. Thus, $Ae^{bx} + C = 0$, so $Ae^{bx} = -C$, and $e^{bx} = -\frac{C}{A}$. From here, we have to take the logarithm of both sides, so $bx = \ln\left(-\frac{C}{A}\right)$, and $x = \frac{1}{b}\ln\left(-\frac{C}{A}\right)$. (Note that the logarithm of a negative number is undefined, so this has a solution only if $-\frac{C}{A} > 0$, i.e. $\frac{C}{A} < 0$. Otherwise, there is no x intercept.) If $f(x) = \frac{1}{2}e^{3x} - 4$, then to find the x intercept we use $\frac{1}{2}e^{3x} - 4 = 0$, so $\frac{1}{2}e^{3x} = 4$, $e^{3x} = 8$, and hence $3x = \ln 8$ and $x = \frac{\ln 8}{3} \approx 0.693$.

<u>Example</u>

Determine the end behavior of an exponential function such as $f(x) = 2e^{2x}$ or $g(x) = -e^{-x}$

The exponential function $y = e^x$ goes to zero as x goes to $-\infty$ and goes to ∞ as x goes to ∞. Multiplying either the exponent or the full exponential by a positive coefficient doesn't change this behavior, so this is the end behavior of $f(x) = 2e^{2x}$: it goes to zero on the left and goes to ∞ on the right.

Negative coefficients, on the other hand, do make a difference. A negative coefficient in the exponent interchanges the left and right side behavior, while a negative coefficient in front of the entire function makes the function go to negative infinity on the right instead of positive infinity. The function $g(x) = -e^{-x}$ has negative coefficients in *both* places, so it goes to $-\infty$ as x goes to $-\infty$, and goes to zero as x goes to ∞.

Example

Determine the end behavior of a logarithmic function such as $f(x) = \ln(-x)$ or $g(x) = -\frac{1}{2}\log_{10}(x + 2)$

Regardless of the base, the logarithmic function $y = \log(x)$ goes to ∞ as x goes to ∞. The domain of $y = \log(x)$ is $(0, \infty)$, so we don't need to consider what happens as x goes to $-\infty$, but as x approaches the vertical asymptote at $x = 0$, $\log(x)$ goes to $-\infty$.

The function $f(x) = \ln(-x)$ has a negative coefficient in front of the x, which means the function is reflected from left to right. This function, therefore, goes to ∞ as x goes to $-\infty$, and on the right $f(x)$ goes to $-\infty$ as x approaches the vertical asymptote at $x = 0$.

The $x + 2$ in the function $g(x) = -\frac{1}{2}\log_{10}(x + 2)$ means the function is shifted two units to the left—which means, in particular, that the vertical asymptote is shifted two units to the left. The negative coefficient in front of the function means the entire graph is flipped vertically. Therefore, $g(x)$ goes to $-\infty$ as x goes to ∞, and goes to ∞ as x approaches the vertical asymptote at $x = -2$.

Example

Given a tangent function such as $f(x) = 2\tan(3x - 4) + 1$, determine how you would find the function's period and midline and use them to graph the function

In the function $f(x) = A\tan(Bx + C) + D$, the midline is $y = D$, and the period is $^{\pi}/_{B}$. Larger values of A stretch the tangent vertically, but since the range of the tangent includes all real numbers, the tangent doesn't have an amplitude in the same sense as the sine and cosine do. If A is negative, the function is flipped vertically. C is related to the *phase shift*, ϕ, which is equal to $-C/B$, and is the amount by which the function is displaced horizontally.

For instance, consider the example function $f(x) = 2\tan(3x - 4) + 1$. Here $A = 2$, $B = 3$, $C = -4$, and $D = 1$, so the midline is at $y = 1$, the period is $\pi/3 \approx 1.05$, and the phase shift is $-(-4/3) = 4/3$. To graph this equation, we start at the point (ϕ, D)—in this case, $(4/3, 1)$—and we draw the tangent shape centered on this point, with a width equal to the period. We then repeat this shape to both sides at regular intervals. The result is as follows:

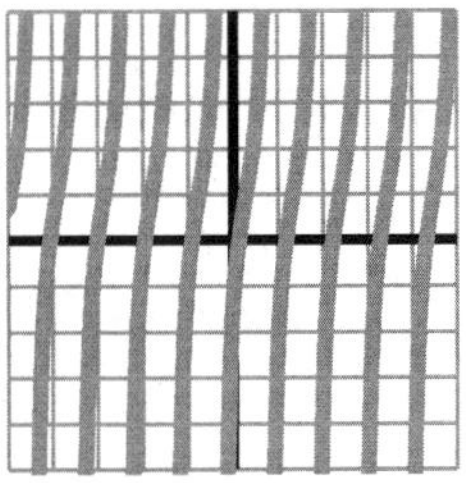

Completing the square of a quadratic function

A quadratic function in the "vertex form" $f(x) = a(x-h)^2 + k$ readily shows the coordinates of the vertex, (h, k). However, quadratic functions are often given in "standard form", $f(x) = ax^2 + bx + c$, which doesn't show the coordinates of the vertex directly. Completing the square is one way to convert the function from standard form to vertex form.

To complete the square, we first factor out the a from the first two terms: $f(x) = a\left(x^2 + \frac{b}{a}x\right) + c$. Now, we have to find a linear expression which, squared, yields a quadratic the first two terms of which match the terms in parentheses. This is probably most easily shown with an example: if $f(x) = 2x^2 + 8x + 6 = 2(x^2 + 4x) + 6$, then a suitable linear expression is $x + 2$, because $(x+2)^2 = x^2 + 4x + 4$. Therefore, we have $f(x) = 2(x+2)^2 + h$. All we have to do now is find a value for h that matches the original equation. Expanding, we have
$f(x) = 2x^2 + 8x + 8 + h$, so we require $8 + h = 6$, thus $h = -2$, and $f(x) = 2(x+2)^2 - 2$.

Factoring a quadratic functions

Factoring a quadratic function of the form $ax^2 + bx + c$ means finding two factors $(px + q)$ and $(rx + s)$ such that $(px+q)(rx+s) = ax^2 + bx + c$. Since $(px+q)(rx+s) = prx^2 + (ps + qr)x + qs$, we're looking specifically for p, q, r, s such that $pr = a$, $ps + qr = b$, and $qs = c$. The matter is much simpler if $a = 1$; then we need only find q and s such that $q + s = b$ and $qs = c$.

<u>Example</u>

Factor quadratic functions $f(x) = x^2 + x - 6$, $g(x) = x^2 - 16$, or $h(x) = 2x^2 + 3x - 7$

For instance, for the first example, $f(x) = x^2 + x - 6$, $b = 1$ and $c = -6$, so we need to find two numbers that add to 1 and multiply to -6. -2 and 3 qualify, so $f(x)$ can be factored to $(x-2)(x+3)$. When the quadratic function has the form $x^2 - c$, we don't even need to do that much work; we know the function's factors are $(x + \sqrt{c})$ and $(x - \sqrt{c})$. So $g(x) = x^2 - 16$ factorizes to

$\left(x+\sqrt{16}\right)\left(x-\sqrt{16}\right)=(x+4)(x-4)$.

Sometimes a quadratic function can't readily be factored by any of these systems. In this case, one can resort to the *quadratic formula*: $x=\frac{-b\pm\sqrt{b^2-4ac}}{2a}$. Note that when you use the quadratic formula to solve the equation $0=ax^2+bx+c$ what you are really solving is $0=x^2+\frac{b}{a}x+\frac{c}{a}$; therefore, when using the quadratic formula to find the factors of ax^2+bx+c you must include the coefficient a as one of your factors. In the case of our third sample function, $h(x)=2x^2+3x-7$, this gives us $x=\frac{-3\pm\sqrt{3^2-4(2)(-7)}}{2\cdot 2}=\frac{-3\pm\sqrt{65}}{4}=-\frac{3}{4}\pm\frac{\sqrt{65}}{4}$, and the factorization is $2\left(x+\frac{3}{4}-\frac{\sqrt{65}}{4}\right)\left(x+\frac{3}{4}+\frac{\sqrt{65}}{4}\right)$.

Finding the extreme values of quadratic functions

A quadratic function of the form ax^2+bx+c has only a single extreme value, at its vertex. Whether this is a maximum or a minimum depends on whether the graph opens upward or downward. This in turn depends on the sign of the coefficient a: if a is positive, then the graph opens upward and the vertex is a minimum, while if a is negative, the graph opens downward and the vertex is a maximum.

Example

Find the extreme values of a quadratic function such as $f(x)=x^2-6x+3$

In the case of the sample function $f(x)=x^2-6x+3$, the coefficient $a=1>0$, so the vertex is a minimum. To find the coordinates of the vertex, we can put the function in *vertex form*, $f(x)=a(x-h)^2+k$. We can do this by completing the square: $(x-3)^2=x^2-6x+9$, so $f(x)=(x-3)^2-6$. The vertex is at the coordinates (h,k)—in this case, $(3,-6)$.

Symmetry of a quadratic functions

Any quadratic function is symmetrical through a vertical line passing through the vertex. When the quadratic function is in vertex form, $f(x)=a(x-h)^2+k$, the coordinates of the vertex can be readily seen from the equation; they are simply (h,k). The axis of symmetry is then $x=h$; the function is unchanged when reflected through this line. If $h=0$, then the axis of symmetry is the line $x=0$, which is the y axis; the function is then symmetrical with respect to reflections through the y axis, which means it is an even function. Quadratic functions with $h\neq 0$ are neither even nor odd.

Example

Symmetry of a $f(x)=3(x-2)^2+5$

In the case of the sample function given here, $f(x)=3(x-2)^2+5$, $h=2$ and $k=5$. This function, therefore, is symmetrical with respect to reflections through the line $x=2$.

Example

Given an exponential equation such as $f(x) = 200 \cdot (1.2)^{3x}$, show how you can determine whether it represents exponential growth or exponential decay

If the coefficient of the exponent is positive (as it is in the sample function given), then the function represents exponential growth if the base of the exponent is greater than 1, and exponential decay if the exponent is less than 1. The sample function therefore represents exponential growth, since the base, 1.2, is greater than 1. An example of a function that would represent exponential decay would be $g(x) = 13 \cdot (0.9)^{2.5x}$, since here the base, 0.9, is less than one.

If the coefficient in the exponent is negative, then this rule of thumb is reversed. Thus, for instance,
$h(x) = 10 \cdot (1.1)^{-2x}$ represents exponential decay, since the coefficient (–2) is negative, and the base (1.1) is greater than 1; $k(x) = 7 \cdot (0.8)^{-1.5x}$ is exponential growth, since the exponent (–1.5) is negative, and the base (0.8) is less than 1.

Example

Finding the percent rate of change of an exponential function such as $f(t) = 70 \cdot (1.4)^{1.05t}$

The percent rate of change is the amount by which a function changes per unit of time, expressed as a percentage. This can be calculated as $\frac{f(t+1)-f(t)}{f(t)}$. For the sample function, $f(t) = 70 \cdot (1.4)^{1.05t}$, this calculation gives $\frac{70\cdot(1.4)^{1.05(t+1)}-70\cdot(1.4)^{1.05t}}{70\cdot(1.4)^{1.05t}} = \frac{70\cdot(1.4)^{1.05(t+1)}}{70\cdot(1.4)^{1.05t}} - 1 = (1.4)^{(1.05(t+1)-1.05t)} - 1 = 1.4^{1.05} - 1 \approx 0.424 = 42.4\%$ per unit of time. Note that the time, t, cancels from the calculation, and therefore the rate of change does not depend on t. This is a characteristic of exponential functions; they have a constant percent rate of change.

The answer we obtained for the sample function can be generalized: in general, the percent rate of change of an exponential function $f(t) = a \cdot b^{ct}$ is equal to $b^c - 1$. Note that if $b^c < 1$, then the percent rate of change is negative. For instance, consider $g(t) = 2 \cdot \left(\frac{1}{2}\right)^t$. The percent rate of change is $\left(\frac{1}{2}\right)^1 - 1 = -\frac{1}{2} = -50\%$. This makes sense, because if $b^c < 1$ then the function represents exponential decay; the function is decreasing, so the percent rate of change is indeed negative.

Important properties of exponents

One important property of exponents is the property that $x^a x^b = x^{a+b}$. This could come into play in a problem in which we have a product of two exponentials, and it simplifies the problem to combine them into one. Conversely, we can use it to simplify an expression with a sum in the exponent, such as $3 \cdot 2^{x+4}$; this simplifies to $3 \cdot 2^x 2^4 = 3 \cdot 2^x \cdot 16 = 48 \cdot 2^x$.

Often given separately is the property $x^a/_{x^b} = x^{a-b}$, but this is really a special case of the previous property where $b < 0$, and applies under similar circumstances.

Another important property of exponents is the property that $(x^a)^b = x^{ab}$. This can be used to simplify expressions in which an exponential is raised to a power, or to simplify an expression with a product in the exponent into a single exponent: for example, $3^{3x} = (3^3)^x = 27^x$.

Determining larger maximum two functions

One algebraically and one graphically

One way to compare the features of two functions represented in different ways is to convert them both to the same manner of representation. If one function is represented algebraically and the other graphically, we can graph the first function on the same axis as the second, enabling us to compare their maxima visually by just observing which one extends farther in the positive *y* direction.

It's also possible to compare their maxima without converting them to the same representation, by simply finding the maximum of each function and comparing them. If the function expressed algebraically is one for which we can find the maximum analytically (for example, a quadratic function), we can compare that value directly with the maximum estimated from the graphed function by observing the *y* coordinate of its highest peak.

One algebraically and one a verbal description

When given two functions in different formats, one way to compare their properties is to convert both functions to the same format. If one of the functions is given in the form of a verbal description, we can write an algebraic expression to represent the described relationship. For instance, if we're told that a function represents the area of a rectangular field for which the total distance around three sides is 40 meters (implying that, if we write *l* as the length and *w* as the width, $l + 2w = 40$), we can write the relationship between the area and the width algebraically as $A = l \cdot w = (40 - 2w)w$. Or, using the more familiar *f* and x, $f(x) = (40 - 2x)x = -2x^2 + 40x$. Completing the square gives us $f(x) = -2(x - 10)^2 + 200$. This function has a maximum when $x = 10$, at which point $f(x) = 200$. We can likewise find the maximum of the other function given algebraically, and we can now compare the maxima directly.

Determining the larger *y* intercept

When given two functions in different formats, one way to compare their properties is to convert both functions to the same format. If one of the functions is given as a table, we can graph that function and then compare it to the graph directly. Conversely, we could determine the values of the graphed function at the *x* values given in the table and therefore express both functions in tabular format.

It's also sometimes possible to compare properties of the functions even without converting them to the same format, and in the case of finding the *y* intercept this isn't difficult (assuming that the *y* intercept of the second function is actually given in the table). We can find the *y* intercept of the graphed function by seeing where the graph crosses the *y*-axis, find the y intercept of the table function by seeing what value of the function corresponds to an x value of 0, and compare these values directly.

Building Functions

Example

Given a description of a relationship, such as a statement that the population of a particular area is 2000 in the year 1980 and doubles every 10 years thereafter, determine how you can write an explicit expression to describe that relationship

The first step in writing an expression to describe a relationship is to pinpoint the variables involved in the expression. In the sample case, the statement describes how the population changes over time, we will write the population P as a function of time, t.

Next, we look for telltale signs that tell us what kind of function we are dealing with. Here, the population increases by a fixed proportion over a specific unit of time, a hallmark of an exponential relationship. Therefore, the expression will take the form $P(t) = P_0A^{ct}$. More specifically, since we're given the population at 1980 as a starting point, we can simplify matters by setting the exponent proportional to the number of years since 1980: $P(t) = P_{1980}A^{c(t-1980)}$.

Finally, we use the given data to put in numbers. When $t = 1980$, $P(t) = 2000$, so $P_{1980} = 2000$. Incorporating the other information gives us $P(t) = 2000 \cdot 2^{(t-1980)/10}$.

Determining kinds of relationships that lend themselves to being written as recursively defined functions

A recursively defined function is generally a *sequence*; that is, its domain consists of a subset of the integers (usually, though not always, the positive integers). Furthermore, the value of the function for a given value of x must be defined in terms of its value for smaller values of x. Often this means $f(x)$ is defined in terms of $f(x-1)$, though it may also be defined in terms of even smaller values. Finally, we need to have $f(x_0)$ explicitly defined for the smallest value or values of x_0 to give us a starting point.

For example, consider the following relationship: A pile of stones starts with three stones, and then every day its size is doubled and then one stone is removed. On day one, then, the size of the pile is $f(1) = 3$. On day x thereafter, we have the relationship $f(x) = 2f(x-1) - 1$. This is a valid recursive definition.

Example

Suppose $f(x) = x^2 - 1$ and $g(x) = x - 1$. How would you find each of the following

$(f+g)(x)$ $(f-g)(x)$ $(f \cdot g)(x)$
$(f/g)(x)$

To combine functions using arithmetic operations, we need only apply the appropriate arithmetic operation to the function's expression. So $(f+g)(x) = f(x) + g(x) = (x^2 - 1) + (x - 1) = x^2 + x - 2$. $(f - g)(x) = (x^2 - 1) - (x - 1) = x^2 - x$. $(f \cdot g)(x) = (x^2 - 1)(x - 1) = x^3 - x^2 - x + 1$.

Finally, $(f/g)(x) = (x^2 - 1)/(x - 1)$. Here we have to be a little more careful. $(x^2 - 1) = (x + 1)(x - 1)$, so it's tempting to cancel out the $(x - 1)$ terms and state simply that $(f/g)(x) = \frac{(x+1)(x-1)}{x-1} = x + 1$. However, this doesn't hold when $x = 1$: $(f/g)(1) = (1^2 - 1)/(1 - 1) = 0/0$, which is undefined, and *not* equal to $1 + 1$. It's more accurate, therefore, to state that $(f/g)(x) = x + 1$ when $x \neq 1$, but is undefined when $x = 1$.

Example

Determine under what circumstances a relationship might be modeled by an arithmetic operation of two functions

A relationship might be modeled by an arithmetic operation of two functions if it represents a sum, product, difference, or quotient of two processes each modeled by a different function. For example, consider the following: A man has \$1000 in one bank account that generates 4% interest, compounded annually, and \$2000 in another bank account that generates 3% annual interest, continually compounded. We want to find the total amount of money he has in the bank after *t* years.

Applying the compound interest formula, $A = P\left(1 + \frac{r}{n}\right)^{nt}$, we find that the amount of money he has in the first account is equal to $f(t) = 1000(1.04)^t$. For continually compounded interest, the formula is $A = Pe^{rt}$, so the amount he has in the second account is equal to $g(t) = 2000e^{0.03t}$. The *total* amount of money he has in the bank is then simply the arithmetic sum of these two: $h(t) = f(t) + g(t) = 1000(1.04)^t + 2000e^{0.03t}$.

Example

Given two functions $f(x)$ and $g(x)$, show how you would determine the domain of each of the following

$(f+g)(x)$ $(f-g)(x)$ $(f \cdot g)(x)$ $(f/g)(x)$

In order for an arithmetic operation of two functions to be defined for a given *x*, each of the two functions themselves must also be defined at that *x*. In other words, in order to be in the domain of $(f+g)(x)$, $(f-g)(x)$, $(f \cdot g)(x)$, or $(f/g)(x)$, a particular number must be in the domain of both $f(x)$ and $g(x)$. For instance, if $f(x) = \ln(x+1)$ and $g(x) = \sqrt{2-x}$, since the domain of $f(x)$ is $(-1, \infty)$ and the domain of $g(x)$ is $(-\infty, 2]$, the domain of $(f+g)(x)$ is the intersection of those two domains, namely $(-1, 2]$.

For $(f/g)(x)$, we also have to take into account the fact that we can't divide by zero. Therefore, any values *x* for which $g(x) = 0$ are excluded from the domain of $(f/g)(x)$. For the sample $f(x)$ and $g(x)$ given above, for instance, the domain of $(f/g)(x)$ would be not $(-1,2]$ but $(-1,2)$, since $g(2) = 0$.

Function composition

Function composition is a process in which the "output" of one function is used as the "input" of another. The composition of two functions $f(x)$ and $g(x)$ can be written as $(f \circ g)(x)$ or as $f(g(x))$.

How to evaluate the composition of two functions

This means we find the value of $f(x')$ at $x' = g(x)$. In other words, to evaluate the function composition $(f \circ g)(x)$ at $x = x_0$, we first find $y_0 = g(x_0)$ and then find $f(y_0)$, which is our final answer. For example, if $f(x) = x^2 + 1$ and $g(x) = x - 1$, then to find $(f \circ g)(3)$, we first find $g(3) = 2$, and then find $f(2) = 5$. So $(f \circ g)(3) = 5$. We can also rewrite the composition of two functions explicitly as a single function by substituting the expression for one function into the other. For instance, for the above functions, $(f \circ g)(x) = f(x - 1) = (x - 1)^2 + 1 = x^2 - 2x + 2$.

Example

Suppose $f(x) = x^2 - x$ and $g(x) = \frac{x}{x+1}$. How you would find each of the following

$(f \circ g)(3)$ $\quad$ $g(f(-1))$ $\quad$ $(f \circ f)(2)$ $\quad$ $f\left(g(f(1))\right)$

All of these expressions indicate function composition, though they use different notations: the notation $(f \circ g)(x)$, for instance, is equivalent to $f(g(x))$. To evaluate a function composition, we can first evaluate the "inner" function expression, and then put that in as the input to the "outer" function. For instance, to evaluate $(f \circ g)(3)$, we first evaluate $g(3) = \frac{3}{3+1} = \frac{3}{4}$, and then $f(g(3)) = f\left(\frac{3}{4}\right) = \left(\frac{3}{4}\right)^2 - \frac{3}{4} = \frac{9}{16} - \frac{12}{16} = -3/16$. Similarly, $g(f(-1)) = g((-1)^2 - (-1)) = g(1 + 1) = g(2) = \frac{2}{2+1} = 2/3$, and $f(f(2)) = f(2^2 - 2) = f(2) = 2^2 - 2 = 2$.

The last expression here can be evaluated similarly; it only takes an extra step: $f\left(g(f(1))\right) = f(g(1^2 - 1)) = f(g(0)) = f\left(\frac{0}{0+1}\right) = f(0) = 0^2 - 0 = 0$. In principle, we could apply the same procedure to a composition of any number of functions, such as $(f \circ g \circ g \circ f \circ g)(4)$.

Example

Suppose $f(x) = x^2 + 1$ and $g(x) = x - 1$. How would you write each of the following as a single function?

$f(g(x))$ $\quad$ $(g \circ f)(x)$ $\quad$ $(g \circ g)(x)$ $\quad$ $g\left(f(g(x))\right)$

All of these expressions indicate function composition, though they use different notations: the notation $(g \circ f)(x)$, for instance, is equivalent to $g(f(x))$. To rewrite a function composition as a single expression, we substitute the expression for one function in for x in the expression for the other. To find $f(g(x))$, for instance, we replace each x in the expression for $f(x)$—that is, $x^2 + 1$—with the expression for $g(x)$ —$(x - 1)$. This gives us $f(g(x)) = f(x - 1) = (x - 1)^2 + 1 = x^2 - 2x + 1 + 1 = x^2 - 2x + 2$. Similarly, $(g \circ f)(x) = g(f(x)) = (x^2 + 1) - 1 = x^2$, and $(g \circ g)(x) = g(g(x)) = (x - 1) - 1 = x - 2$.

The final expression, $g\left(f(g(x))\right)$, looks complex but requires the same procedure, just done in two steps. We've already found $f(g(x)) = x^2 - 2x + 2$. To find $g\left(f(g(x))\right)$, then, we just substitute this into the expression for $g(x)$: $g\left(f(g(x))\right) = g(x^2 - 2x + 2) = (x^2 - 2x + 2) - 1 = x^2 - 2x + 1$.

Relationships modeled by a composition of two functions

A relationship might be modeled by a composition of two functions if it represents a process that depends on the output of another process. For example, consider the following: The population of a town increases exponentially according to the formula $P(t) = 1500e^{0.2t}$, where t is the time in years from a fixed starting year. On average, each person in the town eats 800 kilograms of food per year. We want to find the total amount of food eaten by the entire population of the town in year t.

The relationship between the total amount of food eaten in a year and the population of the town is straightforward: $f(x) = 800x$, where x equals the population. However, x is itself a function: specifically, it's $P(t)$, as given above. Therefore, the total amount of food, as a function of t, is $f(P(t)) = f(1500e^{0.2t}) = 800 \cdot 1500e^{0.2t} = 1200000e^{0.2t}$.

<u>Example</u>

Given two functions $f(x)$ and $g(x)$, show how you would determine the domain and range of $(f \circ g)(x)$

The notation $(f \circ g)(x)$ indicates function composition; this can also be written as $f(g(x))$. $(f \circ g)(x)$ can be evaluated at a point $x = x_0$ by first finding $g(x_0)$ and then putting that as the "input" for $f(x)$. In order for a value x_0 to be in the domain of $(f \circ g)(x)$, then, it's necessary first that x_0 be in the domain of $g(x)$ and second that $g(x_0)$ be in the domain of $f(x)$. For instance, if $f(x) = \sqrt{x}$ and $g(x) = x - 2$, then $x = 1$ is not in the domain of $(f \circ g)(x)$, even though it *is* in the domain of $f(x)$ and $g(x)$, since $g(1) = -1$ is not in the domain of $f(x)$.

Similarly, for a value $y = y_0$ to be in the range of $(f \circ g)(x)$, it's necessary not only that y_0 is in the range of $f(x)$, but that there is at least one value y' in the range of $g(x)$ such that $f(y') = y_0$.

Example

Given an arithmetic sequence expressed recursively, such as $a_1 = 2$, $a_n = a_{n-1} + 3$, explain how to write this sequence in an explicit (nonrecursive) form

An arithmetic sequence is one with a constant difference between consecutive terms: each term is equal to the preceding term plus (or minus) some constant number. An arithmetic sequence can be uniquely characterized by two specific numbers: the first element of the sequence a_1, and the sequence's common difference *d*. The latter is the difference between two consecutive terms of the sequence; *d* is positive if the sequence is increasing and negative if the sequence is decreasing.

An arithmetic sequence can be defined recursively by specifying a_1 and then giving the relationship between consecutive terms, $a_n = a_{n-1} + d$. It can also be defined explicitly with the expression $a_n = a_1 + d(n-1)$ (or, equivalently, $a_n = (a_1 - d) + dn$).

Here, we have a recursive definition; by inspecting it, we see that $a_1 = 2$ and $d = 3$. We can simply put those values into the explicit expression to get $a_n = 2 + 3(n-1)$ (or, equivalently, $a_n = -1 + 3n$).

Example

Given a geometric sequence expressed recursively, such as $a_1 = 3$, $a_n = 2a_{n-1}$, determine how to write this sequence in an explicit (nonrecursive) form

A geometric sequence is one with a constant ratio between consecutive terms: each term is equal to the preceding term multiplied (or divided) by some constant number. A geometric sequence can be uniquely characterized by two specific numbers: the first element of the sequence a_1, and the sequence's common ratio *r*. The latter is the ratio between two consecutive terms of the sequence; *r* is greater than one if the sequence is increasing and less than one if the sequence is decreasing. (If *r* is negative, the terms of the sequence alternate between positive and negative.)

A geometric sequence can be defined recursively by specifying a_1 and then giving the relationship between consecutive terms, $a_n = r \cdot a_{n-1}$. It can also be defined explicitly with the expression $a_n = a_1 \cdot r^{n-1}$ (or, equivalently, $a_n = (a_1/r) \cdot r^n$).

Here, we have a recursive definition; by inspecting it, we see that $a_1 = 3$ and $r = 2$. We can simply put those values into the explicit expression to get $a_n = 3 \cdot 2^{n-1}$ (or, equivalently, $a_n = \frac{3}{2} \cdot 2^n$).

Example

Given an arithmetic sequence defined explicitly, such as $a_n = 3 + 4n$, determine how you can write this sequence in a recursive form

An arithmetic sequence is a sequence in which each term differs from the previous amount by a fixed amount. An arithmetic sequence can be uniquely specified by this fixed difference, *d*, and the first term, a_1. The sequence can be expressed either explicitly, in the form $a_n = a_1 + d(n-1)$, or recursively, in the form $a_n = a_{n-1} + d$ (after specifying the first term).

In this case, being given the sequence in explicit form, we can find a_1 and d by inspection: $a_n = 3 + 4n = 3 + 4(1 + n - 1) = 3 + 4 + 4(n-1) = 7 + 4(n - 1)$. So, comparing this to the general equation $a_n = a_1 + d(n-1)$, we find $a_1 = 7$ and $d = 4$. We can therefore write the sequence recursively as follows: $a_1 = 7, a_n = a_{n-1} + 4$.

Example

Given a geometric sequence defined explicitly, such as $a_n = 3\left(\frac{2}{3}\right)^n$,determine how you can write this sequence in a recursive form

A geometric sequence is a sequence in which each term differs from the previous amount by a fixed ratio. A geometric sequence can be uniquely specified by this fixed ratio, *r*, and the first term, a_1. The sequence can be expressed either explicitly, in the form $a_n = a_1 r^{n-1}$, or recursively, in the form $a_n = r \cdot a_{n-1}$ (after specifying the first term).

In this case, being given the sequence in explicit form, we can find a_1 and r by inspection: $a_n = 3\left(\frac{2}{3}\right)^n = 3\left(\frac{2}{3}\right)^{1+n-1} = 3\left(\frac{2}{3}\right)\left(\frac{2}{3}\right)^{n-1} = 2\left(\frac{2}{3}\right)^{n-1}$. So, comparing this to the general equation $a_n = a_1 r^{n-1}$, we find $a_1 = 2$ and r=$\frac{2}{3}$. We can therefore write the sequence recursively as follows: $a_1 = 2$, $a_n = \frac{2}{3} a_{n-1}$.

Situations modeled by arithmetic sequences

An arithmetic sequence is a good model for any situation that involves a quantity that increases at equal intervals by a constant difference. That is, if the quantity is only defined relative to the positive integers (or technically at any other discrete, evenly spaced intervals), and the difference between the quantity corresponding to any two consecutive integers is the same, then it can be modeled by an arithmetic sequence.

Consider, for instance, the following situation: a large jar initially contains five marbles, and every day three more marbles are added to it. This fits the criteria described above: the quantity is defined relative to the positive integers (number of days), and the difference between the quantity corresponding to consecutive integers (the number of marbles on consecutive days) is constant (three). We can model this situation by the arithmetic sequence
$f(n) = 5 + 3(n - 1)$.

Situations modeled by geometric sequences

A geometric sequence is a good model for any situation that involves a quantity that increases at fixed intervals by a fixed ratio. That is, if the quantity is only defined relative to the positive integers (or technically at any other discrete, evenly spaced intervals), and the ratio of the quantity corresponding to any two consecutive integers is the same, then it can be modeled by a geometric sequence.

Consider, for instance, the following situation: the score for completing level one of a video game is 100, and the score for completing each level afterward is double the score for the previous level. This fits the criteria described above: the quantity is defined relative to the positive integers (levels), and the ratio between the quantity corresponding to consecutive integers (the scores for completing two consecutive levels) is constant (two). We can model this situation by the geometric sequence $f(n) = 100 \cdot 2^{n-1}$.

Example

Graphing of a function $f(x)$ compares with the graph of $f(x) + k$ for some constant k. What about the graph of $f(x + k)$

If we replace $f(x)$ by $(x) + k$, this means the y coordinate of each point on the graph increases by k. This means the graph will be displaced vertically by a value of k: for instance, the graph of $y = x^2 + 1$ will be one unit higher than the graph of $y = x^2$. If k is negative, then the graph will be lowered.

Replacing $f(x)$ by $f(x + k)$ effectively means the x coordinate of each point on the graph *de*creases by k. (Consider that $f\big((x - k) + k\big) = f(x)$, so evaluating $f(x)$ at $x = x_0$ yields the same value as evaluating $f(x + k)$ at $x = x_0 - k$.) This means the graph will be displaced horizontally to the left by a value of k: for instance, the graph of $y = (x + 1)^2$ will be one unit to the left of the graph of $y = x^2$. If k is negative, the graph will be displaced to the right.

Example

Graphing of a function $f(x)$ compares with the graph of $kf(x)$ for some constant k. What about the graph of $f(kx)$

If we replace $f(x)$ by $kf(x)$, this means the y coordinate of each point on the graph is multiplied k. This means the graph will be stretched vertically by a factor of k: for instance, the graph of $y = 2x^2$ will be stretched by a factor of 2 in the vertical direction relative to the graph of $y = x^2$. If k is less than one, then the graph will be compressed; if k is negative, it will be inverted vertically (in addition to the stretch or compression).

Replacing $f(x)$ by $f(kx)$ effectively means the x coordinate of each point on the graph is *divided* by a factor of k. This means the graph will be compressed horizontally by a factor of k (or, if $k < 1$, stretched horizontally by a factor of $1/k$): for instance, the graph of $y = (2x)^2$ will be compressed horizontally by a factor of two relative to the graph of $y = x^2$. If k is negative, the graph will be inverted horizontally (in addition to the stretch or compression).

Determining whether a graph represents an odd or even function

An *odd function* is one for which $f(-x) = -f(x)$. This means that when the x coordinate is inverted, so is the y coordinate. The left half of the graph (to the left of the y-axis) will therefore be an inverted version of the right half (to the right of the y-axis). Rotating the graph by 180° inverts both the x and the y coordinates, so an odd function is symmetrical with respect to 180° rotations around the origin.

An *even function* is one for which $f(-x) = f(x)$. This means that when the x coordinate is inverted, the y coordinate does not change. The left half of the graph is therefore a mirror image of the right half. Reflecting the graph through the y-axis inverts the x coordinate without changing the y coordinate, so an even function is symmetrical with respect to reflections through the y-axis.

A graph that exhibits neither symmetry is neither even nor odd.

Determining whether a function is even or odd

A function $f(x)$ is *even* if it is unchanged when x is replaced by $-x$. It is *odd* if the sign of the function is changed when x is replaced by $-x$. In other words, for an even function, $f(-x) = f(x)$; for an odd function, $f(-x) = -f(x)$. We can therefore check whether a function is even or odd by evaluating $f(-x)$ and checking whether (perhaps after some suitable algebraic manipulation) it is equal to $f(x)$ or $-f(x)$.

For instance, consider the function $f(x) = x^2 + 1$. $f(-x) = (-x)^2 + 1 = x^2 + 1 = f(x)$. $f(-x) = f(x)$, so this function is even. Now consider $g(x) = x^3 + \frac{1}{x}$. $g(-x) = (-x)^3 + \frac{1}{-x} = -x^3 - \frac{1}{x} = -\left(x^3 + \frac{1}{x}\right) = -g(x)$. $g(-x) = -g(x)$, so this function is odd. Finally, consider $h(x) = x - 1$. $h(-x) = -x - 1 = -(x + 1)$. This is equal to neither $h(x)$ nor $-h(x)$, so this function is neither even nor odd.

<u>Example</u>

Given an expression for a function such as $f(x) = x^3 + 1$ or $g(x) = \frac{x}{x-1}$, determine how to find the function's inverse

One algorithm for finding the inverse of the function is as follows: Solve the equation of the function for x—that is, manipulate the equation to get x by itself on one side of the equation. This equation now shows the inverse function of $f(x)$; to write it explicitly as an inverse, change the x to $f^{-1}(x)$ and change each instance of $f(x)$ on the other side of the equation to x.

For instance, we can rewrite our first equation, $f(x) = x^3 + 1$, as $x^3 = f(x) - 1$, so $x = \sqrt[3]{f(x) - 1}$. Writing this explicitly as an inverse function, we can change the x to $f^{-1}(x)$ and the $f(x)$ to x to get $f^{-1}(x) = \sqrt[3]{x - 1}$. Our second example, $g(x) = \frac{x}{x-1}$, takes a little more work: multiplying both sides by $x - 1$ gives $(x - 1)g(x) = x$, which we can rearrange to $xg(x) - x = g(x)$, and finally to $x = \frac{g(x)}{g(x)-1}$. Replacing the x by $g^{-1}(x)$ and the $g(x)$ by x yields $g^{-1}(x) = \frac{x}{x-1}$: this function is its own inverse.

Example

Given a function such as $f(x) = 3x^3 - 4$, determine how you could solve an equation such as $f(x) = 20$

To solve an equation such as $f(x) = 20$, we're not asked to evaluate the function. Rather, we're asked to find a value for x at which the function evaluates to a given value. While in some cases it may be possible to solve such an equation through trial and error, a more reliable method is to use inverse functions (if $f(x)$ is invertible, which is the case here). If we find the inverse $f^{-1}(x)$ of $f(x)$, then we can apply that inverse function to both sides, yielding $f^{-1}(f(x)) = f^{-1}(20)$, which is to say $x = f^{-1}(20)$.

For our sample equation, $f(x) = 3x^3 - 4$, we can find the inverse algebraically. If $y = 3x^3 - 4$, then $3x^3 = y + 4$, $x^3 = \frac{y+4}{3}$, and finally $x = \sqrt[3]{(y+4)/3}$. So $f^{-1}(x) = \sqrt[3]{(x+4)/3}$. We can now find $f^{-1}(20)$: $f^{-1}(20) = \sqrt[3]{(20+4)/3} = \sqrt[3]{24/3} = \sqrt[3]{8} = 2$.

Unique solution for an equation of the form $f(x) = C$

An equation of the form $f(x) = C$ may have one solution, multiple solutions, or no solution. For example, $x + 1 = 1$ has one solution; $x^2 = 1$ has two solutions; $\sin x = 1$ has infinitely many solutions; and $e^x + 2 = 1$ has no solutions.

In order for $f(x) = C$ to have any solutions at all, C must be in the range of $f(x)$. (Note that 1 is not in the range of $f(x) = e^x + 2$.) However, this doesn't guarantee that the solution is unique. If the function $f(x)$ is invertible, then $f(x) = C$ is guaranteed to have a unique solution for all values of C in the range of $f(x)$. If not, then for at least some values of C the solution of $f(x) = C$ will not be unique. For instance, if $f(x) = x^3 - x$, then $f(x) = 0$ has three solutions, since $f(0) = f(1) = f(-1) = 0$, but $f(x) = 6$ has the unique solution $x = 2$.

Example

Given two functions expressed algebraically, explain how to determine whether they are inverses

The simplest way to determine algebraically whether two functions are inverses is to evaluate their composition. If $(f \circ g)(x) = x$ and $(g \circ f)(x) = x$, then $g(x) = f^{-1}(x)$ and vice versa; these two functions are inverses.

For example, consider $f(x) = x^3 + 1$ and $g(x) = \sqrt[3]{x-1}$. $(f \circ g)(x) = f(\sqrt[3]{x-1}) = (\sqrt[3]{x-1})^3 + 1 = (x-1) + 1 = x$, and $(g \circ f)(x) = g(x^3+1) = \sqrt[3]{(x^3+1) - 1} = \sqrt[3]{x^3} = x$.. These two functions, therefore, are inverses. Some functions are their own inverses. Consider $h(x) = \frac{x}{x-1}$: $(h \circ h)(x) = h\left(\frac{x}{x-1}\right) = \frac{x/(x-1)}{x/(x-1)-1} = \frac{x}{x-(x-1)} = \frac{x}{1} = x$. So $h^{-1}(x) = h(x)$.

Example

If $f(g(x)) = x$ for all x in the domain of $g(x)$, and $g(f(x)) = x$ for all x in the domain of $f(x)$, what does this imply about the relationship between $f(x)$ and $g(x)$

If $f(g(x)) = x$ and $g(f(x)) = x$ for all x in the appropriate domains, then this means that $f(x)$ and $g(x)$ are inverse functions, i.e. $f^{-1}(x) = g(x)$ and $g^{-1}(x) = f(x)$. This means that if $f(x_0) = y_0$, then $g(y_0) = x_0$, and vice versa.

Inverse functions are useful because they can be used to solve equations of the form $f(x) = C$. We can get the solution by simply taking the inverse function of both sides: $f^{-1}(f(x)) = f^{-1}(C)$, but $f^{-1}(f(x)) = x$, so $x = f^{-1}(C)$. For example, the exponential function e^x and the logarithm $\ln x$ are inverses, so we can use the exponential to solve logarithmic functions, and vice versa: if $e^x = 3$, then $\ln e^x = \ln 3$, so $x = \ln 3$.

Example

Given a function represented by a table like the one below, determine how you can find the function's inverse

x	0	1	2	3	4	5	6	7
$f(x)$	4	5	0	2	7	1	6	3

To change a function into its inverse, essentially all we need to do is to interchange its domain and range. Therefore, when the function is given in table form, we can just switch the two rows, as follows:

x	4	5	0	2	7	1	6	3
$f^{-1}(x)$	0	1	2	3	4	5	6	7

Putting the domain in ascending order (which isn't technically necessary, but makes the table easier to refer to) gives:

X	0	1	2	3	4	5	6	7
$f^{-1}(x)$	2	5	3	7	0	1	6	4

So, for instance, $f^{-1}(0) = 2$, and $f^{-1}(1) = 5$ —as we would expect, since $f(2) = 0$ and $f(5) = 1$.

Graph of a function vs. graph of its inverse

To convert an invertible function $f(x)$ into its inverse, we interchange the domain and range. This means that the point (x, y) in $f(x)$ maps into the point (y, x) in $f^{-1}(x)$. On a graph, this is equivalent to reflecting the point through the line $y = x$, i.e. flipping it over diagonally, from upper left to lower right. Since this transformation applies to each point, it also applies to the function as a whole: we can get the graph of $f^{-1}(x)$ from the graph of $f(x)$ by just flipping the whole graph over through the diagonal line $y = x$. For example, if the graph of $f(x)$ is the graph shown on the left below, then flipping it over diagonally yields the graph on the right, which is the graph of $f^{-1}(x)$.

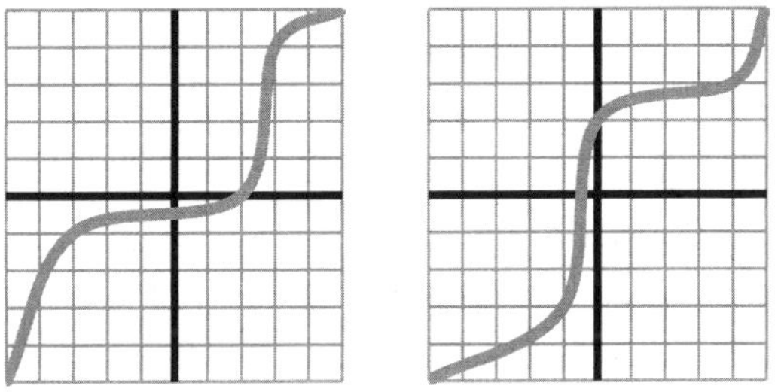

Example

Given a graph of an invertible function $f(x)$ and a value x_0, determine how you can read the value $f^{-1}(x_0)$ from the graph

While it's possible to turn the graph of $f(x)$ into a graph of $f^{-1}(x)$ by simply flipping it over diagonally through the line $y = x$, it's also possible to read values of $f^{-1}(x)$ off the graph of $f(x)$ directly. Just as we can read the value of $f(x_0)$ from a graph by finding the point where the graph intersects the line $x = x_0$ and observing the y coordinate of that point, so we can read the value of $f^{-1}(x_0)$ by the inverse process: We can find the point where the graph intersects the line $y = x_0$, and then read off the point's x-coordinate. The diagram below illustrates this procedure:

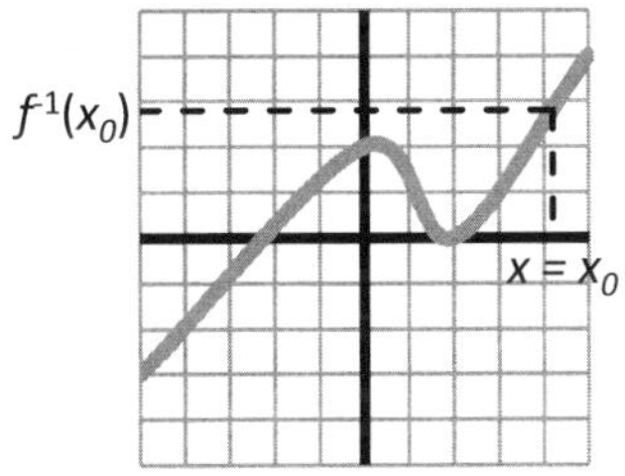

Determining if a function has an inverse

A function has an inverse if and only if each point in the range corresponds to a unique point in the domain. This is similar to the definition of a function itself—in a function, each point in the domain corresponds to a unique point in the range. Therefore, we can use similar guidelines to identify invertible functions. One simple way to tell whether a graph represents a function is the "vertical line test"; we observe whether there exists any vertical line that intersects the graph in more than one point. Similarly, we can check whether a function is invertible from its graph by using a sort of "horizontal line test": we check whether there exists any *horizontal* line that intersects the function in more than one point. If so, then the y coordinate corresponding to that line is matched up with more than one x coordinate, which means that the function is *not* invertible. If no such horizontal line exists, then the function is invertible.

Example

Given a non-invertible function such as $f(x) = x^2 + 1$ or $g(x) = x^3 - x$, determine how you could produce an invertible function by restricting the domain

What makes these functions non-invertible is that there are certain y values that correspond to more than one x value. For instance, $f(1) = f(-1) = 2$, and $g(-1) = g(0) = g(1) = 0$. However, this only occurs because the graph is increasing in some parts of the domain and decreasing in others. If we restrict the domain to regions where the function is only increasing or decreasing, within these regions each y corresponds to a unique x, so this restricted function is invertible.

Our first example, $f(x) = x^2 + 1$, decreases from $-\infty$ to 0, and increases from 0 to ∞. Restricting the domain to either the interval $(-\infty, 0]$ or $[0, \infty)$ produces an invertible function. Finding exactly where $g(x) = x^3 - x$ transitions between increasing and decreasing is difficult without calculus, but we don't need to know the precise transition points; we can choose a smaller interval over which it's clearly increasing or decreasing. For instance, if we graph $g(x)$, we can see it's clearly increasing for all $x > 1$, so we can get an invertible function by restricting its domain to $[1, \infty)$.

Example

Why is it incorrect (or at least incomplete) to say that the functions $f(x) = x^2$ and $g(x) = \sqrt{x}$ are inverses

At first, it might seem obvious that $f(x) = x^2$ and $g(x) = \sqrt{x}$ are inverses. After all, if we take the function composition $f(g(x))$, we find $f(g(x)) = f(\sqrt{x}) = (\sqrt{x})^2 = x$. However, one characteristic of inverse functions is that the domain of the inverse function is the same as the range of the original function, and vice versa. In this case, the range of $f(x)$ is indeed equal to the domain of $g(x)$: $[0, \infty)$. But the domain of $f(x)$ is not equal to the range of $g(x)$: the former is $(-\infty, \infty)$ but the latter only $[0, \infty)$. And, indeed, while $f(g(x)) = x$, we can find points for which $g(f(x)) \neq x$. For example, $g(f(-1)) = g((-1)^2) = g(1) = \sqrt{1} = 1$.

The root of the problem is that the function $f(x)$ is not invertible. There are elements in the range that match up to multiple points in the domain, such as $f(1) = f(-1) = 1$. If we make a new function $f_+(x)$ by restricting the domain of $f(x)$ to the interval $[0, \infty)$, then indeed $g(x) = f_+^{-1}(x)$.

Example

Is it possible that $f(g(x)) = x$ for all x in the domain of $g(x)$, but $g(f(x)) \neq x$ for some x in the domain of $f(x)$

Yes, it's possible that $f(g(x)) = x$ for all x in the domain of $g(x)$ without the same being true for $g(f(x))$. A simple example is $f(x) = x^2$ and $g(x) = \sqrt{x}$. For all x in the domain of $g(x)$, $f(g(x)) = f(\sqrt{x}) = (\sqrt{x})^2 = x$. However, this isn't true for $g(f(x))$: consider $g(f(-1)) = g((-1)^2) = g(1) = \sqrt{1} = 1 \neq -1$.

The reason that occurs is because in this case $f(x)$ is not an invertible function; there are multiple values of x that correspond to the same value of $f(x)$. Accordingly, there can be no function for which $f(g(x)) = x$ and $g(f(x)) = x$, because then the functions would be inverses. If we restrict $f(x)$ to the interval $[0, \infty)$, to produce a new function $f_2(x)$, then $f_2(x)$ is invertible, $f_2(g(x)) = x$, and $g(f_2(x)) = x$.

Example

Given a logarithmic equation such as $3\log_2 2x = 15$, determine how you could solve for x.

To solve a logarithmic equation where the variable appears in the argument of the logarithm, we have to use the fact that the exponential function is the inverse of the logarithmic. First, we rearrange the expression to get the logarithmic expression on a side by itself. After that, we can cancel the logarithm by taking the exponential function of both sides (with the same base as the logarithm). From that point on, solving the equation is a matter of simple algebra.

For instance, we can divide by three both sides of our sample equation, $3\log_2 2x = 15$, to get $\log_2 2x = \frac{15}{3} = 5$. We can now cancel the logarithm with an exponential: $2^{\log_2 2x} = 2^5$, or, simplifying the left hand side, $2x = 2^5$. So $x = \frac{2^5}{2} = \frac{32}{2} = 16$.

Relationship between exponential functions and logarithms

Exponential functions and logarithms are inverse functions. More specifically, an exponential function of a particular base is the inverse of a logarithmic function of the same base. For instance, e^x and $\ln x$ are inverse functions. 10^x and $\log_{10} x$ are inverse functions. And, in general, a^x and $\log_a x$ are inverse functions.

How we can use this relationship to solve problems

This relationship is often useful for solving problems, because we can use it to cancel an exponential or logarithmic function on one side of an equation. For example, given an equation of the form $a^x = C$, we can solve for x by taking the logarithm of both sides: $\log_a(a^x) = \log_a C$, which, since a^x and $\log_a x$ are inverse functions, reduces to $x = \log_a C$. Conversely, given an equation of the form $\log_a x = C$, we can solve for x by taking the exponential of both sides: $a^{\log_a x} = a^C$, which reduces to $x = a^C$.

Using a logarithmic function to solve a problem

The logarithm is the inverse of the exponential, and so can be used to cancel an exponential function. This is useful if a problem involves an exponential equation in which the variable to be solved for is in the exponent; we can then use the logarithmic equation to get the variable out of the exponent. For instance, we can solve the equation $10^x = 20$ by simply taking the logarithm, base 10, of both sides: $\log_{10}(10^x) = \log_{10}(20)$, thus $x = \log_{10} 20$.

More complex equations may require some algebraic manipulation: from $2e^{3x+5} + 6 = 20$, we get $2e^{3x+5} = 14$, then $e^{3x+5} = 7$. We can now take the logarithm of both sides: $\ln(e^{3x+5}) = \ln 7$, hence $3x + 5 = \ln 7$ and finally $x = (\ln 7 - 5)/3$.

Linear, Quadratic, and Exponential Models

Example

Describe what kind of function grows by equal differences over equal intervals, and prove your answer

A function that grows by equal differences over equal intervals is a *linear function*, a function of the form $f(x) = mx + b$.

To prove that a linear function meets this criterion, we can consider some arbitrary interval, Δx, and then show that $f(x + \Delta x) - f(x)$ does not depend on x—hence, that when x increases by an interval of Δx, $f(x)$ grows by a constant amount. Substituting in the linear function, we get$f(x + \Delta x) - f(x) = \big(m(x + \Delta x)\big) + b - (mx + b) = mx + m\Delta x + b - mx - b = m\Delta x$. As expected, this does not depend on x, proving that the linear function grows by equal differences over equal intervals.

Example

Describe what kind of function grows by equal factors over equal intervals, and prove your answer

A function that grows by equal factors over equal intervals is an *exponential function*, a function of the form $f(x) = Ae^{bx}$.

To prove that an exponential function meets this criterion, we can consider some arbitrary interval, Δx, and then show that $f(x + \Delta x)/f(x)$ does not depend on x—hence, that when x increases by an interval of Δx, $f(x)$ grows by a constant factor. Substituting in the exponential function, we get $f(x + \Delta x)/f(x) = Ae^{b(x+\Delta x)}/Ae^{bx} = Ae^{bx}e^{b\Delta x}/Ae^{bx} = e^{b\Delta x}$. As expected, this does not depend on x, proving that the exponential function grows by equal factors over equal intervals.

Phrases in a word problem indicating quantity changes

If one quantity changes at a constant rate relative to another, this means the two quantities have a linear relationship ($y = mx + b$). There are a number of common phrases in a word problem that might indicate this. Rarely are we told directly that the relationship between two quantities is linear, but there are other ways the relationship could be phrased.

Consider the following statement: "For every meter you go deeper underwater, the pressure increases by ten thousand Pascals." This says that one quantity—here the pressure—increases at a constant rate—ten thousand Pascals per meter—relative to another—the depth.

Another common phrasing that indicates a linear relationship is the statement that one quantity is proportional to another. This can be expressed algebraically as $y = mx$. Note that not all linear relationships are proportional—only those in which the y intercept is zero—but all proportional relationships are linear.

Example

Describe what kind of equation you would use to model a relationship in which one quantity changes at a constant rate per unit interval relative to another

A relationship in which one quantity changes at a constant rate per unit interval relative to another is necessarily a *linear relationship*, and can be modeled by a linear equation, of the form $f(x) = mx + b$. In this equation, m is equal to the slope of the line, or to the rate at which $f(x)$ changes per unit interval. This rate may be given directly, or it may be possible to derive it from the given information: if, for example, two points in the relationship are given, we can find m by calculating $\frac{f(x_1)-f(x_2)}{x_1-x_2}$. The constant b is the y intercept, or the value $f(0)$; again, this may be given directly, or may be derivable from given information: if you know m and you're given one data point, you can put these known values into the equation $f(x) = mx + b$ and solve for b.

Example

Suppose you're told an event ticket costs a flat fee of $20 plus $5 per person. Describe how you would write an algebraic expression to describe the total price

To write an expression based on a given situation, the first thing to observe is what quantities we will be concerned with and that will correspond to variables in the expression. In this case, we have a total price that varies by the number of people involved, so we'll be writing $y = f(x)$, where y is the total cost and x is the number of people. Secondly, we can observe exactly how one quantity varies with the other. In this case, the price increases by a fixed amount for each additional person. A situation in which one quantity changes at a constant rate per unit interval relative to the other corresponds to a linear function. In this case, with a flat fee of $20 independent of the number of people, and a fee increase of $5 per person, an appropriate equation is $y = 20 + 5x$.

Phrases in a word problem indicating quantity grows or decays

If one quantity grows or decays by a constant percent rate per unit interval relative to another, this means that the two quantities have an exponential relationship, $y = AB^{Cx}$—or rather, to take into account the percent rate, $y(t) = y_o(1 + P)^{Ct}$, where P is the percent rate.

This relationship may be stated directly, but more often it must be partly inferred by other phrases appearing in the problem. For instance, we may be told the number of bacteria in a culture doubles every ten months—"doubles" indicates a percent rate of 100% ($1 + P = 2$, so $P = 1 = 100\%$).

Some common examples of problems involving exponential relationship involve compound interest and radioactive half-lives. In the former, the interest rate is the percent increase, while the coefficient of the exponent depends on how often the interest is compounded—for interest compounded monthly, the exponent would be $t/12$, assuming that t is measured in months. In the latter, the base of the exponent is always $\frac{1}{2}$, and the exponent is $t/t_{1/2}$, where $t_{1/2}$ is the half-life.

Example

Describe what kind of equation you would use to model a relationship in which one quantity changes by a constant percent rate per unit interval relative to another.

A relationship in which one quantity changes by a constant percent rate per unit interval relative to another is an *exponential relationship*, and can be modeled by an exponential equation, of the form $f(x) = Ae^{bx}$. If the percent rate of change is positive, then b is positive and the equation represents exponential growth; if the percent rate of change is negative, then b is negative and the equation represents exponential decay. Often in such a problem we are given the value of $f(x)$ when $x = 0$; this is simply A, as can be seen as follows: $f(0) = Ae^{b \cdot 0} = Ae^0 = A \cdot 1 = A$. Given this, if we have at least one other data point, we can use it to solve for b.

Example

Suppose you're told that an item initially sold for $200 and its price has increased by 10% per year. Show how you would write an algebraic expression to describe the price

To write an expression based on a given situation, the first thing to observe is what quantities we will be concerned with and that will correspond to variables in the expression. In this case, we have a price that varies by year, so we'll be writing $y = f(t)$, where y is the total cost and t is the time in years from the item's initial sale. Secondly, we can observe exactly how one quantity varies with the other. In this case, the price increases by a fixed percentage per year. A situation in which one quantity changes at a constant percent rate per unit interval relative to the other corresponds to an exponential function. In this case, with an initial cost of $200 at $t = 0$ and an increase of 10% per year, an appropriate equation is $y = 200 \cdot 1.1^t$.

Example

Given two points, such as (1,2) and (3,–1), describe how you can find a linear function that includes those points

A linear function is a function of the form $y = mx + b$, where m is the slope of the line and b is its y intercept. Suppose we are given two points, (x_1, y_1) and

(x_2, y_2). We can find m by calculating the "rise over run": that is, $m = \frac{y_2 - y_1}{x_2 - x_1}$. Knowing m, we can then put the x and y values of one of the points into the equation $y = mx + b$ to solve for b, the only remaining unknown.

For example, using the sample points (1,2) and (3,–1) we have $m = \frac{-1-2}{3-1} = -\frac{3}{2}$. We can now put that into the linear equation along with the coordinates of the first point, (1,2), to yield $2 = -\frac{3}{2}(1) + b$, which we can solve for b to get $b = \frac{7}{2}$. (Had we used the second point instead of the first, we would have arrived at the same answer.) Therefore, the linear function that includes the two given points is $y = -\frac{3}{2}x + \frac{7}{2}$.

Example

Given two points, one of which has an x value of zero, such as (0,2) and (3,20), show how you can find an exponential function that includes those points

An exponential function has the form $y = Ae^{bx}$. (We could use a different base for the exponent rather than e, but in that case, by the properties of exponents, we'd simply have a different value for b; the form of the equation wouldn't change, and neither would the means of solving it.) If one of the given points has an x value of zero, then finding A is easy: we can just put the x and y values of this point into the equation, and we'll find that $y = A$. For the sample points, using (0,2) we find $2 = Ae^{b \cdot 0} = A$, so $A = 2$.

Knowing A, we can now use the x and y values of the other point to solve for b. For the sample points, putting in (3,20) we get $20 = 2e^{b \cdot 3}$. Dividing both sides by 2 yields $10 = e^{3b}$, and now we can take the natural logarithm of both sides, giving $\ln 10 = 3b$, thus $b = \frac{\ln 10}{3}$. Therefore, our final equation is $y = 2e^{\frac{\ln 10}{3}x} = 2\left(e^{\ln 10}\right)^{x/3} = 2 \cdot 10^{\frac{x}{3}}$.

Example

Given two points with nonzero x values, such as (2,4) and (6,60), show how you can find an exponential function that includes both point.

An exponential function has the form $y = Ae^{bx}$. Putting the x and y values for the given points into this equation yields two equations: in the case of the sample points, $4 = Ae^{2b}$ and $60 = Ae^{6b}$. We have two equations and two unknowns (A and b), so in principle it should be possible to solve for the unknowns.

There are many ways of doing this. We could, for instance, solve for A in one equation and substitute that value into the other. Another relatively simple method is to take the ratio of the two equations, thus canceling A: $\frac{60}{4} = \frac{Ae^{6b}}{Ae^{2b}}$, thus $15 = \frac{e^{6b}}{e^{2b}} = e^{6b-2b} = e^{4b}$. Taking the natural logarithm of both sides, $\ln 15 = 4b$, so $b = \frac{\ln 15}{4}$.

Knowing b, we can now use either point to solve for A: using (2,4), we get $4 = Ae^{\frac{\ln 15}{4} \cdot 2} = Ae^{\frac{\ln 15}{2}} = A\left(e^{\ln 15}\right)^{\frac{1}{2}} = A \cdot 15^{1/2} = \sqrt{15}A$, so $A = \frac{4\sqrt{15}}{15}$. Our full equation is then $y = \frac{4\sqrt{15}}{15} e^{\frac{\ln 15}{4}x} = \frac{4\sqrt{15}}{15}\left(e^{\ln 15}\right)^{x/4} = \frac{4\sqrt{15}}{15} \cdot 15^{\frac{x}{4}}$.

Example

Given a graph of a linear function, determine how you can construct an algebraic expression for the function

An algebraic expression for a linear function has the form $y = mx + b$. We can find both m and b from the graph of the function. b is simply equal to the y intercept, and can be read from the graph by observing at what point the graph of the linear function intersects the y-axis. To find m, the slope, we can take from the graph any two points that lie on the line, (x_1, y_1) and (x_2, y_2). The slope m is then equal to $m = \frac{y_1 - y_2}{x_1 - x_2}$.

There are two special cases that must be treated differently: horizontal and vertical lines. A horizontal line has a slope of zero; its equation is $y = b$, where b is, again, the y intercept (or the y coordinate of any other point on the line). Conversely, the slope of a vertical line is undefined; its equation is $x = a$, where a is the x intercept (or the x coordinate of any other point on the line).

Example

Given a graph of an exponential function, describe how you can construct an algebraic expression for the function

An algebraic expression for an exponential function has the form $y = Ae^{bx}$. A can be found directly from the graph; it is simply the graph's y intercept. To see this, consider what happens when we evaluate the expression at $x = 0$: $y = Ae^{b \cdot 0} = Ae^0 = A \cdot 1 = A$. Once we know A, we can choose any other point (x_1, y_1) that lies on the graph of the function *except* the y intercept. We can then use this to solve for b: $y_1 = Ae^{bx_1}$, so $\frac{y_1}{A} = e^{bx_1}$, $\ln\left(\frac{y_1}{A}\right) = \ln\left(e^{bx_1}\right) = bx_1$, and finally $b = \frac{1}{x_1}\ln\left(\frac{y_1}{A}\right)$. For instance, if the y intercept is $(0, 2)$ and the graph also passes through the point (5,4), then we have $4 = 2e^{b \cdot 5}$, hence $2 = e^{5b}$, $\ln 2 = 5b$, and $b = \frac{\ln 2}{5}$. So an algebraic expression for the function is $y = 2e^{\frac{\ln 2}{5}x}$. This can be simplified: $2e^{\frac{\ln 2}{5}x} = 2\left(e^{\ln 2}\right)^{\frac{1}{5}x} = 2 \cdot 2^{\frac{1}{5}x} = 2^{\frac{1}{5}x+1}$. So $y = 2 \cdot 2^{\frac{1}{5}x}$ and $y = 2^{\frac{1}{5}x+1}$ are both acceptable ways to write the expression.

Example

Describe how you can write an algebraic expression for an arithmetic sequence given two (not necessarily consecutive) terms of the sequence

An arithmetic sequence is a sequence in which there is a constant difference d between consecutive terms. It can be expressed by the formula $f(n) = a_1 + d(n-1)$. Suppose we are given two terms of the sequence, $f(n_1)$ and $f(n_2)$. Since the difference between consecutive terms is d, the difference between terms Δn terms apart is simply $\Delta n \cdot d$. In this case, $\Delta n = (n_2 - n_1)$, so $f(n_2) - f(n_1) = (n_2 - n_1)d$, and $d = \frac{f(n_2)-f(n_1)}{n_2-n_1}$. Knowing d, we can use one of the given terms to solve for a_1: $f(n_1) = a_1 + d(n_1 - 1)$, so $a_1 = f(n_1) - d(n_1 - 1)$.

For example, suppose we are told that the third term of an arithmetic sequence is 5 and the seventh term is 17—that is, $f(3) = 5$ and $f(7) = 17$. Then $17 - 5 = (7 - 3)d$, hence $d = \frac{17-5}{7-3} = \frac{12}{4} = 3$. We can now solve for a_1: $5 = a_1 + 3(3 - 1)$, so $a_1 = 5 - 3(3 - 1) = 5 - 3(2) = -1$. So an expression for this arithmetic sequence is $f(n) = -1 + 3(n - 1)$.

Example

Describe how you can write an algebraic expression for a geometric sequence given two (not necessarily consecutive) terms of the sequence

A geometric sequence is a sequence in which there is a constant ratio r between consecutive terms. It can be expressed by the formula $f(n) = a_1 r^{n-1}$. Suppose we are given two terms of the sequence, $f(n_1)$ and $f(n_2)$. Since the ratio of consecutive terms is r, the ratio of terms Δn terms apart is simply $r^{\Delta n}$. In this case, $\Delta n = (n_2 - n_1)$, so $f(n_2)/f(n_1) = r^{n_2-n_1}$, and $r = \left(f(n_2)/f(n_1)\right)^{1/(n_2-n_1)}$. Knowing r, we can use one of the given terms to solve for a_1: $f(n_1) = a_1 r^{n_1-1}$, so $a_1 = f(n_1)/r^{n_1-1}$.

For example, suppose we are told that the ninth term of an arithmetic sequence is 40 and the fifteenth term is 5—that is, $f(9) = 40$ and $f(15) = 5$. Then $\frac{5}{40} = r^{15-9} = r^6$, hence $r = \left(\frac{5}{40}\right)^{1/6} = \left(\frac{1}{8}\right)^{1/6} = \frac{1}{8^{\frac{1}{6}}} = \frac{1}{\sqrt[6]{8}} = \frac{1}{\sqrt{2}} = \frac{\sqrt{2}}{2}$. We can now solve for a_1: $40 = a_1\left(\frac{\sqrt{2}}{2}\right)^{9-1} = a_1\left(\frac{\sqrt{2}}{2}\right)^{8} = a_1\left(\frac{1}{16}\right)$, so $a_1 = 40/(1/16) = 40 \cdot 16 = 640$. So an expression for this arithmetic sequence is $f(n) = 640 \cdot \left(\frac{\sqrt{2}}{2}\right)^{n-1}$.

Exponential functions (with a positive exponent) eventually exceeds any polynomial function

An exponential function has the form $y = Ae^{bx}$. A polynomial function has the form $y = a_n x^n + a_{n-1}x^{n-1} + \cdots + a_1 x + a_0$. The exponential always exceeds the polynomial for sufficiently large x, regardless of the values of A, b, n, and $a_0 \ldots a_n$.

One way to see this is to consider the rate of change. One characteristic of an exponential function is that over a fixed interval it changes by a constant ratio: when x increases by 1, Ae^{bx} increases by e^b. This isn't true of polynomials; for large x, when only the leading term of the polynomial is significant, when x increases by 1 the polynomial increases by a ratio of $\frac{(x+1)^n}{x^n} = \left(\frac{x+1}{x}\right)^n$, which *decreases* as x increases, converging at very large x to 1. Therefore, eventually the rate of change of the polynomial will drop below the rate of change of the exponential, and thereafter at some point the exponential will surpass the polynomial.

Example

The graph below shows a cubic function, an exponential function, a linear function, a logarithmic function, and a quadratic function

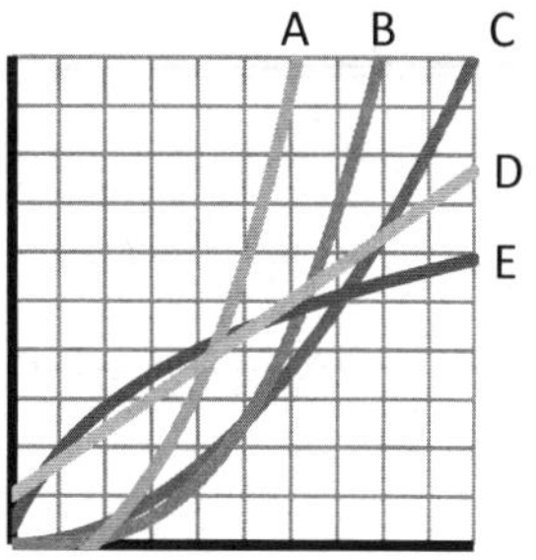

All of these functions tend toward infinity in their right end behavior, but some of them do so more rapidly than others. An exponential equation eventually increases more rapidly than any polynomial, and certainly increases more rapidly than a logarithmic function. The function that, in the end, increases most rapidly must therefore be the exponential, namely A. Conversely, the logarithmic function, the inverse of the exponential, must eventually increase more *slowly* than any polynomial. The logarithmic function must be the one that increases the most slowly in the end, namely E.

This leaves B, C, and D as the cubic, linear, and quadratic. These are all polynomial functions, and in its end behavior a polynomial of a larger order (largest exponent) increases more rapidly than one of a smaller order. This means B must be the cubic (order 3), C the quadratic (order 2), and D the linear (order 1).

Determining how to tell which is a cubic function, an exponential function, a linear function, a logarithmic function, and a quadratic function

x	1	2	3	4	5	6	7	8	9	10
$f(x)$	0.00	0.60	1.60	3.00	4.80	7.00	9.60	12.60	16.00	19.80
$g(x)$	2.00	2.12	2.43	3.05	4.07	5.58	7.70	10.52	14.13	18.65
$h(x)$	4.00	5.39	6.20	6.77	7.22	7.58	7.89	8.16	8.39	8.61
$j(x)$	0.03	0.09	0.27	0.81	2.43	7.29	21.87	65.61	196.83	590.49
$k(x)$	0.50	1.00	1.50	2.00	2.50	3.00	3.50	4.00	4.50	5.00

$k(x)$ increases by a constant rate (0.5) per unit interval, and consecutive terms of $j(x)$ differ by a constant ratio (3), so $k(x)$ must be the linear function and $j(x)$ the exponential. However, we can also determine which function is which by comparing their end behavior. The function that, in the end, increases most rapidly must be the exponential, namely $j(x)$. Conversely, the logarithmic function, the inverse of the exponential, must eventually increase more *slowly* than any polynomial. Although $k(10) < h(10)$, it's clear that $h(x)$ is increasing at a much slower rate than $k(x)$, and for sufficiently large x in the end $k(x) > h(x)$. $h(x)$ is therefore the logarithmic function.

The remaining functions are all polynomials of varying degrees. In its end behavior a polynomial of a larger order (largest exponent) increases more rapidly than one of a smaller order. Observing the end behavior of $f(x)$, $g(x)$, and $k(x)$, we therefore conclude that $k(x)$ must be the lowest degree (linear), $f(x)$ the next (quadratic), and $g(x)$ the highest degree (cubic).

Determining how to express the solution of an equation of the form $ab^{ct} = d$ in terms of a logarithm

To express the solution of an equation of the form $ab^{ct} = d$ in terms of a logarithm, we'll have to take the logarithm of both sides of the equation. Before doing that, though, we'd have to isolate the exponential on a side by itself. We can do that by dividing both sides by a: $b^{ct} = d/a$. To cancel an exponential with a base of b, we have to use a logarithm with the base of b: $\log_b b^{ct} = \log_b(d/a)$. Since the logarithm is the inverse of the exponential, the left side, $\log_b b^{ct}$, reduces to just ct. So $ct = \log_b(d/a)$, so $t = \frac{\log_b(d/a)}{c}$. (Using the rule $\log(\alpha/\beta) = \log\alpha - \log\beta$, we can also rewrite this as $t = \frac{\log_b d - \log_b a}{c}$.)

<u>Example</u>

Given an exponential equation such as $20 = 4 \cdot 2^{3x}$, show how you could solve for x

To solve an exponential equation where the variable appears in the exponent, we have to use the fact that the logarithmic function is the inverse of the exponential. First, we rearrange the expression to get the exponential expression on a side by itself. After that, we can cancel the exponential by taking the logarithm of both sides (with the same base as the exponential). From that point on, solving the equation is a matter of simple algebra.

For instance, we can divide by four both sides of our sample equation, $20 = 4 \cdot 2^{3x}$, to get $2^{3x} = \frac{20}{4} = 5$. We can now cancel the exponential with a logarithm: $\log_2 2^{3x} = \log_2 5$, or, simplifying the left hand side, $3x = \log_2 5$. So $x = \frac{1}{3}\log_2 5$.

Using a calculator to evaluate logarithms such as $\log_e 2$, $\log_{10} 7$, and $\log_2 5$

The logarithm base *e* is also called the natural logarithm, abbreviated *ln*: so $\log_e 2$ is the same thing as $\ln 2$. Scientific calculators generally have an "ln" button, so evaluating natural logarithms is straightforward: to evaluate $\ln 2$ on a TI-84 calculator, for instance, just involves hitting "LN", "2", "ENTER". Similarly, most scientific calculators have a button to calculate logarithms base 10, though it often just says "log" without the base. On a TI-84, $\log_{10} 7$ can be evaluated by hitting "LOG", "7", "ENTER".

Evaluating logarithms with bases other than 10 and e is not quite as straightforward, but still possible using the relation $\log_a b = \frac{\log_c b}{\log_c a}$ (for any base c). Therefore $\log_2 5 = \ln 5 / \ln 2$ or $\log_{10} 5 / \log_{10} 2$, either of which is readily evaluable with a calculator.

Example

In the equation of a linear function, $y = mx + b$, what is the physical significance of the parameters m and b

The parameter m is the slope of the line. Regarding the relationship between the physical quantities symbolized by x and y , m is the *rate of change* of y with respect to x: specifically, when x increases by 1, y increases by the amount m.

b is often known as the *y-intercept* of the line: it represents the y coordinate of the point where the line crosses the y-axis. Another way of saying this, and one that makes its physical significance clearer, is that b is the value of y when $x = 0$. When x represents time (as is frequently the case), then b is the *initial value* of y.

Example

Given an exponential equation such as the compound interest equation $A = P\left(1 + \frac{r}{n}\right)^{nt}$, determine how to interpret its parameters in terms of the context

While we could memorize the meaning of each parameter in the compound interest equation $A = P\left(1 + \frac{r}{n}\right)^{nt}$, it's also possible to figure out what they mean by examining the exponential equation. The amount of money in an account with compound interest rises exponentially as a function of time. The quantity that rises exponentially in this equation is A, so that must be the total amount of money in the account. The variable in the exponent is t, so that must be time. (There's also an n in the exponent, but that appears elsewhere as well.) P is the amount of money in the account when $t = 0$, so that must be the initial amount of money deposited in the account (the *principal*).

Two parameters of compound interest remain: the interest rate and the interval over which it's compounded (monthly, quarterly, etc.) The latter must be n, since it affects the exponent: interest compounded monthly would rise exponentially faster than interest compounded quarterly, for instance. That leaves r for the interest rate.

Example

Given a logarithmic equation such as the equation for the loudness of a sound in decibels in terms of its intensity, $\beta = 10\log_{10}\left(\frac{I}{I_0}\right)$, determine how to interpret its parameters in terms of the context

Even if we're not familiar with this equation, we can figure out what its parameters mean by examining the equation. Since the equation is for the loudness of a sound, that must be what the β stands for. This means the intensity, the other quantity mentioned, must be either I or I_0. If the intensity were I_0, that would mean that as the sound intensity increases, the loudness decreases, which seems illogical. It stands to reason, then that I represents the sound intensity. As for I_0, since it doesn't correspond to one of the variables, it must just be a constant factor.

As it happens, I_0 is defined as 10^{-12} watts, but even without knowing that, we can still get useful information from this equation; for instance, we can tell that if a sound's intensity increases by a factor of 100, then its loudness increases by 20 decibels.

Trigonometric Functions

Radian

A *radian* is a unit of angle measurement often used by mathematicians and scientists; one radian is equal to $180/\pi$ degrees. (The reason why radians are more useful than degrees may not be immediately obvious, but in calculus in particular, radians make calculations involving trigonometric functions much simpler.)

One way to define the radian measurement of an angle relates to the unit circle: if we place an angle with its vertex at the center of the circle, then the length of the arc subtended by the angle is equal to the measurement of the angle in radians. For example, a right angle subtends a quarter of the circle; the arc length is therefore one quarter of the circle's circumference, or $\frac{2\pi(1)}{4} = \frac{\pi}{2}$. So a right angle measures $\frac{\pi}{2}$ radians.

Converting an angle between angles and radians, and vice versa

An angle's measurement in radians can be equated to the length of an arc of the unit circle subtended by an angle based at its center. Since the circumference of a full circle is 2π, this must correspond to 360°. The arc of a semicircle is just π, which must correspond to 180°. The arc of a quarter circle (the amount subtended by a right angle) is $\pi/2$, which must correspond to the number of degrees in a right angle, 90°. The conversion factor between degrees and radians must therefore be $\frac{2\pi}{360} = \frac{\pi/2}{90} = \frac{\pi}{180}$. So, for instance, 30° corresponds to $30\left(\frac{\pi}{180}\right) = \pi/6$ radians, 45° to $45\left(\frac{\pi}{180}\right) = \pi/4$ radians, and 60° to $60\left(\frac{\pi}{180}\right) = \pi/3$ radians. To convert from radians to degrees, we just *divide* by $\frac{\pi}{180}$, or multiply by $\frac{180}{\pi}$; thus, for instance, $\pi/5$ radians equals $(\pi/5)\left(\frac{180}{\pi}\right) = 36°$.

Making sense of trigonometric functions of angles less than 0 or greater than 90°

Trigonometric functions such as sine and cosine are often defined in terms of the ratio of sides of a right triangle. Obviously, a right triangle cannot have any angles less than 0 or greater than 90°. So there must be a more general definition of the trigonometric functions that doesn't rely on angles in a right triangle. The functions can instead be defined relative to a unit circle (a circle with radius 1), centered at the origin. If we start with a ray oriented along the positive *x* axis, and then rotate that ray by an angle θ counter-clockwise about the origin (or clockwise if θ is negative), then we can consider the point where that ray intersects the unit circle, defining cos θ to be equal to the *x* coordinate of this point and sin θ to be its *y* coordinate. For an angle between 0 and 90°, this definition coincides with the definition in terms of sides of a right triangle, but unlike that definition, the definition in terms of the unit circle allows us to make sense of trigonometric functions of any real number.

Trigonometric functions relation to the unit circle

To relate the trigonometric functions of an angle θ to the unit circle, first consider a ray that coincides with the x-axis, and then rotate that ray counterclockwise through the angle θ. Now, consider the x and y coordinates of the point where the rotated ray intersects a unit circle centered on the origin. (See the diagram below.)

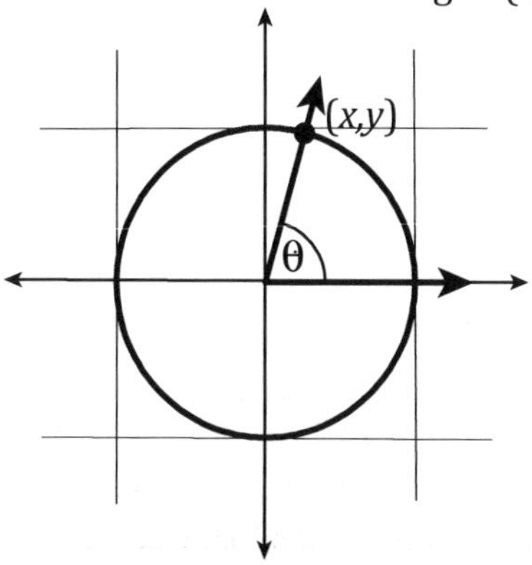

All six trigonometric functions can be described in terms of those coordinates. $\sin\theta = y$, $\cos\theta = x$, $\tan\theta = y/x$, $\sec\theta = 1/x$, $\csc\theta = 1/y$, and $\cot\theta = x/y$. If the denominator of any of these expressions is zero, then the corresponding function is undefined. For example, if $\theta = \pi/2$, then $x = 0$ and $y = 1$, so $\sin(\pi/2) = 1$, $\cos(\pi/2) = 0$, $\csc(\pi/2) = 1/1 = 1$, and $\cot(\pi/2) = 0/1 = 0$. Both $\tan(\pi/2)$ and $\sec(\pi/2)$ are undefined, since the expressions $1/x$ and y/x both have zeroes in their denominators.

Unit circle vs. right triangles

Students first learn the trigonometric functions in terms of right triangles: the sine is equal to the length of the opposite leg divided by the length of the hypotenuse, the cosine to the length of the adjacent leg divided by the length of the hypotenuse, and the tangent to the length of the opposite leg divided by the length of the adjacent leg. While this method of determining the trigonometric functions remains often useful, it has its limitations. Namely, it only makes sense for angles between 0 and 90 degrees (0 and $\pi/2$ radians), since a right triangle can't have any angles with measurements outside this range. However, the trigonometric functions can also be defined in terms of the arc of a unit circle subtended by an angle at the circle's center. For angles between 0 and 90 degrees, this matches the right angle definition, but it also applies to angle measurements of any real number.

Finding the sine, cosine, and tangent of $\pi - x$ in terms of the respective functions of x

$\sin(\pi - x) = \sin(x)$, $\cos(\pi - x) = -\cos(x)$, and $\tan(\pi - x) = -\tan(x)$. While it's possible to memorize these relationships, it is unnecessary, since they can easily be derived from the unit circle. Consider the relationship between the angles θ and $\pi - \theta$ on the unit circle:

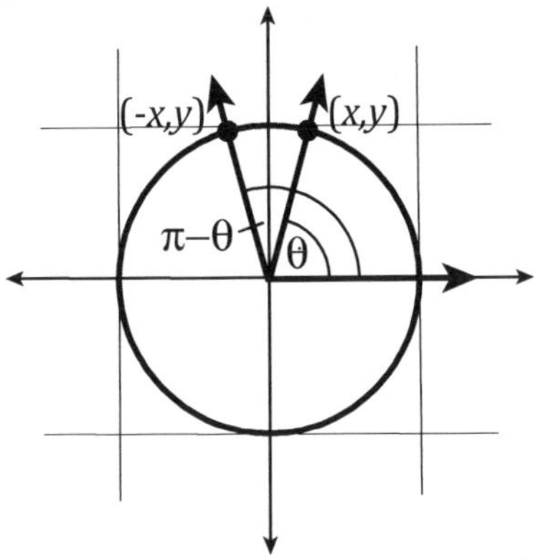

Replacing θ by $\pi - \theta$ is equivalent to a reflection through the y-axis: the x coordinate is inverted, and the y coordinate is unchanged. This means that the cosine is inverted (since it's equal to the x coordinate), the sine is unchanged (since it's equal to the y coordinate), and the tangent is inverted (since it's equal to the ratio y / x, and if one side of the ratio is inverted the ratio is inverted).

Finding the sine, cosine, and tangent of $\pi + x$ in terms of the respective functions of x

$\sin(\pi + x) = -\sin(x)$, $\cos(\pi + x) = -\cos(x)$, and $\tan(\pi + x) = \tan(x)$. While it's possible to memorize these relationships, it is unnecessary, since they can easily be derived from the unit circle. Consider the relationship between the angles θ and $\pi + \theta$ on the unit circle:

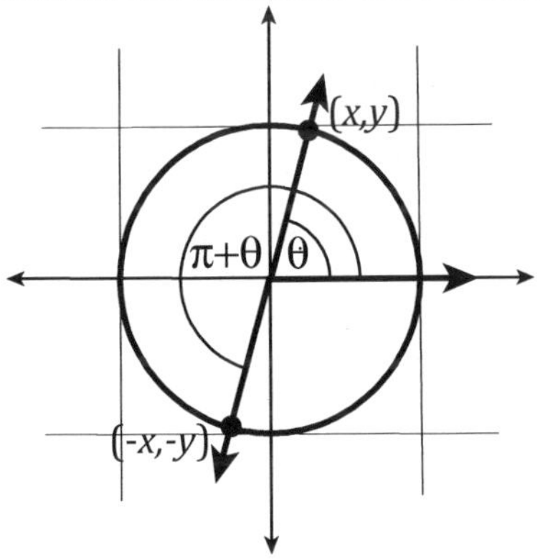

Replacing θ by $\pi + \theta$ means a rotation by π radians (or 180°), which is equivalent to reflections through both the x and y axes: the x and y coordinates are both inverted. This means that the cosine is inverted (since it's equal to the x coordinate), the sine is inverted (since it's equal to the y coordinate), and the tangent is unchanged (since it's equal to the ratio y / x, and the inversion of one side of the ratio cancels the inversion of the other).

Finding the sine, cosine, and tangent of 2π – x in terms of the respective functions of x

$\sin(2\pi - x) = -\sin(x)$, $\cos(2\pi - x) = \cos(x)$, and $\tan(2\pi - x) = -\tan(x)$. While it's possible to memorize these relationships, it is unnecessary, since they can easily be derived from the unit circle. Consider the relationship between the angles θ and $2\pi - \theta$ on the unit circle:

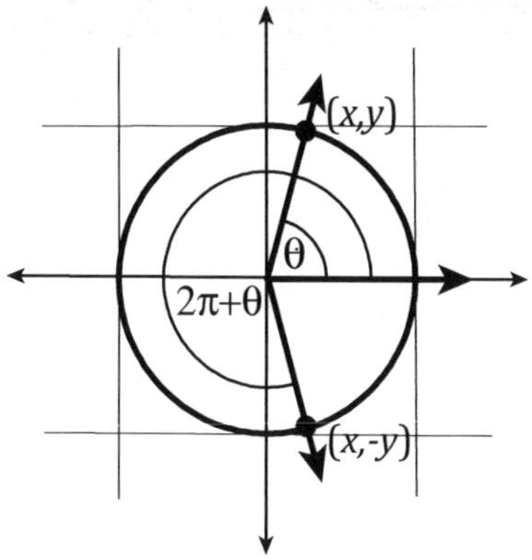

Replacing θ by $2\pi - \theta$ is equivalent to a reflection through the *x*-axis: the *y* coordinate is inverted, and the *x* coordinate is unchanged. This means that the cosine is unchanged (since it's equal to the *x* coordinate), the sine is inverted (since it's equal to the *y* coordinate), and the tangent is inverted (since it's equal to the ratio y / x, and if one side of the ratio is inverted the ratio is inverted).

Finding the sine, cosine, and tangent of $\pi/3$ without using technology

The angle $\pi/3$ comes up often enough in problems that its trigonometric functions may be worth memorizing. However, if you don't memorize them, they're still not hard to find. If $\pi/3$ doesn't seem familiar, try converting it from radians to degrees: $\pi/3$ radians is equal to $(\pi/3)(180/\pi) = 60$ degrees. Now, consider a right triangle with one angle of 60°. This should sound familiar; a "30/60/90" triangle is one of the most familiar kinds of right triangles, and you should have learned that its hypotenuse is always twice as long as its shorter leg. Since the cosine of an angle in a right triangle is equal to the length of the adjacent leg divided by the length of the hypotenuse, and the adjacent leg to the 60° angle is the shorter leg, this means the cosine of 60°, and therefore of $\pi/3$, must be equal to ½. Therefore $\sin(\pi/3) = \sqrt{1 - (^1/_2)^2} = {}^{\sqrt{3}}/_2$, and $\tan(\pi/3) = (\sqrt{3}/2)/(1/2) = \sqrt{3}$.

Finding the sine, cosine, and tangent of $\pi/6$ without using technology

The angle $\pi/6$ comes up often enough in problems that its trigonometric functions may be worth memorizing. However, if you don't memorize them, they're still not hard to find. If $\pi/6$ doesn't seem familiar, try converting it from radians to degrees: $\pi/6$ radians is equal to $(\pi/6)(180/\pi) = 30$ degrees. Now, consider a right triangle with one angle of 30°. This should sound familiar; a "30/60/90" triangle is one of the most familiar kinds of right triangles, and you should have learned that its hypotenuse is always twice as long as its shorter leg. Since the sine of an angle in a right triangle is equal to the length of the opposite leg divided by the length of the hypotenuse, and the opposite leg to the 30° angle is the shorter leg, this means the sine of 30°, and therefore of $\pi/6$, must be equal to ½. Therefore $\cos(\pi/6) = \sqrt{1 - (^1/_2)^2} = {}^{\sqrt{3}}/_2$, and $\tan(\pi/6) = (1/2)/(\sqrt{3}/2) = \sqrt{3}/3$.

Finding the sine, cosine, and tangent of $\pi/4$ without using technology

The angle $\pi/4$ comes up often enough in problems that its trigonometric functions may be worth memorizing. However, if you don't memorize them, they're still not hard to find. If $\pi/4$ doesn't seem familiar, try converting it from radians to degrees: $\pi/4$ radians is equal to $(\pi/4)(180/\pi) = 45$ degrees. Now, consider a right triangle with one angle of 45°. This should sound familiar; a "45/45/90" triangle is one of the most familiar kinds of right triangles, and you should have learned that its legs are equal in length. This means if each leg has length 1, the hypotenuse, by the Pythagorean theorem, has length $\sqrt{1^2 + 1^2} = \sqrt{2}$. Since the sine of an angle in a right triangle is equal to the length of the opposite leg divided by the length of the hypotenuse, this means the sine of 45°, and therefore of $\pi/4$, must be equal to $1/\sqrt{2} = \sqrt{2}/2$. Similarly, $\cos(\pi/4) = 1/\sqrt{2} = \sqrt{2}/2$, and $\tan(\pi/4) = 1/1 = 1$.

Determining which of the six trigonometric functions are odd, and which are even

An *odd* function is a function that is inverted when its argument is inverted: $f(x) = -f(-x)$. An *even* function is a function that is unchanged when its argument is inverted: $f(x) = f(-x)$. To see which trigonometric functions are odd and which are even, consider the unit circle: inverting the angle is equivalent to tracing the angle around the unit circle in the opposite direction.

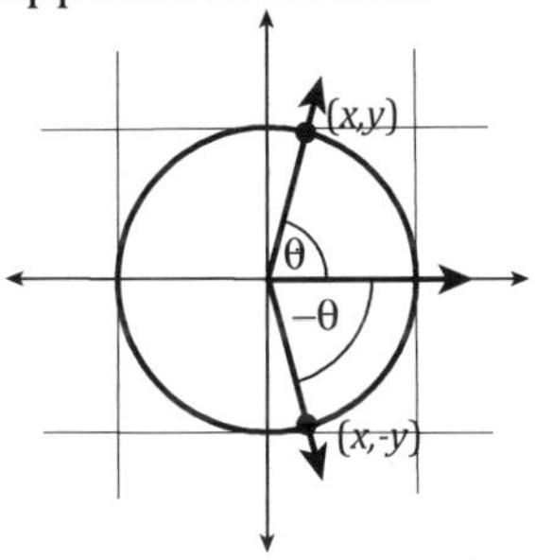

As is clear from the diagram, inverting the angle inverts the y coordinate (the sine) while leaving the x coordinate (the cosine) unchanged, so the sine is odd and the cosine even. The tangent, the ratio of the sine and cosine, is also inverted and therefore odd. If a function is odd or even, so is its reciprocal, so the cosecant and the cotangent are odd (as the reciprocals of the sine and tangent, respectively) and the secant is even (as the reciprocal of the cosine).

Periodicity of the sine, cosine, and tangent functions

The sine and cosine functions are periodic with a period of 2π radians (360°): $\sin(\theta + 2\pi) = \sin(\theta)$, and $\cos(\theta + 2\pi) = \cos(\theta)$. This can be seen from their relation to the unit circle: since the sine and cosine of θ can be equated to the y and x coordinates of a point originally at (1,0) after it rotates by an angle θ about the origin, we would expect that after one full rotation—2π radians—the values would repeat.

The tangent is also periodic, but with a different period. Consider that the tangent is the ratio of the sine and the cosine. After a rotation of π radians—halfway around the unit circle—the sine and the cosine have both changed in sign: $\sin(\theta + \pi) = -\sin(\theta)$, and $\cos(\theta + \pi) = -\cos(\theta)$. But if both the sine and cosine change in sign, then their ratio is unchanged; the sign changes cancel out. Therefore $\tan(\theta + \pi) = \tan(\theta)$, and the period of the tangent is π.

Example

What kind of function would best model periodic data such as the graph shown below

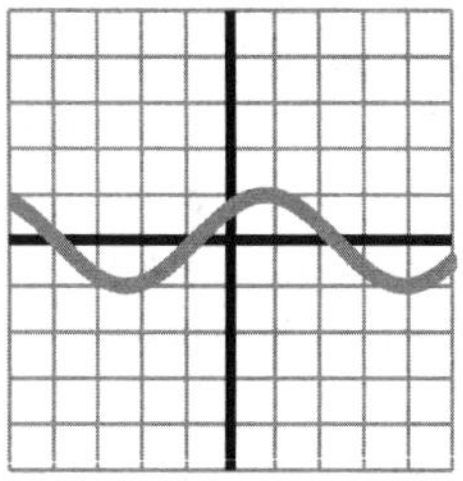

A periodically oscillating graph like the one pictured here is best modeled by a sine wave or a cosine wave. Generally, if at $x = 0$ the wave is at its center and increasing, it's best modeled by $y = \sin(x)$ (or, more generally, $y = A(\sin bx) + C$, depending on the amplitude, period, and vertical displacement, but in the case shown here $A = b = 1$ and $C = 0$). If at $x = 0$ the wave is at its center and decreasing, the best model is $y = -\sin(x)$. If at $x = 0$ the graph is at its maximum, the appropriate function is $y = \cos(x)$. If at $x = 0$ the graph is at its minimum, the appropriate function is $y = -\cos(x)$.

In a case like the one here where none of these apply, we require an appropriate *phase shift*. We can use either the sine or the cosine, since they differ only in phase; $\sin(x) = \cos\left(x + \frac{\pi}{2}\right)$. The particular graph shown here can be modeled by either $y = \sin\left(x + \frac{\pi}{4}\right)$ or $y = \cos\left(x - \frac{\pi}{4}\right)$; the two expressions are equivalent.

Writing a trigonometric equation to represent a sine graph like the one shown here

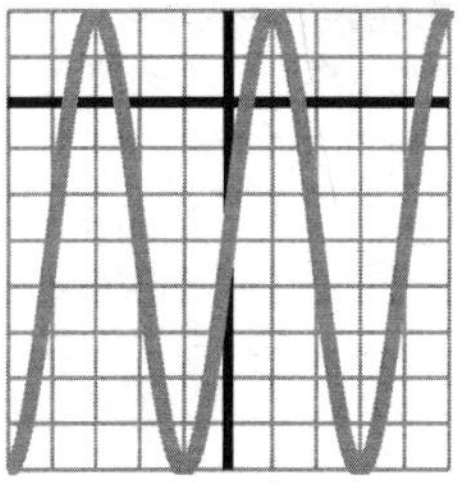

A sine function in its most general form takes the form $y = A\sin(bx + \phi) + C$. When the graph starts at the center line, as here, the phase shift ϕ is equal to zero. However, the other three parameters we still have to determine.

C here is the vertical displacement, that is, the distance between the center line of the graph and the x axis. In this case, the center line of the graph is 3 units below the x axis, so $C = -3$. A is the amplitude, the vertical distance between the center line and the maximum (or minimum) of the graph, or, equivalently, half the vertical distance between the maximum or minimum: in this case, $A = 5$. Finally, b is related to the period of the graph: more specifically, the period is equal to ${}^{2\pi}/_{b}$. In this case, the period (the horizontal distance between successive maxima or minima) is equal to 4, so $b = {}^{2\pi}/_{4} = \frac{\pi}{2}$. The full equation is therefore $y = 5\sin\left(\frac{\pi}{2}x\right) - 3$.

Example

Given the coordinates of an adjacent maximum and minimum of a periodic phenomenon, show how to determine the parameters of a trigonometric function that models the phenomenon

The fact that the phenomenon *has* a maximum and minimum implies it's best modeled by a sine or cosine, not a tangent. A sine or cosine function has four parameters: amplitude, period, vertical shift, and phase shift. The amplitude is half the difference between the y coordinates of the two points, while the period is twice the difference between the x coordinates. The vertical shift is the average of the y coordinates. As for the phase shift, it would be equal to the position of the maximum minus one quarter of the period.

For instance, suppose a function has a maximum at $(\pi/4, 5)$ and a minimum at $(7\pi/4, 1)$. The amplitude is then $\frac{5-1}{2} = 2$, the period is $2(7\pi/4 - \pi/4) = 3\pi$, the vertical shift is $\frac{5+1}{2} = 3$, and the phase shift is $\pi/4 - \frac{1}{4}(3\pi) = -\frac{\pi}{2}$.

Example

Given that $\sin(x)$ is defined for any real value of x, explain why $\sin^{-1}(x)$ is always between $-\frac{\pi}{2}$ and $\frac{\pi}{2}$

It's true that $y = \sin(x)$ is defined for any real number x, but each value of x does not correspond to a unique value of y. For instance, $\sin\left(\frac{\pi}{4}\right) = \sin\left(\frac{3\pi}{4}\right) = \sin\left(\frac{9\pi}{4}\right)$. Because of this, if we take the domain to include all real numbers, $\sin(x)$ is not invertible. To make a suitable invertible function, we have to restrict the domain to an interval where the function is strictly increasing or strictly decreasing. $\left[-\frac{\pi}{2}, \frac{\pi}{2}\right]$ is such an interval; between $-\frac{\pi}{2}$ and $\frac{\pi}{2}$ the function $\sin(x)$ is strictly increasing, and therefore invertible. It's not the *only* such interval—$\left[\frac{\pi}{2}, \frac{3\pi}{2}\right]$ or $\left[\frac{3\pi}{2}, \frac{5\pi}{2}\right]$ also qualify—but it makes sense to choose a domain that includes 0. Since inverting a function involves interchanging the range and the domain, if we restrict the original function to the domain $\left[-\frac{\pi}{2}, \frac{\pi}{2}\right]$, then this will be the range of the inverse function.

Ranges of $\sin^{-1}(x)$, $\cos^{-1}(x)$, and $\tan^{-1}(x)$

The trigonometric functions in their standard form are not invertible; there are multiple values of x that would give the same value for $\sin(x)$, $\cos(x)$, and $\tan(x)$. In order to produce invertible functions, we must restrict their domains to intervals in which they are strictly increasing or strictly decreasing. Although there are infinitely many such intervals we could choose for each function, it makes sense for simplicity's sake to choose continuous intervals that include zero and that include positive numbers. Such an interval for $\sin(x)$ is $\left[-\frac{\pi}{2}, \frac{\pi}{2}\right]$, for $\cos(x)$ is $[0, \pi]$, and for $\tan(x)$ is $\left[-\frac{\pi}{2}, \frac{\pi}{2}\right]$.

The range of an inverse function is equal to the domain of the original function. So the range of $\sin^{-1}(x)$ is $\left[-\frac{\pi}{2}, \frac{\pi}{2}\right]$, the range of $\cos^{-1}(x)$ is $[0, \pi]$, and the range of $\tan^{-1}(x)$ is $\left[-\frac{\pi}{2}, \frac{\pi}{2}\right]$.

Example

Given an equation with an unknown in the argument of a sine or cosine function, such as $3 = 6\cos(2x)$, show how you can solve for the unknown

To solve for an unknown in the argument of a trigonometric function, we have to cancel the function by using the appropriate inverse trigonometric function. We first manipulate the equation to get the trigonometric function on a side by itself; we can then take the corresponding inverse trigonometric function of both sides. For instance, for our sample equation, $3 = 6\cos(2x)$, we first divide by 6 to get $^1/_2 = \cos(2x)$, hence $2x = \cos^{-1}\left(\frac{1}{2}\right) = \frac{\pi}{3}$, and $x = \frac{\pi}{6}$.

This is not, however, the only solution. Recall that $\cos(x) = \cos(x + 2\pi n) = \cos(-x + 2\pi n)$ for any integer n. The equation, therefore, has infinitely many solutions: not only can $2x$ equal $\frac{\pi}{3}$, but it can also be $\frac{\pi}{3} + 2\pi n$ or $-\frac{\pi}{3} + 2\pi n$, and so $x = \frac{1}{2}\left(\pm\frac{\pi}{3} + 2\pi n\right) = \pm\frac{\pi}{6} + \pi n$ for any integer n. Similar considerations apply for other trigonometric functions: $\sin(x) = \sin(x + 2\pi n) = \sin(\pi - x + 2\pi n)$, and $\tan(x) = \tan(x + \pi n)$.

Example

Given an equation with an unknown in the argument of a tangent function, such as $\tan^2(x + 1) = 3$, show how you can solve for the unknown

To solve for an unknown in the argument of a trigonometric function, we have to cancel the function by using the appropriate inverse trigonometric function. We first manipulate the equation to get the trigonometric function on a side by itself; we can then take the corresponding inverse trigonometric function of both sides. For instance, for our sample equation, $\tan^2(x + 1) = 3$, we first take the square root of both sides to get $\tan(x + 1) = \pm\sqrt{3}$, hence $x + 1 = \tan^{-1}\sqrt{3} =$ or $\tan^{-1}(-\sqrt{3})$, and so $x + 1 = \pm\frac{\pi}{3}$.

This is not, however, the only solution. Recall that $\tan(x) = \tan(x + \pi n)$ for any integer n. The equation, therefore, has infinitely many solutions: not only can $x + 1$ equal $\pm\frac{\pi}{3}$, but it can also be $\pm\frac{\pi}{3} + \pi n$, and so $x = \pm\frac{\pi}{3} + \pi n - 1$ for any integer n. Similar considerations apply for other trigonometric functions: $\sin(x) = \sin(x + 2\pi n) = \sin(\pi - x + 2\pi n)$, and $\cos(x) = \cos(x + 2\pi n) = \cos(-x + 2\pi n)$.

Proving the Pythagorean identity, $\sin^2(\theta) + \cos^2(\theta) = 1$

There are many different ways to prove the Pythagorean identity. Probably the simplest method not using calculus or infinite series, however, relies on the well-known Pythagorean theorem that the sum of the squares of the legs of a right triangle is equal to the square of the hypotenuse. First of all, we can plot the angle on the unit circle, and then draw an appropriate triangle as shown below:

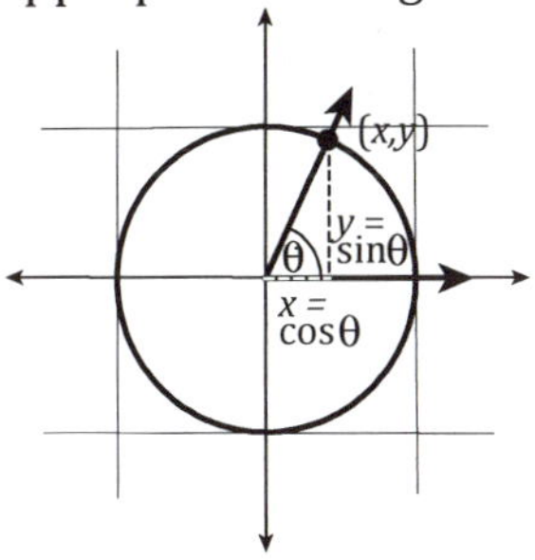

Notice that the hypotenuse is a radius of the circle, which by definition of a unit circle is equal to 1. The legs of the right triangle are equal to $|\sin\theta|$ and $|\cos\theta|$. The sum of the squares of the legs is then $\sin^2\theta + \cos^2\theta$, and the square of the hypotenuse is $1^2 = 1$. Thus, $\sin^2(\theta) + \cos^2(\theta) = 1$.

If you're given the value of one trigonometric function of an angle, what other information you would need in order to find the value of another trigonometric function of the same angle

If the two trigonometric functions are reciprocals, no further information is needed. If we're given $\sin\theta$ and asked to find $\csc\theta$, or vice versa, all we have to do is take the reciprocal, since $\sin\theta = 1/\csc\theta$. The same goes for $\cos\theta$ and $\sec\theta$, or $\tan\theta$ and $\cot\theta$.

In other cases, however, the one function alone is insufficient. We can use the Pythagorean identities such as $\sin^2\theta + \cos^2\theta = 1$ or $1 + \cot^2\theta = \csc^2\theta$, but these identities alone will give us only the *absolute value* of the unknown function; it won't tell us whether it's positive or negative. For that, we need more information, such as the quadrant of the angle—then we can use the Pythagorean identities to find the magnitude of the function and the quadrant to determine the sign.

<u>Example</u>

If you're given the value of $\sin\theta$ and the quadrant of the angle, show how you can find $\cos\theta$ and $\tan\theta$

Given the value of $\sin\theta$, we can find $\cos\theta$ using the Pythagorean identity, $\sin^2(\theta) + \cos^2(\theta) = 1$. Solving for $\cos\theta$, we get $\cos^2\theta = 1 - \sin^2\theta$, and $\cos\theta = \pm\sqrt{1 - \sin^2\theta}$. For instance, if $\sin\theta = \frac{3}{5}$, then $\cos\theta = \pm\sqrt{1 - \left(\frac{3}{5}\right)^2} = \pm\sqrt{1 - \frac{9}{25}} = \pm\sqrt{\frac{16}{25}} = \pm\frac{4}{5}$. To decide whether the cosine is positive or negative, we take into account the quadrant of the angle: if the angle is in quadrant 1 or 4, $\cos\theta$ is positive, and if the angle is in quadrant 2 or 3, $\cos\theta$ is negative.

Since the tangent is equal to the sine divided by the cosine, once we know the sine and the cosine finding the tangent is simple. Again, if $\sin\theta = \frac{3}{5}$, and if the angle is in quadrant 2 so the cosine is negative, then $\tan\theta = \frac{3/5}{-4/5} = -\frac{3}{4}$.

Example

If you're given the value of $\cos\theta$ and the quadrant of the angle, show how you can find $\sin\theta$ and $\tan\theta$

Given the value of $\cos\theta$, we can find $\sin\theta$ using the Pythagorean identity, $\sin^2(\theta)+\cos^2(\theta)=1$. Solving for $\sin\theta$, we get $\sin^2\theta = 1-\cos^2\theta$, and $\sin\theta = \pm\sqrt{1-\cos^2\theta}$. For instance, if $\cos\theta = \frac{12}{13}$, then $\sin\theta = \pm\sqrt{1-\left(\frac{12}{13}\right)^2} = \pm\sqrt{1-\frac{144}{169}} = \pm\sqrt{\frac{25}{169}} = \pm\frac{5}{13}$. To decide whether the sine is positive or negative, we take into account the quadrant of the angle: if the angle is in quadrant 1 or 2, $\sin\theta$ is positive, and if the angle is in quadrant 3 or 4, $\sin\theta$ is negative.

Since the tangent is equal to the sine divided by the cosine, once we know the sine and the cosine finding the tangent is simple. Again, if $\cos\theta = \frac{12}{13}$, and if the angle is in quadrant 1 so the sine is positive, then $\tan\theta = \frac{5/13}{12/13} = \frac{5}{12}$.

Example

If you're given the value of $\tan\theta$ and the quadrant of the angle, show how you can find $\sin\theta$ and $\cos\theta$

Given the value of $\tan\theta$, one way we can find $\sin\theta$ and $\cos\theta$ is by using the identity $1+\tan^2\theta = \sec^2\theta$. So $\sec\theta = \pm\sqrt{1+\tan^2\theta}$, and since $\cos\theta = 1/\sec\theta$, $\cos\theta = \pm(1+\tan^2\theta)^{-1/2}$. For instance, if $\tan\theta = \frac{15}{8}$, then $\cos\theta = \pm\left(1+\left(\frac{15}{8}\right)^2\right)^{-1/2} = \pm\left(1+\frac{225}{64}\right)^{-1/2} = \pm\left(\frac{289}{64}\right)^{-1/2} = \pm\sqrt{\frac{64}{289}} = \pm\frac{8}{17}$. To decide whether the cosine is positive or negative, we take into account the quadrant of the angle: if the angle is in quadrant 1 or 4, $\cos\theta$ is positive, and if the angle is in quadrant 2 or 3, $\cos\theta$ is negative.

Since the tangent is equal to the sine divided by the cosine, once we know the cosine and the tangent finding the sine is simple: we just multiply the cosine by the tangent. Again, if $\tan\theta = \frac{15}{8}$, and if the angle is in quadrant 1 so the cosine is positive, then $\sin\theta = \left(\frac{15}{8}\right)\left(\frac{8}{17}\right) = \frac{15}{17}$.

Deriving the addition formula for the sine function

The addition formula for the sine function is $\sin(a+b) = \sin a\cos b + \sin b\cos a$. There are many different ways this can be proven. One proof (at least for a and b between 0 and $\frac{\pi}{2}$) uses the following diagram:

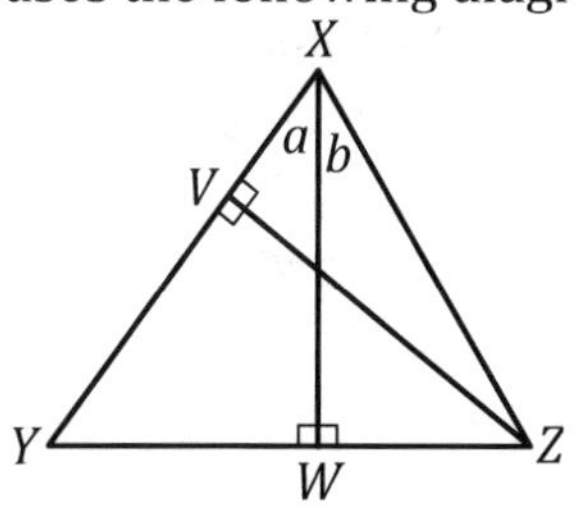

Consider first right triangle XWZ. By the right-triangle definition of the sine and cosine, $WZ = XZ \sin b$ and $WX = XZ \cos b$. Similarly, considering right triangle XWY, we find that $WY = XY \sin a$ and $WX = XY \cos a$. Since the area of a triangle is one half the base times the height, the area of triangle XWZ is $\frac{1}{2} WZ \cdot WX = \frac{1}{2}(XZ \sin b)(XY \cos a)$, and the area of triangle XWY is $\frac{1}{2} WY \cdot WX = \frac{1}{2}(XY \sin a)(XZ \cos b)$. Now, from right triangle XVZ, we see that $VZ = XZ \sin(a + b)$. If we take XY to be the base of triangle XYZ, we therefore find that the area of triangle XYZ is equal to $\frac{1}{2} XY \cdot VZ = \frac{1}{2} XY(XZ \sin(a + b))$. Since the area of XYZ must be the sum of the areas of XWY and XWZ, we find $\frac{1}{2} XY(XZ \sin(a + b)) = \frac{1}{2}(XY \sin a)(XZ \cos b) + \frac{1}{2}(XZ \sin b)(XY \cos a)$, or, canceling $\frac{1}{2} XY \cdot XZ$ from each term, $\sin(a + b) = \sin a \cos b + \sin b \cos a$.

Deriving the addition formula for the cosine function

The addition formula for the cosine function is $\cos(a + b) = \cos a \cos b - \sin a \sin b$. There are many different ways this can be proven; one uses the unit circle, as follows:

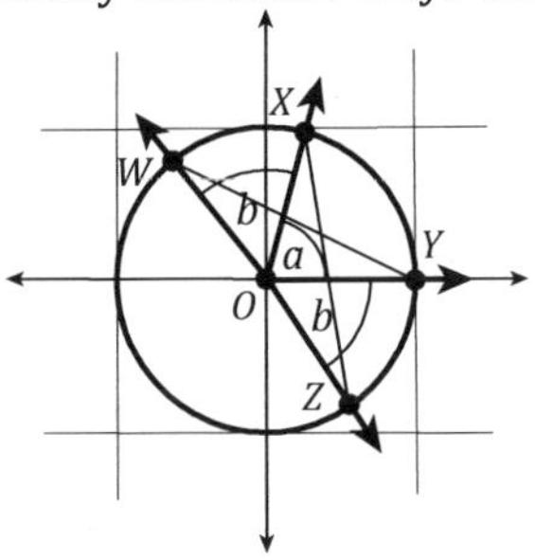

Note that the angles between OX and OZ and between OW and OY are both equal to $a + b$, so $XZ = WY$. By the distance formula, $XZ^2 = (\cos a - \cos b)^2 + (\sin a + \sin b)^2 = \cos^2 a + \cos^2 b - 2 \cos a \cos b + \sin^2 a + \sin^2 b + 2 \sin a \sin b = (\sin^2 a + \cos^2 a) + (\sin^2 b + \cos^2 b) + 2(\sin a \sin b - \cos a \cos b) = 2 + 2(\sin a \sin b - \cos a \cos b)$. Similarly, $WY^2 = (1 - \cos(a + b))^2 + (\sin(a + b))^2 = 1 + \cos^2(a + b) - 2 \cos(a + b) + \sin^2(a + b) = 1 + (\sin^2(a + b) + \cos^2(a + b)) - 2 \cos(a + b) = 2 - 2 \cos(a + b)$. Setting these equal to each other, we get $2 + 2(\sin a \sin b - \cos a \cos b) = 2 - 2\cos(a + b)$, so $\cos(a + b) = \cos a \cos b - \sin a \sin b$.

Deriving the addition formula for the tangent function

The addition formula for the tangent function is $\tan(a + b) = \frac{\tan a + \tan b}{1 - \tan a \tan b}$. This can be proven by taking the ratio of the addition formulas for the sine and cosine formulas: $\tan(a + b) = \frac{\sin(a+b)}{\cos(a+b)} = \frac{\sin a \cos b + \cos a \sin b}{\cos a \cos b - \sin a \sin b}$. If we divide both the numerator and the denominator by $\cos a \cos b$, the numerator becomes $\frac{\sin a \cos b}{\cos a \cos b} + \frac{\cos a \sin b}{\cos a \cos b} = \frac{\sin a}{\cos a} + \frac{\sin b}{\cos b} = \tan a + \tan b$, and the denominator becomes $\frac{\cos a \cos b}{\cos a \cos b} - \frac{\sin a \sin b}{\cos a \cos b} = 1 - \tan a \tan b$, giving a ratio of $\frac{\tan a + \tan b}{1 - \tan a \tan b}$. (There are ways of proving the addition formula for the tangent function directly without relying on the formulas for the sine and cosine, but they're substantially more complicated.)

Example

Determine how you could use trigonometric identities to solve a problem such as finding the sine of θ in the diagram below

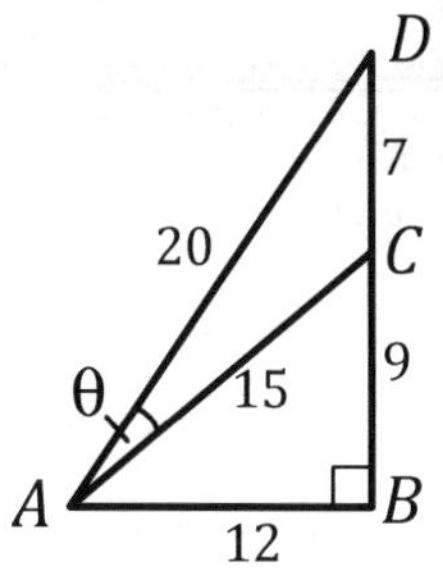

One way to find $\sin\theta$ in the given diagram is by using the sine subtraction formula. We may not be able to find $\sin\theta$ directly, since it's not part of a right triangle, but we can find the sines of angles DAB and CAB, which *are* angles in right triangles. Using the fact that the sine of an angle in a right triangle is equal to the length of the opposite leg divided by the length of the hypotenuse, we find $\sin(\angle DAB) = (7+9)/20 = 4/5$, and $\sin(\angle CAB) = 9/15 = 3/5$. Likewise, by dividing the length of the *adjacent* leg by the length of the hypotenuse, we find $\cos(\angle DAB) = 12/20 = 3/5$, and $\cos(\angle CAB) = 12/15 = 4/5$. So, using the subtraction formula for the sine, $\sin(\alpha - \beta) = \sin\alpha\cos\beta - \cos\alpha\sin\beta$, we have $\sin\theta = \sin(\angle DAB - \angle CAB) = \sin(\angle DAB)\cos(\angle CAB) - \cos(\angle DAB)\sin(\angle CAB) = (4/5)(4/5) - (3/5)(3/5) = (16/25) - (9/25) = 7/25$.

Evaluating a trigonometric function such as $\cos 15°$ or $\tan 7\pi/12$

Although 15° and $7\pi/12$ are not angles the trigonometric functions of which are commonly memorized, they can be written as sums or differences of angles with trigonometric functions that *are* well known: $15° = 45° - 30°$, and $7\pi/12 = \pi/3 + \pi/4$. (These sums or differences are not unique; we could also have used, for instance, $15° = 60° - 45°$ or $7\pi/12 = 3\pi/4 - \pi/6$.) We can therefore use the sum and difference formulas to solve for the trigonometric functions of these angles.

The cosine difference formula is $\cos(a-b) = \cos a \cos b + \sin a \sin b$. In this case, $\cos(45° - 30°) = (\cos 45°)(\cos 30°) + (\sin 45°)(\sin 30°) = \left(\frac{\sqrt{2}}{2}\right)\left(\frac{1}{2}\right) + \left(\frac{\sqrt{2}}{2}\right)\left(\frac{\sqrt{3}}{2}\right) = (\sqrt{2} + \sqrt{6})/4$. The tangent sum formula is $\tan(a+b) = \frac{\tan a + \tan b}{1 - \tan a \tan b}$. In this case, $\tan(\pi/3 + \pi/4) = \frac{\tan(\pi/3) + \tan(\pi/4)}{1 - (\tan\pi/3)(\tan\pi/4)} = \frac{\sqrt{3}+1}{1-(\sqrt{3})(1)} = \frac{1+\sqrt{3}}{1-\sqrt{3}}$.

Conditional Probability and the Rules of Probability

Sample space of a statistical experiment

The sample space of a statistical experiment is the set of all possible distinct outcomes of the experiment. If the experiment comprises the flip of a coin, for example, there are only two elements in the sample space: either the coin will come up heads, or the coin will come up tails. For the roll of a standard die, there are six possible outcomes in the sample space, one for each number that could come up on the die. When drawing a card from a full deck (without jokers), there are 52 possible outcomes.

The elements of the sample space need not all have the same probability. If you roll a weighted die that comes up 1 50% of the time, the sample space is the same as for the roll of an ordinary, unweighted die; only the probabilities of the elements in the sample space differ.

Event in a statistical experiment

In a statistical experiment, an event can be defined as a subset of the sample space—that is, an event is a particular collection of possible outcomes. The event may have only one element, or it may have many different elements. For instance, suppose the statistical experiment in question is the draw of a card from a deck. One event is the draw of the ace of spades—this is one possible outcome from the draw. Another could be the draw of a jack—this event comprises four possible outcomes, since there are four jacks in the deck. Still another could be the draw of a black card—twenty-six of the cards in the deck are black, so this event comprises twenty-six different outcomes.

Union and intersection of two sets of outcomes

Let A and B each be a set of elements or outcomes. Since the application is probability theory, we will use the term "outcomes".

The union (symbol ∪) of two sets is the set of elements found in Set A or Set B. For example, if A={2,3,4} and B={3,4,5}, $A \cup B = \{2, 3, 4, 5\}$. Note that the outcomes 3 and 4 appear only once in the union. For statistical events, the union is equivalent to "or"; $P(A \cup B)$ is the same thing as P(A or B).

The intersection (symbol ∩) of two sets is the set of outcomes common to both sets. For the above sets A and B, $A \cap B = \{3, 4\}$. For statistical events, the intersection is equivalent to "and"; $P(A \cap B)$ is the same thing as P(A and B).

The union and intersection commute: $A \cup B = B \cup A$and$A \cap B = B \cap A$.The union of sets is left and right distributive over intersection, $A \cup (B \cap C) = (A \cup B) \cap (A \cup C)$and $(B \cap C) \cup A = (B \cup A) \cap (C \cup A)$. Likewise, the intersection of sets is left and right distributive over union: $A \cap (B \cup C) = (A \cap B) \cup (A \cap C)$ and $(B \cup C) \cap A = (B \cap A) \cup (C \cap A)$.

Complement of a set of outcomes

In general, the complement of a set is the set of all possible elements not in the set. This requires first defining the set of all possible elements under consideration, known as the universe. In probability theory, however, this is already defined; the universe under consideration is the sample space. The complement of a set of outcomes is therefore the set of all outcomes in the sample space that are not in the original set.

For example, suppose that an integer is randomly chosen between 1 and 7. The sample space is then {1, 2, 3, 4, 5, 6, 7}. Consider the set of outcomes A = {1, 3, 4}. Then its complement $A^C = \{2, 5, 6, 7\}$—all the possible outcomes in the sample set that do not appear in A.

The complement of a union of two sets is the intersection of their complements, and vice versa: $(A \cup B)^C = A^C \cap B^C$, and $(A \cap B)^C = A^C \cup B^C$.

Defining events in terms of other events

Consider the draw of a card from a deck. Drawing the ace of spades is one possible event; drawing a red card is another; drawing a face card is still another. Still another event is the drawing of either the ace of spades or a red card—since both the outcomes of the two events "ace of spades" and "red card" are included, this event is the union of those two events. We can also consider drawing a red face card, i.e. a card that is both a red card and a face card. The set of outcomes in this event is the intersection of those in the two events "red card" and "face card". The drawing of a card that is not a face card is also an event, the complement of the face card event. In general, "or" indicates a union, "and" an intersection, and "not" a complement of events.

Independent events

Two events are independent if the occurrence of one event has no effect on the probability of the other event occurring. For example, for two successive coin flips, the coin comes up heads on the first flip and the coin coming up heads on the second flip are independent events: whether the coin comes up heads or tails on the first flip has no effect on whether it comes up heads or tails on the second. However, if you draw two cards from a deck, while not replacing the first card, the probability of the first and second cards being red represents dependent events. In this case, the number of possible outcomes and the sample space, in the second event, are each decreased by 1.

Proving independence with the product of the probabilities
For two independent events, and only for independent events, the product of the probabilities of each event is equal to the probability that both events will occur: $P(A)P(B) = P(A \cap B)$. If we know these probabilities, then, we can use this equation to check whether the events are independent. Conversely, if we know the probabilities of two events that we know are independent, we can use this equation to find the probability that both will occur.

For example, suppose you're programming a computer game in which there's a random chance of finding a certain item at the end of each level. You want the chances at each level to be independent. Suppose you find after running some trials that the chances of finding the item at the end of the first level are $\frac{1}{3}$, at the end of the second level are $\frac{1}{4}$, and at the end of both the first and the second level are $\frac{1}{12}$. Since $\left(\frac{1}{3}\right)\left(\frac{1}{4}\right) = \left(\frac{1}{12}\right)$, this proves that the events are indeed independent.

Conditional probability

Given two events A and B, the conditional probability P(A|B)is the probability that event B will occur, given that event A has occurred. For instance, suppose you have a jar containing two red marbles and two blue marbles, and you draw two marbles at random. Note. The first drawn marble is not replaced. Consider event A being the event that the first marble drawn is red, and event B being the event that the second marble drawn is blue. With no conditions set, both P(A) and P(B) are equal to $\frac{1}{2}$. However, if we know that the first marble drawn was red—that is, that event A occurred—then that leaves one red marble and two blue marbles in the jar. In that case, the probability that the second marble is blue given that the first marble was red—that is, P(A|B)—is equal to $\frac{2}{3}$.

Calculating the conditional probability P(A|B) in terms of the probabilities of events A and B and their union and/or intersection

The conditional probability P(A|B) is the probability that event B will occur given that event A occurs. This cannot be calculated simply from P(A) and P(B); these probabilities alone do not give sufficient information to determine the conditional probability. It can, however, be determined given also $P(A \cap B)$, the probability that events A and B both occur. Specifically, $P(A|B) = \frac{P(A \cap B)}{P(B)}$.

For instance, suppose you have a jar containing two red marbles and two blue marbles, and you draw two marbles at random. Consider event A being the event that the first marble drawn is red, and event B being the event that the second marble drawn is blue. P(A) is $\frac{1}{2}$, and $P(A \cap B)$ is $\frac{1}{3}$. (The latter may not be obvious, but may be determined by finding the product of $\frac{1}{2}$ and $\frac{2}{3}$) Therefore $P(A|B) = \frac{1/3}{1/2} = \frac{2}{3}$.

Conditional probability in everyday situations

Conditional probability often arises in everyday situations in, for example, estimating the risk or benefit of certain activities. The conditional probability of having a heart attack given that you exercise daily may be smaller than the overall probability of having a heart attack. The conditional probability of having lung cancer given that you are a smoker is larger than the overall probability of having lung cancer.

Note that changing the order of the conditional probability changes the meaning: the conditional probability of having lung cancer given that you are a smoker is a very different thing from the probability of being a smoker given that you have lung cancer. In an extreme case, suppose that a certain rare disease is caused only by eating a certain food, but even then is unlikely. Then the conditional probability of having that disease given that you eat the dangerous food is nonzero but low, but the conditional probability of having eaten that food given that you have the disease is 100%!

Independent events

The conditional probability P(A|B) is the probability that event B will occur given that event A occurs. If the two events are independent, we do not expect that whether or not event A occurs should have any effect on whether or not event B occurs. In other words, we expect P(A|B)=P(A).

This can be proven using the usual equations for conditional probability and the joint probability of independent events. The conditional probability $P(A|B) = \frac{P(A \cap B)}{P(B)}$. But if A and B are independent, then $P(A \cap B) = P(A)P(B)$. So $P(A|B) = \frac{P(A)P(B)}{P(B)} = P(A)$.

By similar reasoning, if A and B are independent then P(B|A)=P(B).

Independence

Determining independence from a two-way frequency table

If we have a two-way frequency table, it is generally a straightforward matter to read off the probabilities of any two events A and B, as well as the joint probability of both events occurring, $P(A \cap B)$. We can then check whether or not the events are independent by verifying whether $P(A)P(B) = P(A \cap B)$.

For example, consider the following table, showing a certain store's recent T-shirt sales, categorized by size and color:

		Size			
		Small	Medium	Large	Total
Color	Blue	25	40	35	100
	White	27	25	22	74
	Black	8	23	15	26
	Total	60	88	72	220

Suppose we want to check whether the event A that a customer buys a blue shirt is independent of the event B that a customer buys a medium shirt. From the table, $P(A) = \frac{100}{220} = \frac{5}{11}$ and $P(B) = \frac{88}{220} = \frac{4}{10}$. Also, $P(A \cap B) = \frac{40}{220} = \frac{2}{11}$. Since $\left(\frac{5}{11}\right)\left(\frac{4}{10}\right) = \frac{20}{220} = \frac{2}{11}$, $P(A)P(B) = P(A \cap B)$ and these two events are indeed independent.

Estimating a conditional probability from a two-way frequency table

If we have a two-way frequency table, it is generally a straightforward matter to read off the probabilities of any two events A and B, as well as the joint probability of both events occurring, $P(A \cap B)$. We can then find the conditional probability P(A|B) by calculating $P(A|B) = \frac{P(A \cap B)}{P(B)}$.

For example, a certain store's recent T-shirt sales:

		Size			
		Small	Medium	Large	Total
Color	Blue	25	40	35	100
	White	27	25	22	74
	Black	8	23	15	26
	Total	60	88	72	220

Suppose we want to find the conditional probability that a customer buys a black shirt (event A), given that the shirt he buys is size small (event B). From the table, the probability P(A) that a customer buys a small shirt is $\frac{60}{220} = \frac{3}{11}$. The probability $P(A \cap B)$ that he buys a small, black shirt is $\frac{8}{220} = \frac{2}{55}$. The conditional probability P(A|B) that he buys a black shirt, given that he buys a small shirt, is therefore $P(A|B) = \frac{2/55}{3/11} = \frac{2}{15}$.

Everyday situations
Even if we don't necessarily think of it in those terms, we often use independence of events in everyday situations. We know when playing a board game, for instance, that each roll of the die is independent, and is unaffected by previous rolls.

Sometimes, however, our intuition fails us and we tend to think of independent events as influencing each other; if we flip a coin and it comes up heads three times in a row, we may erroneously believe on some level that the next flip is more likely to come up tails because a tails is "overdue". Many gamblers make this mistake, seeing meaningful streaks in random results, and expecting certain results on the basis of previous events. Remembering what it means for events to be random helps avoid this error.

Uniform probability model

A uniform probability model is a model in which the probabilities of all outcomes are equally likely. For example, the roll of a fair die can be simulated by such a model; it's equally likely that any face of the die come up on top. Likewise, the draw of a card from a well-shuffled deck can be represented by a uniform probability model; it's equally likely for any card to be drawn.

One useful feature of a uniform probability model is that probabilities can be determined by simply counting outcomes. The probability of an event A occurring is equal to the total number of outcomes in event A divided by the total number of outcomes in the sample set. For example, suppose we want to know the probability of drawing a face card from a well-shuffled deck of cards (without jokers). There are fifty-two cards in the deck, twelve of which are face cards. The probability of drawing a face card from the deck is therefore $\frac{12}{52} = \frac{3}{13}$.

When plotted, a uniform distribution is rather flat, in appearance. Uniform distribution results when plotting the sampling distribution of a large number of samples, thus illustrating the Central Limit Theorem.

Finding the conditional probability P(A|B)
Although one way of finding the conditional probability is to calculate $P(A|B) = \frac{P(A \cap B)}{P(B)}$, this is not the only way. For a uniform probability model, it's possible to find the conditional probability even without knowing the overall probability of any event, just knowing all the outcomes included in event B. To see this, consider that the probability of event B occurring is equal to the number of outcomes in event B, which we can call X_B, divided by the total number of outcomes in the sample space, X_{TOTAL}. Similarly, the probability of events A and B both occurring is equal to the number of outcomes in the intersection of A and B, $X_{A \cap B}$, divided by the total number of outcomes in the sample space, X_{TOTAL}. So the conditional probability $P(A|B) = \frac{P(A \cap B)}{P(B)} = \frac{X_{A \cap B}/X_{TOTAL}}{X_B/X_{TOTAL}} = \frac{X_{A \cap B}}{X_B}$. In other words, we can find the conditional probability $P(A|B)$ by simply dividing the number of outcomes that belong to both A and B by the number of outcomes that belong to B: $P(A|B)$ is the fraction of B's outcomes that also belong to A.

Interpreting a conditional probability
A conditional probability $P(A|B)$ is the probability that event A will occur given that event B occurs. For a uniform probability model, this is equal to the fraction of B's outcomes that also belong to A. For instance, suppose we are interested in knowing the number of students of each grade at a certain school who buy their lunch at the school and who take their lunch from home. We will call the event that a randomly chosen student is in the ninth grade event A, and the event that he buys his lunch at school event B. Since the students are randomly chosen with equal probability, this is a uniform probability model. The probability that a student buys his lunch at school, given that he is in the ninth grade, is $P(A|B)$, and is simply equal to the fraction of ninth-grade students who buy their lunches at the school.

Addition rule

The addition rule for probabilities is $P(A \cup B) = P(A) + P(B) - P(A \cap B)$. In other words, the probability that either event A or event B will occur is equal to the sum of the probabilities of each event, minus the probability that they will both occur.

For example, suppose you want to find the probability that, when you roll two dice, either their numbers will match (event A) or they will add to eight (event B). $P(A) = \frac{6}{36} = \frac{1}{6}$, since there are six possible combinations of matching dice ((1,1), (2,2), (3,3), (4,4), (5,5), or (6,6)), and thirty-six combinations total. $P(B) = \frac{5}{36}$; there are five combinations that add to 8 ((2,6), (3,5), (4,4), (5,3), or (6,2)). $P(A \cap B) = \frac{1}{36}$; there is only one combination of matching dice that add to 8 (that is, (4,4)). So $P(A \cup B) = \frac{1}{6} + \frac{5}{36} - \frac{1}{36} = \frac{5}{18}$.

Interpreting the result in terms of a uniform probability model
The addition rule states that $P(A \cup B) = P(A) + P(B) - P(A \cap B)$. The result of the equation gives the probability that either event A or B will occur, which for a uniform probability distribution is equal to the fraction of outcomes in either A or B.

Suppose, for example, we are told that of the books on a certain shelf, $\frac{1}{3}$ are paperbacks, $\frac{1}{2}$ are fiction, and $\frac{1}{4}$ are paperback fiction books. We can call event A the event that a randomly chosen book is a paperback and event B the event that a randomly chosen book is fiction. Since we are randomly choosing the books, this is a uniform probability model. From the given information, $P(A) = \frac{1}{3}$, $P(B) = \frac{1}{2}$, and $P(A \cap B)$—the probability that a randomly chosen book is both paperback and fiction—is equal to $\frac{1}{4}$. So $P(A \cup B) = \frac{1}{3} + \frac{1}{2} - \frac{1}{4} = \frac{7}{12}$. This indicates in this case that $\frac{7}{12}$ of the books are either paperback or fiction.

General multiplication rule

The general multiplication rule for probabilities states that $P(A \cap B) = P(A)P(B|A) = P(B)P(A|B)$. In other words, the probability that events A and B will both occur is equal to the probability that event A will occur times the probability that event B will occur on the condition that A occurs; or, equivalently, it is equal to the to the probability that event B will occur times the probability that event A will occur on the condition that B occurs.

For example, suppose we're told that a certain cat is in a certain yard half the time, and when it is in the yard there is a $\frac{1}{3}$ chance that a second cat will be with it. We will call the event of the first cat being in the yard A, and the event of the second cat being in the yard B. Then from the given information, P(A) = $\frac{1}{2}$ and $P(B|A) = \frac{1}{3}$. The probability that both cats are in the yard is then $P(A \cap B) = P(A)P(B|A) = \left(\frac{1}{2}\right)\left(\frac{1}{3}\right) = \frac{1}{6}$.

Interpreting the result in terms of a uniform probability model

The general multiplication rule states that $P(A \cap B) = P(A)P(B|A) = P(B)P(A|B)$. The result of this rule is the probability that events A and B will both occur, which for a uniform probability model is equal to the fraction of outcomes that are in both events A and B.

For example, suppose we are told that $\frac{1}{4}$ of the insects in a certain woman's insect collection are butterflies, and that $\frac{1}{5}$ of those butterflies are blue. We can call event A the event that a randomly chosen insect from the collection is a butterfly and event B the event that it is blue. So P(A) = $\frac{1}{4}$, and $P(B|A) = \frac{1}{5}$—the fraction of butterflies in the collection that are blue is equal to the probability that a randomly chosen insect in the collection is blue, given that it is a butterfly. Then by the multiplication rule, $P(A \cap B) = P(A)P(B|A) = \left(\frac{1}{4}\right)\left(\frac{1}{5}\right) = \frac{1}{20}$. So the probability that a randomly selected insect from the collection is both blue and a butterfly is $\frac{1}{20}$; $\frac{1}{20}$ of the insects are blue butterflies.

Permutations and combinations

Both combinations and permutations are used when it is required to determine the number of ways that k elements can be chosen (without repetition) out of a larger set of n elements. In general, a permutation is used when the order of the elements matters, and a combination when it doesn't. For instance, if we wanted to calculate how many different five-letter sequences are possible (with no letters repeated), the order matters, so we would want the permutation of five elements out of the twenty-six-letter alphabet, ${}_{26}P_5$(which is equal to $\frac{26!}{(26-5)!} = 7{,}893{,}600$). If we wanted to calculate how many different hands of four cards we could draw from a deck of 52 cards, the order doesn't matter, so we would want the combination of four elements out of the fifty-two, ${}_{52}C_4$ (which is equal to $\frac{52!}{4!(52-4)!} =$ 270,725.

Permutation

A permutation is a way of selecting k elements out of a larger group of n elements, in which the order matters: (1, 2, 3) is considered a different permutation from (2, 3, 1). The number of permutations of k elements out of n can be written as ${}_nP_k$, and is equal to $\frac{n!}{(n-k)!}$. When k is small, this is more easily calculated as $(n)(n-1)\dots(n-k+1)$. For instance, there are six possible ways to choose two (ordered) elements out of three: (1, 2), (2, 1), (1, 3), (3, 1), (2, 3), (3, 2). And, accordingly, ${}_3P_2 = \frac{3!}{(3-2)!} = \frac{6}{1} = 6$. The number of ways to choose five (ordered) elements out of a hundred is much harder to enumerate, but not hard to calculate: ${}_{100}P_5 = \frac{100!}{(100-5)!} = (100)(99)(98)(97)(96) = 9{,}034{,}502{,}400$. The number of ways to choose 95 (ordered) elements out of 100 is much larger, equal to ${}_{100}P_{95} = \frac{100!}{(100-95)!} = \frac{100!}{5!}$, which turns out to be a number with more than 150 digits.

Combination

A combination is a way of selecting k elements out of a larger group of n elements, in which the order doesn't matter: (1, 2, 3) and (2, 3, 1) are considered the same combination. The number of permutations of k elements out of n can be written as ${}_nC_k$, and is equal to $\frac{n!}{k!(n-k)!}$. For instance, there are three possible ways to choose two (unordered) elements out of three: (1, 2), (2, 3), or (1, 3). And, accordingly, ${}_3C_2 = \frac{3!}{2!(3-2)!} = \frac{6}{2 \cdot 1} = 3$. The number of ways to choose five (unordered) elements out of a hundred is much harder to enumerate, but not hard to calculate: ${}_{100}C_5 = \frac{100!}{5!(100-5)!} = \frac{100!}{5! \cdot 95!} = 75{,}287{,}520$. Similarly, the number of ways to choose 95 (unordered) elements out of 100 is equal to ${}_{100}C_{95} = \frac{100!}{95!(100-95)!} = \frac{100!}{95! \cdot 5!} = 75{,}287{,}520$. This illustrates a general rule: ${}_nC_k = {}_nC_{n-k}$, for any positive integer values of n and k such that $k \leq n$.

Calculating the number of possible sequences of six letters, with no letters repeated

The total number of possible sequences of six letters, with no letters repeated, is equal to the number of permutations of 6 elements out of 26, or ${}_{26}P_6$. This can be calculated as ${}_{26}P_6 = \frac{26!}{(26-6)!} = \frac{26!}{20!} = 165{,}765{,}600$. There are almost 166 million possible sequences of six letters, with no letters repeated.

If repetitions are allowed, then the permutation formula no longer applies. Rather, now each letter can be treated as an independent event, since choosing one letter has no bearing on the possible choices for the others. Since there are 26 possible choices for the first letter, 26 for the second, 26 for the third, and so on, the total number of combinations is $26 \cdot 26 \cdot 26 \cdot 26 \cdot 26 \cdot 26 = 26^6 = 308{,}915{,}776$.

Probability problem solved with a permutation

A permutation can be used to solve a problem that involves finding the probability of one or more particular ordered arrangements of elements occurring. The permutation can be used to find the total number of outcomes in the sample space, and then the probability is the number of outcomes in the event in question divided by that number.

For example, suppose you had twelve tiles labeled with the numbers one through twelve, and you wanted to find the probability that, if you drew three tiles at random, they would be consecutive numbers in ascending order. There are ten arrangements that fit those criteria: (1, 2, 3), (2, 3, 4), (3, 4, 5), (4, 5, 6), (5, 6, 7), (6, 7, 8), (7, 8, 9), (8, 9, 10), (9, 10, 11), and (10, 11, 12). The total number of possible outcomes is ${}_{12}P_3 = \frac{12!}{(12-3)!} = 1320$. The probability that they will fulfill the criteria is then $\frac{10}{1320} = \frac{1}{132}$.

Probability problem that can be solved with a combination

A combination can be used to solve a problem that involves finding the probability of one or more particular unordered arrangements of elements occurring. The combination can be used to find the total number of outcomes in the sample space, and then the probability is the number of outcomes in the event in question divided by that number.

For example, suppose you wanted to find the probability of drawing a royal flush (a ten, ace, jack, queen, and king all of the same suit) from a standard deck of 52 cards. There are four suits in a standard deck, thus four possible royal flushes. Since the order of the cards doesn't matter, the total number of possible outcomes—sets of five cards that can be drawn—is equal to ${}_{52}C_5 = \frac{52!}{5!(52-5)!} = 2{,}598{,}960$. The probability of drawing a royal flush is therefore $\frac{4}{2{,}598{,}960} = \frac{1}{649{,}740}$.

<u>Deriving formulas for permutations and combinations</u>
The number of permutations of k elements out of n, ${}_nP_k$, is equal to the number of ways we can choose k elements, in order, from a larger set of n. The first element can be any of the n elements of the larger set. Once we've chosen it, however, there are only $n-1$ elements left to choose for the second element, then $n-2$ for the third, and so on down to $n-k+1$ for the kth element. The total number of possibilities is then the product of all of these numbers, $n(n-1)(n-2)\ldots(n-k+1)$, which is equal to $\frac{n(n-1)(n-2)\ldots(n-k+1)(n-k)(n-k-1)\ldots(2)(1)}{(n-k)(n-k-1)\ldots(2)(1)} = \frac{n!}{(n-k)!}$.
The number of combinations of k elements out of n, ${}_nC_k$ is equal to the number of ways we can choose k elements out of a larger set of n, disregarding the order. This is similar to ${}_nP_k$ except that the order doesn't matter. Essentially, then, we can get ${}_nP_k$ from ${}_nC_k$ by multiplying by the number of possible orders of the k elements, which is ${}_kP_k = k!$. So ${}_nP_k = {}_nC_k \cdot k!$; solving for ${}_nC_k$ we get ${}_nC_k = \frac{{}_nP_k}{k!} = \frac{n!}{k!(n-k)!}$.

Interpreting Categorical and Quantitative Data

Dot plot, histogram, and box plot

Dot plots, histograms, and box plots are three different methods of representing data sets in graphical form. While they all have similar purposes, some are more suitable for some data sets than others. Dot plots represent each data point as a separate dot, and are most useful for relatively small data sets with a small number of possible values. When the data set contains more than a few dozen points, dot plots may become unwieldy. For larger data sets, where the data distribution is continuous rather than discrete, histograms may be more practical. Histograms are especially useful to estimate the density of the data, and to estimate probability density functions. Box plots may be used to summarize the shape of a larger number of univariate data values; they are most useful for comparing separate groups of data, such as the results of several different experiments, or the statistics of several discrete populations.

Dot plot

A dot plot is a representation of a data set in which each data point is represented by a dot or similar marking, with matching data points grouped in columns. For instance, the data set {2, 1, 3, 1, 1, 5, 4, 4, 3, 3, 3, 4, 1, 5} can be represented as a dot plot as follows:

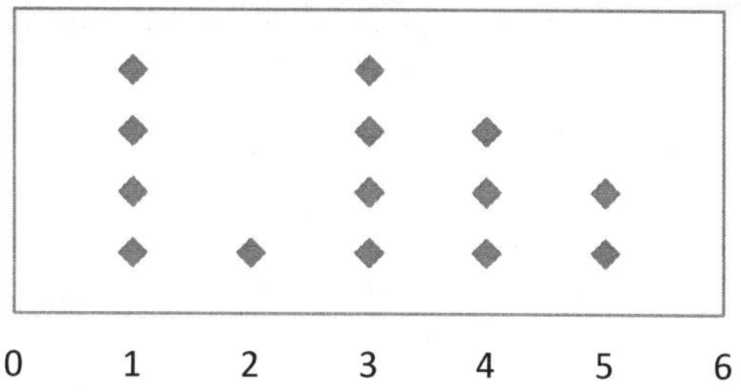

For large data sets, it is possible for each dot in a dot plot to represent more than one data point. However, for such data sets other representations may be more suitable.

Histogram

A histogram is a representation of a data set in which the data are represented by bars corresponding to discrete intervals, with the height of each bar representative of the number of data points falling in the corresponding interval. For example, the data set {101, 141, 105, 159, 122, 107, 145, 153, 183, 172, 164, 162, 144, 132, 138, 116, 155, 147, 141, 129, 168, 145, 152} can be represented by a histogram as follows:

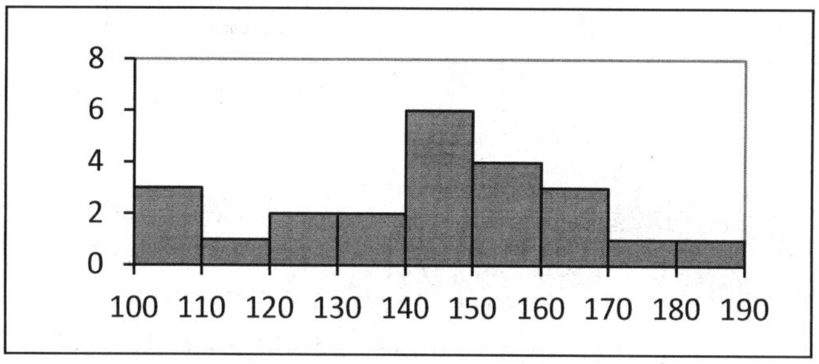

Histograms are useful for large data sets with values that may range continuously over intervals rather than being confined to discrete possibilities.

Box plot

A *box plot*, or box-and-whisker plot, is a representation of one or more data sets in which each data set is represented by a box with a bar in the middle and a "whisker" on each side. The bar represents the *median* of the data, and the edges of the box represent the first and third quartiles. The ends of the whiskers may represent the maximum and minimum data values, although often outliers are excluded and are represented instead as discrete points.

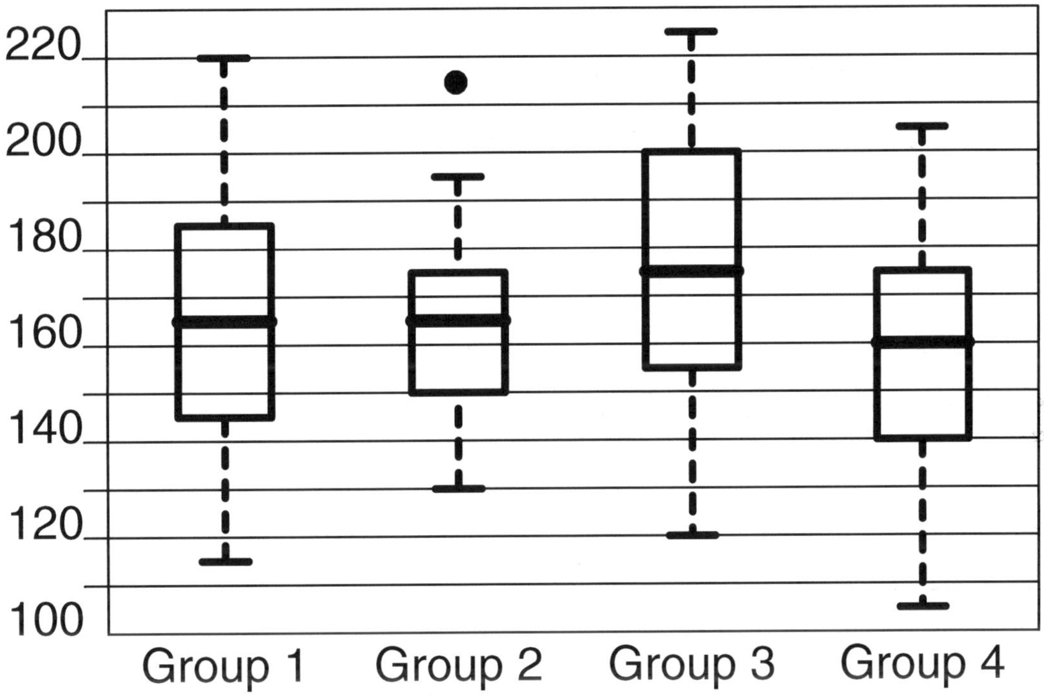

For example, given the data, 5, 5, 6, 9, 12, 14, 15, 17, 17, 21, 24, 26, 29, 31, 36, 38, 39, 46, 47, 49, the following summary statistics may be recorded: Median = 22.5, Q1 = 13, Q3 = 37, minimum = 5, and maximum = 49. Thus, a box plot of this data will show a box, with a middle bar at the value, 22.5, edges of the box at the values, 13 and 37, and whiskers at the values, 5 and 49. Box plots are useful when it is desired to compare the statistics of multiple related data sets, such as several different groups of experimental subjects.

Measures of central tendency

Mean

The mean is the average of the data points; that is, it is the sum of the data points divided by the number of data points. Mathematically, the mean of a set of data points $\{x_1, x_2, x_3, \ldots x_n\}$can be written as$\bar{X} = \sum \frac{X}{N}$. For instance, for the data set (1, 3, 6, 8, 100, 800), the mean is $\frac{1+3+6+8+100+800}{6} = 153$.

The mean is most useful, when data is approximately normal and does not include extreme outliers. In the above example, the data shows much variation. Thus, the mean is not the best measure of central tendency to use, when interpreting the data. With this data set, the median will give a more complete picture of the distribution.

Median
The median is the value in the middle of the data set, in the sense that 50% of the data points lie above the median and 50% of the data points lie below. The median can be determined by simply putting the data points in order, and selecting the data point in the middle. If there is an even number of data points, then the median is the average of the middle two data points. For instance, for the data set {1, 3, 6, 8, 100, 800}, the median is $\frac{6+8}{2} = 7$.

For distributions with widely varying data points, especially those with large outliers, the median is a more appropriate measure of central tendency, and thus gives a better idea of a "typical" data point. Notice in the data set above, the mean is 153, while the median is 7.

Mode
The mode is the value that appears most often in the data set. For instance, for the data set {2, 6, 4, 9, 4, 5, 7, 6, 4, 1, 5, 6, 7, 5, 6}, the mode is 6: the number 6 appears four times in the data set, while the next most frequent values, 4 and 5, appear only three times each. It is possible for a data set to have more than one mode: in the data set {11, 14, 17, 16, 11, 17, 12, 14, 17, 14, 13}, 14 and 17 are both modes, appearing three times each. In the extreme case of a uniform distribution—a distribution in which all values appear with equal probability—all values in the data set are modes.

The mode is useful to get a general sense of the shape of the distribution; it shows where the peaks of the distribution are. More information is necessary to get a more detailed description of the full shape.

Relation to shape of measurement
The measurement of central tendency with the most clearly visible relationship to the shape is the mode. The mode defines the peak of the distribution, and a distribution with multiple modes has multiple peaks. The relationship of the shape to the other measurements of central tendency is more subtle. For a symmetrical distribution with a single peak, the mode, median, and mean all coincide. For a distribution skewed to the left or right, however, this is not generally the case. One rule of thumb often given is that the median is displaced from the mode in the same direction as the skew of the graph, and the mean in the same direction farther still.

First quartile

The first quartile of a data set is a value greater than or equal to one quarter of the data points (and less than the other three quarters). Various methods exist for defining the first quartile precisely; one of the simplest is to define the first quartile as the median of the first half of the ordered data (excluding the median if there are an odd number of data points).

Applying this method, for example, to the data set {3, 1, 12, 7, 17, 4, 10, 8, 9, 20, 4}, we proceed as follows: Putting the data in order, we get {1, 3, 4, 4, 7, 8, 9, 10, 12, 17, 20}. The first half (excluding the median) is {1, 3, 4, 4, 7}, which has a median of 4. Therefore the first quartile of this data set is 4.

Third quartile

The third quartile of a data set is a value greater than or equal to three quarters of the data points (and less than the remaining quarter). Various methods exist for defining the third quartiles precisely; one of the simplest is to define the third quartile as the median of the second half of the ordered data (excluding the median if there are an odd number of data points). Applying this method, for example, to the data set {3, 1, 12, 7, 17, 4, 10, 8, 9, 20, 4}, we proceed as follows: Putting the data in order, we get {1, 3, 4, 4, 7, 8, 9, 10, 12, 17, 20}. The second half (excluding the median) is {9, 10, 12, 17, 20}, which has a median of 12. Therefore the third quartile of this data set is 12.

Interquartile range of a data set

The interquartile range of a data set is the difference between the third and first quartiles. That is, one quarter of the data fall below the interquartile range and one quarter of the data above it. Exactly half of the data points fall within the interquartile range, half of those above the median and half below. (This is, of course, why the quartile points are called "quartiles", because they divide the data into quarters: one quarter of the data points are below the first quartile, one quarter between the first and second quartile (the median), and so on.) The interquartile range is useful to get a rough idea of the spread of the data. The median by itself shows where the data are centered (or rather, shows one measure of central tendency); the interquartile range gives a better idea of how much the data points vary from this center.

Standard deviation

The standard deviation of a data set is a measurement of how much the data points vary from the mean. More precisely, it is equal to the square root of the average of the squares of the differences between each point and the mean: $s_x = \sqrt{\frac{\sum(X-\bar{X})^2}{N-1}}$.

The standard deviation is useful for determining the spread, or dispersion, of the data, or how far they vary from the mean. The smaller the standard deviation, the closer the values tend to be to the mean; the larger the standard deviation, the more they tend to be scattered far from the mean.

Outlier

An outlier is an extremely high or extremely low value in the data set. It may be the result of measurement error, in which case, the outlier is not a valid member of the data set. However, it may also be a valid member of the distribution. Unless a measurement error is identified, the experimenter cannot know for certain if an outlier is or is not a member of the distribution. There are arbitrary methods that can be employed to designate an extreme value as an outlier. One method designates an outlier (or possible outlier) to be any value less than $Q_1 - 1.5(IQR)$ or any value greater than $Q_3 + 1.5(IQR)$, where Q_1 and Q_3 are the first and third quartiles and IQR is the interquartile range. For instance, in the data set {42, 71, 22, 500, 33, 38, 62, 44, 58, 37, 61, 25}, the point 500 may be considered an outlier, since 500 is greater than 101.25 (61.5 + 1.5(26.5) = 101.25).

Effect on measurements of the center and spread of a data distribution

Regarding measurements of the center, outliers tend to have little or no effect on the mode, and in general little effect on the median, though their effects may be magnified for very small distributions. Means, however, are very sensitive to outliers; a single data point that lies far outside the range of the others may leave the mode and median almost unchanged while drastically altering the mean. For instance, the data set {2, 2, 5, 5, 5, 8, 11} has a mode and median of 5 and a mean of approximately 5.4; adding the outlying value 650 to the data set leaves the mode and median unchanged but increases the mean to 86.

Like the median, the interquartile range is little affected by outliers, though, again, the effect may be greater for small data sets. The standard deviation, like the mean, is much more sensitive to outliers, and may be significantly increased by a single outlier that lies far from the spread of the rest of the points.

Two data sets with the same center but different spreads

It's certainly possible for two data sets to have the same center but different spreads; all that's necessary is for the points in one set to be clustered closer to the center than the other. Consider, for instance, two data sets that both have the normal distribution with the same mean but different standard deviations: all usual measurements of central tendency would match—the mean, mode, and median—but their spread, as measured by either interquartile range or by standard deviation, would differ. The graph below shows the distributions of two such data sets:

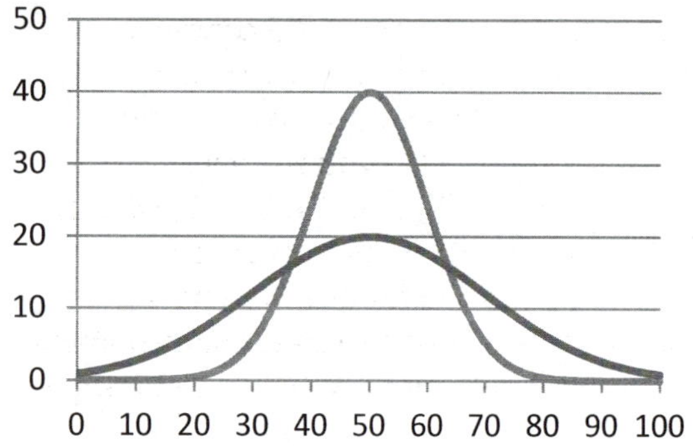

Two data sets with the same spread but different centers

It's certainly possible for two data sets to have the same spread but different centers; nothing prevents the data points of two sets from being equally near the center even if the center differs. Consider, for instance, two data sets that both have the normal distribution with the same standard deviation but different means: their spread, as measured by either interquartile range or by standard deviation, would match, but the measures of central tendency, mean, mode, and median—would differ between the data sets. The graph below shows the distributions of two such data sets:

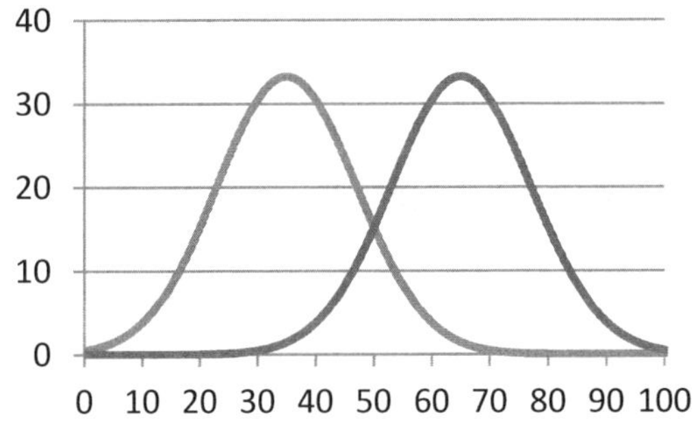

Two data distributions with the same spread and center but different shapes

It's certainly possible for two data distributions to have the same spread and center but different shapes. While the spread and the center are significant characteristics of a distribution, they are not sufficient to uniquely determine the distribution; two distributions may very well have the same spread and center but differ in the details. Consider, for instance, the data sets {5, 10, 15, 20, 25, 30, 35} and {7, 10, 11, 20, 29, 30, 33}: both these data sets have a mean and median of 20, an interquartile range of 20, and a standard deviation of approximately 10.8; yet clearly they are not identical, and have different shapes. For another example, consider an asymmetric distribution reflected about its mean; despite their different shapes, the distribution and its reflection have the same mean and necessarily the same spread.

Normal distribution

A normal distribution is a symmetrical, bell-shaped distribution that can be used to model real-world situations. In particular, the normal distribution is a good match for data that represents the sum or the mean of a large number of similar variables acting independently. If you roll a large number of dice, for instance, their mean will tend to follow close to a normal distribution. The normal distribution has a number of useful properties. Perhaps the most notable is that the distribution of the sum or difference of two variables each of which follows the normal distributions is itself another normal distribution, with the mean equal to the sum or difference of the means of the distributions of the original variables, and the standard deviation equal to the square root of the sum of the squares of the standard deviations of the original distributions.

Circumstances not appropriate for normal distribution

Many data sets that arise in real-world problems can be fit to or at least approximated by a normal distribution, and given the useful properties of this distribution it's often useful to do so. However, the normal distribution is not a good fit for all data sets. In general, if a data set seems to follow a symmetrical bell curve, it is likely (though not necessarily the case) that it can be usefully fit to a normal distribution. For a data sets that is clearly skewed and asymmetrical, however, such a fit is not suitable. Nor is it appropriate to try to fit to a normal distribution data sets that have no peaks or multiple peaks (though it may be possible to fit such data to a sum of normal distributions).

Generating normal distribution from the given mean and standard deviation

The normal distribution is defined by the normal equation, $f(x) = \frac{1}{\sigma\sqrt{2\pi}} e^{-\frac{1}{2}\left(\frac{x-\mu}{\sigma}\right)^2}$, where μ is the mean and σ is the standard deviation. Generating a normal equation corresponding to a given mean and standard deviation, then, is as simple as putting the appropriate values for μ and σ into this equation. A standard deviation with a mean of 100 and a standard deviation of 10, for instance, would have a normal equation $f(x) = \frac{1}{10\sqrt{2\pi}} e^{-\frac{1}{2}\left(\frac{x-100}{10}\right)^2}$. The probability that the data lies within a certain range can be found by determining the area under the normal curve—the graph of the normal function—within the given range.

It's often simpler, however, to consider the standard normal distribution, with the equation $f(z) = \frac{1}{\sqrt{2\pi}} e^{-\frac{1}{2}z^2}$. This is simply a normal distribution with a mean of 0 and a standard deviation of 1. A standard z-distribution is represented by the formula, $z = \frac{X-\mu}{\sigma}$.

Estimating population percentages

The population percentages falling within certain ranges in a normal distribution can be estimated by finding the area under the normal curve. This can either be estimated by inspection or determined using a calculator. For certain values, however, the population percentages can be estimated more directly. About 68% of the data points in a normal distribution lie within one standard deviation of the mean, about 95% within two standard deviations, and about 99.9% within three. For a normal distribution with a mean of 100 and a standard deviation of 10, for instance, we would expect 68% of the data points to lie between 90 and 110 (100 ± 10), and 95% of the data points to lie between 80 and 120. Because of the normal distribution's symmetry, half of these would lie on each side of the mean, so, for instance, about 34% of the data points would lie between 90 and 100 and 34% between 100 and 110; about 2.5% of the data points (½(100% – 95%)) would exceed 120.

Estimating area under a normal curve

Using a calculator

Most scientific calculators have statistical functions that allow the easy calculation of probabilities related to common probability distributions, including the normal distribution. The details depend on the particular model of calculator. In the TI-84, one of the most commonly used calculators today, the appropriate function can be accessed from the DISTR button (press "2nd", and then "VARS"). This will bring up a menu of distribution-related functions; select "normalcdf". The parameters of this function are, in order, the lower bound, the upper bound, the mean, and the standard deviation. For a normal distribution with a mean of 100 and a standard deviation of 10, for instance, to find the probability that a data point lies between 105 and 115 you would enter "normalcdf(105, 115, 100, 10)", yielding an answer of about 0.242, or 24.2%.

If you desire to see the area visually, you can hit the right arrow from the DISTR menu to get to the DRAW menu, and choose "ShadeNorm". The parameters are the same as for the "normalcdf" function.

Using a spreadsheet
Most modern spreadsheet programs include functions that allow the user to find the area under a normal curve. In Microsoft Excel, the appropriate function is NORMDIST, which gives the total area of the graph to the left of a particular value. The first parameter of this function is the value in question, the second is the mean, and the third the standard deviation. The fourth parameter should be simply set to TRUE. (If it's set to FALSE, Excel will return the value of the normal function at that point rather than the area under the curve.) For instance, for a normal distribution with a mean of 100 and a standard deviation of 10, to find the area under the curve to the left of 115, you would enter into the cell "=NORMDIST(115,100,10,TRUE)".

To find the area within a given interval, you can simply take the difference of two results. For instance, for the previous example, the area of the curve between 105 and 115 would be generated by "=NORMDIST(115,100,10,TRUE)-NORMDIST(105,100,10,TRUE)".

Using a table
Z-tables are available and give the total area under a normal curve to the left of a given value (or the larger portion). The area within an interval can be found by taking the difference between the areas for the right and left endpoints. A mean to z table is also available and may be used to find the area between the mean and a given value. This table may also be used, in order to find the area to the left (or right) or a value, by adding half the area under the normal curve (0.5), to the mean to z area represented by the given value.

Z-tables represent standardized values. The raw values are not represented by the table. Instead, the table represents standardized z-scores. A z-score is written as: $z = \frac{X-\mu}{\sigma}$, where X represents the particular value, μ represents the population mean, and σ represents the population standard deviation. (Literally translated, a z-score represents the number of standard deviations a value is above, or below, the mean.)For instance, if we wanted to find the area under the curve between 105 and 115 for a normal distribution with a mean of 100 and a standard deviation of 10, we would first convert our values to those appropriate for a normal distribution, $\frac{105-100}{10} = 0.5$ and $\frac{115-100}{10} = 1.5$, and then look up 1.5 and 0.5 in the table and subtract the results.

# of students	SPANISH	FRENCH	GERMAN
MALE	30	20	25
FEMALE	26	28	21

Two-way frequency table

A two-way frequency table is a table that shows the number of data points falling into each combination of two categories in the form of a table, with one category on each axis.

Creating a two-way frequency table is simply a matter of drawing a table with each axis labeled with the possibilities for the corresponding category, and then filling in the numbers in the appropriate cells. For instance, suppose you're told that at a given school, 30 male students take Spanish, 20 take French, and 25 German, while 26 female students take Spanish, 28 French, and 21 German. These data can be represented by the following two-way frequency table:

		Category #1 (Color)			TOTALS
		yellow	grey	black	
Category #2 (Vehicle)	truck	2	5	20	27
	car	2	25	3	30
	motorcycle	15	4	3	22
TOTALS		19	34	26	79

Joint and marginal frequencies

The joint frequency, $P(X,Y)$, is the probability of belonging to two specific subcategories. It's also known as a joint probability or joint relative frequency. The marginal frequency, $P(X)$, is the probability of belonging in a specific subcategory. It's also known as a marginal probability or marginal relative frequency. For example,

The joint frequency that a vehicle is a yellow truck is equal to $\frac{2}{79}$, where 2 is the number in the table cell corresponding to both "truck" and "yellow" and 79 is the total number of all vehicles of all colors.

The marginal frequency that a vehicle is a truck is equal to the sum of the probabilities of its being a yellow truck, a grey truck, or a black truck, $P(truck) = \frac{2}{79} + \frac{5}{79} + \frac{20}{79} = \frac{27}{79}$.

Conditional frequency

The conditional frequency, $P(X|Y)$, is the probability that X is a certain value on the condition that Y is a certain value. It's also known as a conditional probability or conditional relative frequency. The conditional frequency is related to the joint frequency and the marginal frequency by the relation $P(X,Y) = P(X|Y)P(Y)$; thus knowing the joint and marginal frequencies we can find the conditional frequency.

For example, consider the two-way frequency table below.

		Category #1 (Color)			TOTALS
		yellow	grey	black	
Category #2 (Vehicle)	truck	2	5	20	27
	car	2	25	3	30
	motorcycle	15	4	3	22
TOTALS		19	34	26	79

The joint frequency that a vehicle is a yellow truck is equal to $\frac{2}{79}$, and the marginal frequency that a vehicle is a truck is $\frac{27}{79}$. Therefore, the conditional frequency that a vehicle is yellow on the condition that it is a truck (the probability that a given truck in the data set is yellow) is equal to $\frac{2}{79} \div \frac{27}{79} = \frac{2}{27}$.

Scatter plots

Representing data on two quantitative variables

Data sets on two quantitative variables can be represented on a scatter plot by plotting each data point as a separate point on the chart. One axis of the chart corresponds to each variable, and then the data points are plotted accordingly in the appropriate positions on each axis. For instance, if 50 widgets cost \$500, 100 widgets cost \$800, and 200 widgets cost \$1500, this can be plotted on a scatter plot as follows:

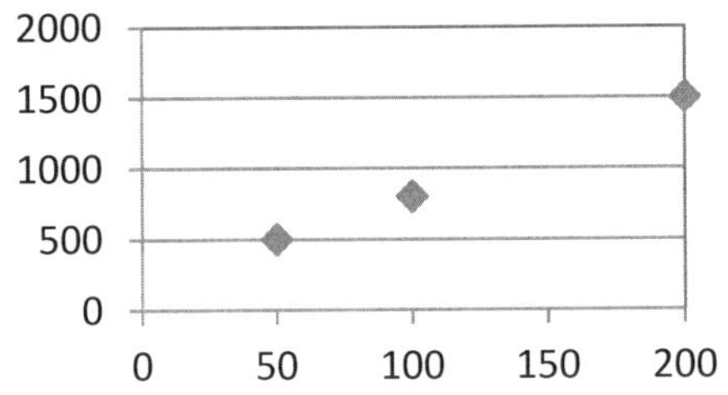

Normally, of course, a scatter plot would be used for larger data sets than this. A scatter plot is useful for seeing the relationship between the variables; one can often see at a glance if the variables have a linear or other simple relationship.

Determining the function that fits the data for two variables

It's often possible from examining a scatter plot to see roughly what relationship exists between the data by estimating what kind of smooth curve would best fit the data points. Linear relationships are particularly easy to spot—do the data points look like they're roughly arranged in a straight line?—but other functions may also fit the data. Actually finding the parameters of the function for the most precise fit is a more complex matter, though most calculators and spreadsheets have the capability of performing the necessary calculations. Qualitatively judging what kind of function fits the data, however, is simpler. Below are examples of scatter plots fit to quadratic and exponential functions, respectively:

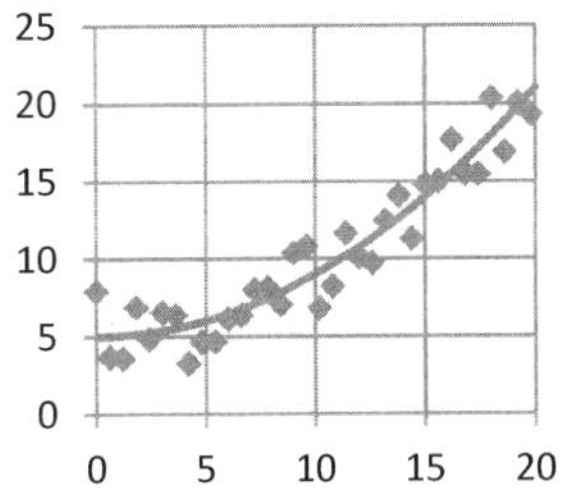

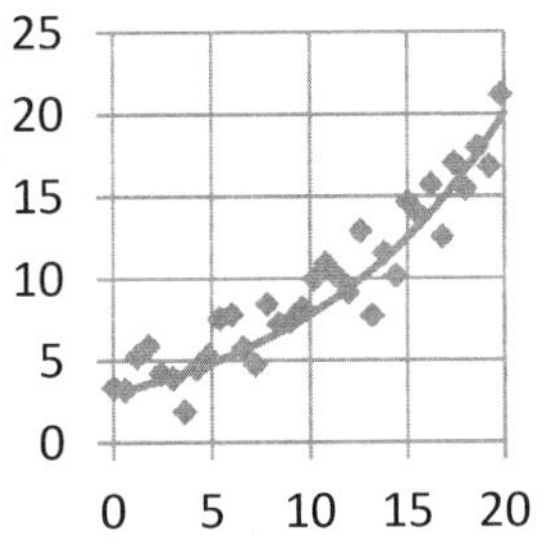

Using a linear function to solve problems in the context of the data
Once you have a function fitted to the scatter plot, you can use the equation of that function to solve problems regarding the data. For instance, suppose the scatter plot on the left below represents the number of bacteria that grow in a petri dish after one week, in millions, versus the amount of a certain nutrient added, in milligrams. The graph on the right shows a linear function fitted to the data.

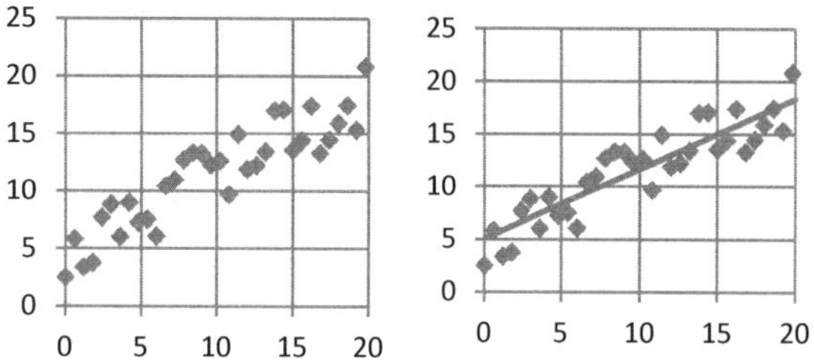

The equation of the line of best fit is $y = \frac{2}{3}x + 5$, where y is the bacteria count in millions and x is the amount of nutrient added, in milligrams. We can then use this function to solve problems; for instance, if we want to estimate how many bacteria to expect if we add 30 milligrams of nutrient, we solve $y = \frac{2}{3}(30) + 5 = 25$, or about 25 million bacteria.

Using a quadratic function to solve problems in the context of the data
Once you have a function fitted to the scatter plot, you can use the equation of that function to solve problems regarding the data. For instance, suppose the scatter plot on the left below represents the area covered by a certain patch of mold, in square centimeters, versus the time in days. The graph on the right shows a quadratic function fitted to the data.

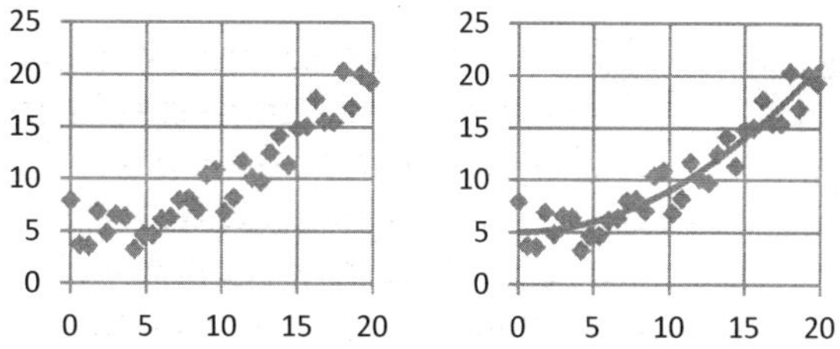

The equation of the quadratic trendline is $y = \frac{1}{25}x^2 + 5$, where x is the time in days and y is the area in square centimeters. We can then use this function to solve problems; for instance, if we want to estimate how much area to expect the mold to cover after 30 days, we solve $y = \frac{1}{25}(30^2) + 5 = 41$, or 41 square centimeters.

Using an exponential function to solve problems in the context of the data
Once you have a function fitted to the scatter plot, you can use the equation of that function to solve problems regarding the data. For instance, suppose the scatter plot on the left below represents the total assets of a certain company in millions of dollars, versus the time in years since 1990. The graph on the right shows an exponential function fitted to the data.

The equation of the trendline is $y = 3e^{0.095t}$, where t is the time in years and y is the company's assets, in millions of dollars. We can then use this function to solve problems;

for instance, if we want to estimate the company's projected assets in the year 2020 (30 years after 1990), we solve $y = 3e^{0.095 \cdot 30} \approx 51.9$, or 51.9 million dollars.

Residuals of a fit to a data set

The residuals of a fit to a data set are the differences between the observed values of the data and the predicted values based on the fit. For example, consider the data set {(6,6), (8,12), (10,20), (12,30)}, shown in the scatter plot on the left below A linear fit to the graph is shown on the right:

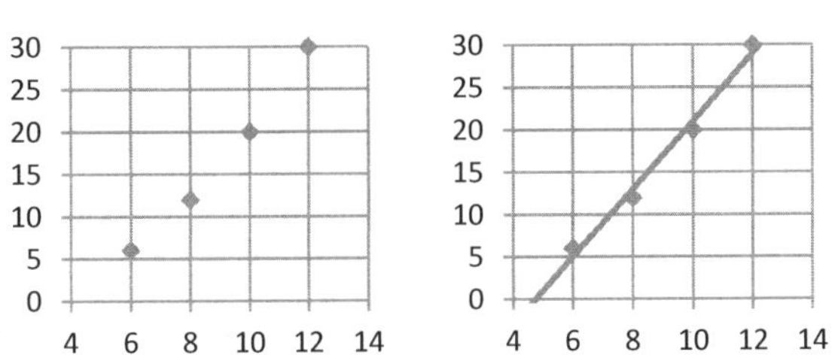

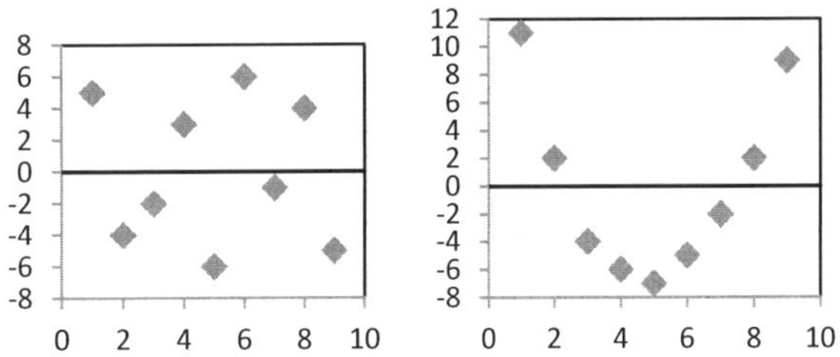

The line of best fit has the equation$y = 4x - 19$. The predicted value for x = 6 is then $4(6) - 19 = 5$, and the residual at x = 6 is $6 - 5 = 1$. At x = 8, the predicted value is $4(8) - 19 = 13$, and the residual at x = 8 is $12 - 13 = -1$. Similarly, the residuals at x = 10 and x = 12 are -1 and 1, respectively.

Note that these residuals add to 0 $(1 + (-1) + (-1) + 1 = 0)$. For the best fit curve, this is always the case; the sum and mean of the residuals will always be zero.

Residual plot

A residual plot is simply the plot of the residuals of a fit to a data set versus the independent variable (the x coordinates of the points). If the residual plot looks random—if the residuals seem to bear no relation to the independent variable—then the function fit to the model was probably a good choice. If the residual plot shows a definite pattern, then the data is probably better suited to a different kind of curve. Consider, for instance, the two residual plots shown below, both corresponding to linear fits. The plot on the left shows no obvious pattern, indicating that the linear fit in question is appropriate to the data. The plot on the left, however, shows a pronounced U shape, indicating that a nonlinear function would be a better fit to the data.

Calculating a fit to a linear function

Without technology

Although it's complicated to calculate an exact fit to a linear function without the aid of technology, finding an approximate fit is feasible. To produce such a fit, first draw a line that seems to follow the data points as closely as possible, probably with about as many data points above the line as below it. Then find the equation for this linear fit the same way as you would find the equation of any graphed line: choose two points on the line, (x_1, y_1) and (x_2, y_2), and then find the slope of the line as $m = \frac{y_2 - y_1}{x_2 - x_1}$. Then use this value of m and one of the known points in the equation $y = mx + b$ to solve for b (it doesn't matter which of the two points you use).

Because this method involves some eyeballing and approximation, it will generally not be completely optimal, and two people may get slightly different results. However, this approximate result will typically be good enough to find estimated solutions to problems.

Using technology

Most modern calculators and spreadsheets have the functionality to calculate linear fits to data sets. On a TI-84, you can find the fit as follows: First, press "STAT", select "EDIT", and enter your data into the table, with the independent variable in the L1 column and the dependent in the L2. Then press "STAT" again, select "CALC", and select "LinReg(ax+b)". The screen will display the coefficients a and b of the linear fit.

In recent versions of Microsoft Excel, you can put the independent and dependent variables in adjacent columns, select all the data, and insert a scatter plot. Then right-click on one of the data points of the graph and select "Add Trendline". Select "Linear", and be sure to check "Display Equation on chart" before clicking OK. The linear plot should be displayed on the graph, along with the corresponding equation of the line.

Slope

In the case of a linear fit to a data set, of the form $y = mx + b$, the slope m corresponds to the rate of change of the dependent variable y with respect to the independent variable x. This can often be expressed in a form similar to "y per x". For instance, if the data represents the distance of an object from some point as a function of time, with the distance as y and the time as x, then the slope of the linear model represents the change in distance with respect to the corresponding change in time—i.e., the velocity. If the data represents the cost to produce various quantities of products, then the slope of the linear model is the change in the cost with respect to the quantity of products produced—i.e., the production cost per unit of product.

Intercept

In the case of a linear fit to a data set, of the form $y = mx + b$, the intercept b corresponds to the value of the dependent variable y when the independent variable x is equal to zero. This often can be expressed as the "initial value" of the variable, or as its offset. For instance, if the data represents the distance of an object from some point as a function of time, with the distance as y and the time as x, then the intercept of the linear model represents the object's distance at time zero—i.e., its initial distance. If the data represents the cost to produce various quantities of products, then the intercept of the linear model is the cost when no units are being produced—in other words, the overhead cost involved in the production.

Correlation coefficient of a linear fit

The correlation coefficient of a linear fit is a number that expresses how closely the linear fit approximates the function. The coefficient is negative if the line of best fit has a negative slope—the dependent variable decreases as the independent variable increases, and positive if the best fit has a positive slope—the dependent variable increases as the independent variable increases. The linear fit is most closely correlated to the data if the correlation coefficient is equal to ± 1; this means that all the data points lie exactly on the best fit line. If the correlation coefficient is equal to 0, then the data are completely uncorrelated; there is no relationship between the dependent and the independent variable. More often, the correlation coefficient is somewhere in between 0 and 1, indicating a fit that reveals some correlation between the variables.

Most modern calculators and spreadsheets have the functionality to calculate the correlation coefficients of linear fits to data sets. On a TI-84, you can find the fit as follows: First, press "STAT", select "EDIT", and enter your data into the table, with the independent variable in the L1 column and the dependent in the L2. Then press "STAT" again, select "CALC", and select "LinReg(ax+b)". In addition to the coefficients a and b of the linear fit, the screen will display the correlation coefficient, r.

In recent versions of Microsoft Excel, you can put the independent and dependent variables in adjacent columns, then in another cell type "CORREL(". Select the cells containing the independent variables, then type a comma, select the cells containing the dependent variables and type a closing parenthesis. The cell should contain something like "CORREL(A1:A10,B1:B10)", though the letters and numbers may differ. Press ENTER and the cell will show the correlation coefficient of a linear fit to the data.

Correlation

Two variables are correlated if some nonrandom relationship exists between them: if a change in one variable tends to correspond to a change in the other. While many relationships may exist between variables—they may have a quadratic relationship, or an exponential, for example—"correlation" often refers to linear correlation, the existence of a linear relationship $y = mx + b$ between the variables. The data points need not perfectly follow that line; if they do, they are perfectly correlated, but data that approximately follow close to a line may still be said to be correlated. The degree of correlation may be quantified by a value called the correlation coefficient.

Note that correlation is not the same thing as causation; just because two variables are correlated does not necessarily mean that one is the cause of the other.

<u>Correlation and causation</u>
Two variables are correlated if a change in one variable is accompanied by a change in the other, especially if the two variables have a linear relationship. Causation exists if one variable directly depends on the other; a change in one variable causes a change in the other. Note that correlation does not imply causation. If two variables x and y are correlated, it could be because x causes y. However, it could also be that the apparent correlation is coincidental, or that y causes x, or it could be that both x and y are influenced by a third variable separate from both x and y.

<u>Correlation not linked by causation</u>
Many examples could be constructed of data sets with variables that are correlated but in which one variable is not the cause of the other. One way to construct such a data set is to consider two variables that might both be affected by a third. For example, suppose a survey at a given school indicates that students' shoe sizes are correlated with their spelling; the students with larger shoe sizes tend to have better spelling. Clearly it would seem strange that larger feet would lead to better spelling. In fact, there's a third variable at play here: older students would tend to have larger feet, and likewise older students will

tend to have better spelling. The larger shoe sizes don't cause the better spelling, nor does the better spelling cause the larger shoe sizes; rather, both are caused by a third variable that wasn't measured.

Success Strategies

The most important thing you can do is to ignore your fears and jump into the test immediately. Do not be overwhelmed by any strange-sounding terms. You have to jump into the test like jumping into a pool—all at once is the easiest way.

Make Predictions

As you read and understand the question, try to guess what the answer will be. Remember that several of the answer choices are wrong, and once you begin reading them, your mind will immediately become cluttered with answer choices designed to throw you off. Your mind is typically the most focused immediately after you have read the question and digested its contents. If you can, try to predict what the correct answer will be. You may be surprised at what you can predict.

Quickly scan the choices and see if your prediction is in the listed answer choices. If it is, then you can be quite confident that you have the right answer. It still won't hurt to check the other answer choices, but most of the time, you've got it!

Answer the Question

It may seem obvious to only pick answer choices that answer the question, but the test writers can create some excellent answer choices that are wrong. Don't pick an answer just because it sounds right, or you believe it to be true. It MUST answer the question. Once you've made your selection, always go back and check it against the question and make sure that you didn't misread the question and that the answer choice does answer the question posed.

Benchmark

After you read the first answer choice, decide if you think it sounds correct or not. If it doesn't, move on to the next answer choice. If it does, mentally mark that answer choice. This doesn't mean that you've definitely selected it as your answer choice, it just means that it's the best you've seen thus far. Go ahead and read the next choice. If the next choice is worse than the one you've already selected, keep going to the next answer choice. If the next choice is better than the choice you've already selected, mentally mark the new answer choice as your best guess.

The first answer choice that you select becomes your standard. Every other answer choice must be benchmarked against that standard. That choice is correct until proven otherwise by another answer choice beating it out. Once you've decided that no other answer choice seems as good, do one final check to ensure that your answer choice answers the question posed.

Valid Information

Don't discount any of the information provided in the question. Every piece of information may be necessary to determine the correct answer. None of the information in the question is there to throw you off (while the answer choices will certainly have information to throw you off). If two seemingly unrelated topics are discussed, don't ignore either. You can be confident there is a relationship, or it wouldn't be included in the question, and you are probably going to have to determine what is that relationship to find the answer.

Avoid "Fact Traps"

Don't get distracted by a choice that is factually true. Your search is for the answer that answers the question. Stay focused and don't fall for an answer that is true but irrelevant. Always go back to the question and make sure you're choosing an answer that actually answers the question and is not just a true statement. An answer can be factually correct, but it MUST answer the question asked. Additionally, two answers can both be seemingly correct, so be sure to read all of the answer choices, and make sure that you get the one that BEST answers the question.

Milk the Question

Some of the questions may throw you completely off. They might deal with a subject you have not been exposed to, or one that you haven't reviewed in years. While your lack of knowledge about the subject will be a hindrance, the question itself can give you many clues that will help you find the correct answer. Read the question carefully and look for clues. Watch particularly for adjectives and nouns describing difficult terms or words that you don't recognize. Regardless of whether you completely understand a word or not, replacing it with a synonym, either provided or one you more familiar with, may help you to understand what the questions are asking. Rather than wracking your mind about specific detailed information concerning a difficult term or word, try to use mental substitutes that are easier to understand.

The Trap of Familiarity

Don't just choose a word because you recognize it. On difficult questions, you may not recognize a number of words in the answer choices. The test writers don't put "make-believe" words on the test, so don't think that just because you only recognize all the words in one answer choice that that answer choice must be correct. If you only recognize words in one answer choice, then focus on that one. Is it correct? Try your best to determine if it is correct. If it is, that's great. If not, eliminate it. Each word and answer choice you eliminate increases your chances of getting the question correct, even if you then have to guess among the unfamiliar choices.

Eliminate Answers

Eliminate choices as soon as you realize they are wrong. But be careful! Make sure you consider all of the possible answer choices. Just because one appears right, doesn't mean that the next one won't be even better! The test writers will usually put more than one good answer choice for every question, so read all of them. Don't worry if you are stuck between two that seem right. By getting down to just two remaining possible choices, your odds are now 50/50. Rather than wasting too much time, play the odds. You are guessing, but guessing wisely because you've been able to knock out some of the answer choices that you know are wrong. If you are eliminating choices and realize that the last answer choice you are left with is also obviously wrong, don't panic. Start over and consider each choice again. There may easily be something that you missed the first time and will realize on the second pass.

Tough Questions

If you are stumped on a problem or it appears too hard or too difficult, don't waste time. Move on! Remember though, if you can quickly check for obviously incorrect answer choices, your chances of guessing correctly are greatly improved. Before you completely give up, at least try to knock out a couple of possible answers. Eliminate what you can and then guess at the remaining answer choices before moving on.

Brainstorm

If you get stuck on a difficult question, spend a few seconds quickly brainstorming. Run through the complete list of possible answer choices. Look at each choice and ask yourself, "Could this answer the question satisfactorily?" Go through each answer choice and consider it independently of the others. By systematically going through all possibilities, you may find something that you would otherwise overlook. Remember though that when you get stuck, it's important to try to keep moving.

Read Carefully

Understand the problem. Read the question and answer choices carefully. Don't miss the question because you misread the terms. You have plenty of time to read each question thoroughly and make sure you understand what is being asked. Yet a happy medium must be attained, so don't waste too much time. You must read carefully, but efficiently.

Face Value

When in doubt, use common sense. Always accept the situation in the problem at face value. Don't read too much into it. These problems will not require you to make huge leaps of logic. The test writers aren't trying to throw you off with a cheap trick. If you have to go beyond creativity and make a leap of logic in order to have an answer choice answer the question, then you should look at the other answer choices. Don't overcomplicate the problem by creating theoretical relationships or explanations that will warp time or space. These are normal problems rooted in reality. It's just that the applicable relationship or explanation may not be readily apparent and you have to figure things out. Use your common sense to interpret anything that isn't clear.

Prefixes

If you're having trouble with a word in the question or answer choices, try dissecting it. Take advantage of every clue that the word might include. Prefixes and suffixes can be a huge help. Usually they allow you to determine a basic meaning. Pre- means before, post- means after, pro - is positive, de- is negative. From these prefixes and suffixes, you can get an idea of the general meaning of the word and try to put it into context. Beware though of any traps. Just because con- is the opposite of pro-, doesn't necessarily mean congress is the opposite of progress!

Hedge Phrases

Watch out for critical hedge phrases, led off with words such as "likely," "may," "can," "sometimes," "often," "almost," "mostly," "usually," "generally," "rarely," and "sometimes." Question writers insert these hedge phrases to cover every possibility. Often an answer choice will be wrong simply because it leaves no room for exception. Unless the situation calls for them, avoid answer choices that have definitive words like "exactly," and "always."

Switchback Words

Stay alert for "switchbacks." These are the words and phrases frequently used to alert you to shifts in thought. The most common switchback word is "but." Others include "although," "however," "nevertheless," "on the other hand," "even though," "while," "in spite of," "despite," and "regardless of."

New Information

Correct answer choices will rarely have completely new information included. Answer choices typically are straightforward reflections of the material asked about and will directly relate to the question. If a new piece of information is included in an answer choice that doesn't even seem to relate to the topic being asked about, then that answer choice is likely incorrect. All of the information needed to answer the question is usually provided for you in the question. You should not have to make guesses that are unsupported or choose answer choices that require unknown information that cannot be reasoned from what is given.

Time Management

On technical questions, don't get lost on the technical terms. Don't spend too much time on any one question. If you don't know what a term means, then odds are you aren't going to get much further since you don't have a dictionary. You should be able to immediately recognize whether or not you know a term. If you don't, work with the other clues that you have—the other answer choices and terms provided—but don't waste too much time trying to figure out a difficult term that you don't know.

Contextual Clues

Look for contextual clues. An answer can be right but not the correct answer. The contextual clues will help you find the answer that is most right and is correct. Understand the context in which a phrase or statement is made. This will help you make important distinctions.

Don't Panic

Panicking will not answer any questions for you; therefore, it isn't helpful. When you first see the question, if your mind goes blank, take a deep breath. Force yourself to mechanically go through the steps of solving the problem using the strategies you've learned.

Pace Yourself

Don't get clock fever. It's easy to be overwhelmed when you're looking at a page full of questions, your mind is full of random thoughts and feeling confused, and the clock is ticking down faster than you would like. Calm down and maintain the pace that you have set for yourself. As long as you are on track by monitoring your pace, you are guaranteed to have enough time for yourself. When you get to the last few minutes of the test, it may seem like you won't have enough time left, but if you only have as many questions as you should have left at that point, then you're right on track!

Answer Selection

The best way to pick an answer choice is to eliminate all of those that are wrong, until only one is left and confirm that is the correct answer. Sometimes though, an answer choice may immediately look right. Be careful! Take a second to make sure that the other choices are not equally obvious. Don't make a hasty mistake. There are only two times that you should stop before checking other answers. First is when you are positive that the answer choice you have selected is correct. Second is when time is almost out and you have to make a quick guess!

Check Your Work

Since you will probably not know every term listed and the answer to every question, it is important that you get credit for the ones that you do know. Don't miss any questions through careless mistakes. If at all possible, try to take a second to look back over your answer selection and make sure you've selected the correct answer choice and haven't made a costly careless mistake (such as marking an answer choice that you didn't mean to mark). The time it takes for this quick double check should more than pay for itself in caught mistakes.

Beware of Directly Quoted Answers

Sometimes an answer choice will repeat word for word a portion of the question or reference section. However, beware of such exact duplication. It may be a trap! More than likely, the correct choice will paraphrase or summarize a point, rather than being exactly the same wording.

Slang

Scientific sounding answers are better than slang ones. An answer choice that begins "To compare the outcomes…" is much more likely to be correct than one that begins "Because some people insisted…"

Extreme Statements

Avoid wild answers that throw out highly controversial ideas that are proclaimed as established fact. An answer choice that states the "process should used in certain situations, if…" is much more likely to be correct than one that states the "process should be discontinued completely." The first is a calm rational statement and doesn't even make a definitive, uncompromising stance, using a hedge word "if" to provide wiggle room, whereas the second choice is a radical idea and far more extreme.

Answer Choice Families

When you have two or more answer choices that are direct opposites or parallels, one of them is usually the correct answer. For instance, if one answer choice states "x increases" and another answer choice states "x decreases" or "y increases," then those two or three answer choices are very similar in construction and fall into the same family of answer choices. A family of answer choices consists of two or three answer choices, very similar in construction, but often with directly opposite meanings. Usually the correct answer choice will be in that family of answer choices. The "odd man out" or answer choice that doesn't seem to fit the parallel construction of the other answer choices is more likely to be incorrect.

How to Overcome Test Anxiety

The very nature of tests caters to some level of anxiety, nervousness, or tension, just as we feel for any important event that occurs in our lives. A little bit of anxiety or nervousness can be a good thing. It helps us with motivation, and makes achievement just that much sweeter. However, too much anxiety can be a problem, especially if it hinders our ability to function and perform.

"Test anxiety," is the term that refers to the emotional reactions that some test-takers experience when faced with a test or exam. Having a fear of testing and exams is based upon a rational fear, since the test-taker's performance can shape the course of an academic career. Nevertheless, experiencing excessive fear of examinations will only interfere with the test-taker's ability to perform and chance to be successful.

There are a large variety of causes that can contribute to the development and sensation of test anxiety. These include, but are not limited to, lack of preparation and worrying about issues surrounding the test.

Lack of Preparation

Lack of preparation can be identified by the following behaviors or situations:

- Not scheduling enough time to study, and therefore cramming the night before the test or exam
- Managing time poorly, to create the sensation that there is not enough time to do everything
- Failing to organize the text information in advance, so that the study material consists of the entire text and not simply the pertinent information
- Poor overall studying habits

Worrying, on the other hand, can be related to both the test taker, or many other factors around him/her that will be affected by the results of the test. These include worrying about:

- Previous performances on similar exams, or exams in general
- How friends and other students are achieving
- The negative consequences that will result from a poor grade or failure

There are three primary elements to test anxiety. Physical components, which involve the same typical bodily reactions as those to acute anxiety (to be discussed below). Emotional factors have to do with fear or panic. Mental or cognitive issues concerning attention spans and memory abilities.

Physical Signals

There are many different symptoms of test anxiety, and these are not limited to mental and emotional strain. Frequently there are a range of physical signals that will let a test taker know that he/she is suffering from test anxiety. These bodily changes can include the following:

- Perspiring
- Sweaty palms
- Wet, trembling hands
- Nausea
- Dry mouth
- A knot in the stomach
- Headache
- Faintness
- Muscle tension
- Aching shoulders, back and neck
- Rapid heart beat
- Feeling too hot/cold

To recognize the sensation of test anxiety, a test-taker should monitor him/herself for the following sensations:

- The physical distress symptoms as listed above
- Emotional sensitivity, expressing emotional feelings such as the need to cry or laugh too much, or a sensation of anger or helplessness
- A decreased ability to think, causing the test-taker to blank out or have racing thoughts that are hard to organize or control.

Though most students will feel some level of anxiety when faced with a test or exam, the majority can cope with that anxiety and maintain it at a manageable level. However, those who cannot are faced with a very real and very serious condition, which can and should be controlled for the immeasurable benefit of this sufferer.

Naturally, these sensations lead to negative results for the testing experience. The most common effects of test anxiety have to do with nervousness and mental blocking.

Nervousness

Nervousness can appear in several different levels:

- The test-taker's difficulty, or even inability to read and understand the questions on the test
- The difficulty or inability to organize thoughts to a coherent form
- The difficulty or inability to recall key words and concepts relating to the testing questions (especially essays)
- The receipt of poor grades on a test, though the test material was well known by the test taker

Conversely, a person may also experience mental blocking, which involves:

- Blanking out on test questions
- Only remembering the correct answers to the questions when the test has already finished.

Fortunately for test anxiety sufferers, beating these feelings, to a large degree, has to do with proper preparation. When a test taker has a feeling of preparedness, then anxiety will be dramatically lessened.

The first step to resolving anxiety issues is to distinguish which of the two types of anxiety are being suffered. If the anxiety is a direct result of a lack of preparation, this should be considered a normal reaction, and the anxiety level (as opposed to the test results) shouldn't be anything to worry about. However, if, when adequately prepared, the test-taker still panics, blanks out, or seems to overreact, this is not a fully rational reaction. While this can be considered normal too, there are many ways to combat and overcome these effects.

Remember that anxiety cannot be entirely eliminated, however, there are ways to minimize it, to make the anxiety easier to manage. Preparation is one of the best ways to minimize test anxiety. Therefore the following techniques are wise in order to best fight off any anxiety that may want to build.

To begin with, try to avoid cramming before a test, whenever it is possible. By trying to memorize an entire term's worth of information in one day, you'll be shocking your system, and not giving yourself a very good chance to absorb the information. This is an easy path to anxiety, so for those who suffer from test anxiety, cramming should not even be considered an option.

Instead of cramming, work throughout the semester to combine all of the material which is presented throughout the semester, and work on it gradually as the course goes by, making sure to master the main concepts first, leaving minor details for a week or so before the test.

To study for the upcoming exam, be sure to pose questions that may be on the examination, to gauge the ability to answer them by integrating the ideas from your texts, notes and lectures, as well as any supplementary readings.

If it is truly impossible to cover all of the information that was covered in that particular term, concentrate on the most important portions, that can be covered very well. Learn these concepts as best as possible, so that when the test comes, a goal can be made to use these concepts as presentations of your knowledge.

In addition to study habits, changes in attitude are critical to beating a struggle with test anxiety. In fact, an improvement of the perspective over the entire test-taking experience can actually help a test taker to enjoy studying and therefore improve the overall experience. Be certain not to overemphasize the significance of the grade - know that the result of the test is neither a reflection of self worth, nor is it a measure of intelligence; one grade will not predict a person's future success.

To improve an overall testing outlook, the following steps should be tried:

- Keeping in mind that the most reasonable expectation for taking a test is to expect to try to demonstrate as much of what you know as you possibly can.
- Reminding ourselves that a test is only one test; this is not the only one, and there will be others.
- The thought of thinking of oneself in an irrational, all-or-nothing term should be avoided at all costs.

- A reward should be designated for after the test, so there's something to look forward to. Whether it be going to a movie, going out to eat, or simply visiting friends, schedule it in advance, and do it no matter what result is expected on the exam.

Test-takers should also keep in mind that the basics are some of the most important things, even beyond anti-anxiety techniques and studying. Never neglect the basic social, emotional and biological needs, in order to try to absorb information. In order to best achieve, these three factors must be held as just as important as the studying itself.

Study Steps

Remember the following important steps for studying:

- Maintain healthy nutrition and exercise habits. Continue both your recreational activities and social pass times. These both contribute to your physical and emotional well being.
- Be certain to get a good amount of sleep, especially the night before the test, because when you're overtired you are not able to perform to the best of your best ability.
- Keep the studying pace to a moderate level by taking breaks when they are needed, and varying the work whenever possible, to keep the mind fresh instead of getting bored.
- When enough studying has been done that all the material that can be learned has been learned, and the test taker is prepared for the test, stop studying and do something relaxing such as listening to music, watching a movie, or taking a warm bubble bath.

There are also many other techniques to minimize the uneasiness or apprehension that is experienced along with test anxiety before, during, or even after the examination. In fact, there are a great deal of things that can be done to stop anxiety from interfering with lifestyle and performance. Again, remember that anxiety will not be eliminated entirely, and it shouldn't be. Otherwise that "up" feeling for exams would not exist, and most of us depend on that sensation to perform better than usual. However, this anxiety has to be at a level that is manageable.

Of course, as we have just discussed, being prepared for the exam is half the battle right away. Attending all classes, finding out what knowledge will be expected on the exam, and knowing the exam schedules are easy steps to lowering anxiety. Keeping up with work will remove the need to cram, and efficient study habits will eliminate wasted time. Studying should be done in an ideal location for concentration, so that it is simple to become interested in the material and give it complete attention. A method such as SQ3R (Survey, Question, Read, Recite, Review) is a wonderful key to follow to make sure that the study habits are as effective as possible, especially in the case of learning from a textbook. Flashcards are great techniques for memorization. Learning to take good notes will mean that notes will be full of useful information, so that less sifting will need to be done to seek out what is pertinent for studying. Reviewing notes after class and then again on occasion will keep the information fresh in the mind. From notes that have been taken summary sheets and outlines can be made for simpler reviewing.

A study group can also be a very motivational and helpful place to study, as there will be a sharing of ideas, all of the minds can work together, to make sure that everyone understands, and the studying will be made more interesting because it will be a social occasion.

Basically, though, as long as the test-taker remains organized and self confident, with efficient study habits, less time will need to be spent studying, and higher grades will be achieved.

To become self confident, there are many useful steps. The first of these is "self talk." It has been shown through extensive research, that self-talk for students who suffer from test anxiety, should be well monitored, in order to make sure that it contributes to self confidence as opposed to sinking the student. Frequently the self talk of test-anxious students is negative or self-defeating, thinking that everyone else is smarter and faster, that they always mess up, and that if they don't do well, they'll fail the entire course. It is important to decreasing anxiety that awareness is made of self talk. Try writing any negative self thoughts and then disputing them with a positive statement instead. Begin self-encouragement as though it was a friend speaking. Repeat positive statements to help reprogram the mind to believing in successes instead of failures.

Helpful Techniques

Other extremely helpful techniques include:

- Self-visualization of doing well and reaching goals
- While aiming for an "A" level of understanding, don't try to "overprotect" by setting your expectations lower. This will only convince the mind to stop studying in order to meet the lower expectations.
- Don't make comparisons with the results or habits of other students. These are individual factors, and different things work for different people, causing different results.
- Strive to become an expert in learning what works well, and what can be done in order to improve. Consider collecting this data in a journal.
- Create rewards for after studying instead of doing things before studying that will only turn into avoidance behaviors.
- Make a practice of relaxing - by using methods such as progressive relaxation, self-hypnosis, guided imagery, etc - in order to make relaxation an automatic sensation.
- Work on creating a state of relaxed concentration so that concentrating will take on the focus of the mind, so that none will be wasted on worrying.
- Take good care of the physical self by eating well and getting enough sleep.
- Plan in time for exercise and stick to this plan.

Beyond these techniques, there are other methods to be used before, during and after the test that will help the test-taker perform well in addition to overcoming anxiety.

Before the exam comes the academic preparation. This involves establishing a study schedule and beginning at least one week before the actual date of the test. By doing this, the anxiety of not having enough time to study for the test will be automatically eliminated.

Moreover, this will make the studying a much more effective experience, ensuring that the learning will be an easier process. This relieves much undue pressure on the test-taker.

Summary sheets, note cards, and flash cards with the main concepts and examples of these main concepts should be prepared in advance of the actual studying time. A topic should never be eliminated from this process. By omitting a topic because it isn't expected to be on the test is only setting up the test-taker for anxiety should it actually appear on the exam. Utilize the course syllabus for laying out the topics that should be studied. Carefully go over the notes that were made in class, paying special attention to any of the issues that the professor took special care to emphasize while lecturing in class. In the textbooks, use the chapter review, or if possible, the chapter tests, to begin your review.

It may even be possible to ask the instructor what information will be covered on the exam, or what the format of the exam will be (for example, multiple choice, essay, free form, true-false). Additionally, see if it is possible to find out how many questions will be on the test. If a review sheet or sample test has been offered by the professor, make good use of it, above anything else, for the preparation for the test. Another great resource for getting to know the examination is reviewing tests from previous semesters. Use these tests to review, and aim to achieve a 100% score on each of the possible topics. With a few exceptions, the goal that you set for yourself is the highest one that you will reach.

Take all of the questions that were assigned as homework, and rework them to any other possible course material. The more problems reworked, the more skill and confidence will form as a result. When forming the solution to a problem, write out each of the steps. Don't simply do head work. By doing as many steps on paper as possible, much clarification and therefore confidence will be formed. Do this with as many homework problems as possible, before checking the answers. By checking the answer after each problem, a reinforcement will exist, that will not be on the exam. Study situations should be as exam-like as possible, to prime the test-taker's system for the experience. By waiting to check the answers at the end, a psychological advantage will be formed, to decrease the stress factor.

Another fantastic reason for not cramming is the avoidance of confusion in concepts, especially when it comes to mathematics. 8-10 hours of study will become one hundred percent more effective if it is spread out over a week or at least several days, instead of doing it all in one sitting. Recognize that the human brain requires time in order to assimilate new material, so frequent breaks and a span of study time over several days will be much more beneficial.

Additionally, don't study right up until the point of the exam. Studying should stop a minimum of one hour before the exam begins. This allows the brain to rest and put things in their proper order. This will also provide the time to become as relaxed as possible when going into the examination room. The test-taker will also have time to eat well and eat sensibly. Know that the brain needs food as much as the rest of the body. With enough food and enough sleep, as well as a relaxed attitude, the body and the mind are primed for success.

Avoid any anxious classmates who are talking about the exam. These students only spread anxiety, and are not worth sharing the anxious sentimentalities.

Before the test also involves creating a positive attitude, so mental preparation should also be a point of concentration. There are many keys to creating a positive attitude. Should fears become rushing in, make a visualization of taking the exam, doing well, and seeing an A written on the paper. Write out a list of affirmations that will bring a feeling of confidence, such as "I am doing well in my English class," "I studied well and know my material," "I enjoy this class." Even if the affirmations aren't believed at first, it sends a positive message to the subconscious which will result in an alteration of the overall belief system, which is the system that creates reality.

If a sensation of panic begins, work with the fear and imagine the very worst! Work through the entire scenario of not passing the test, failing the entire course, and dropping out of school, followed by not getting a job, and pushing a shopping cart through the dark alley where you'll live. This will place things into perspective! Then, practice deep breathing and create a visualization of the opposite situation - achieving an "A" on the exam, passing the entire course, receiving the degree at a graduation ceremony.

On the day of the test, there are many things to be done to ensure the best results, as well as the most calm outlook. The following stages are suggested in order to maximize test-taking potential:

- Begin the examination day with a moderate breakfast, and avoid any coffee or beverages with caffeine if the test taker is prone to jitters. Even people who are used to managing caffeine can feel jittery or light-headed when it is taken on a test day.
- Attempt to do something that is relaxing before the examination begins. As last minute cramming clouds the mastering of overall concepts, it is better to use this time to create a calming outlook.
- Be certain to arrive at the test location well in advance, in order to provide time to select a location that is away from doors, windows and other distractions, as well as giving enough time to relax before the test begins.
- Keep away from anxiety generating classmates who will upset the sensation of stability and relaxation that is being attempted before the exam.
- Should the waiting period before the exam begins cause anxiety, create a self-distraction by reading a light magazine or something else that is relaxing and simple.

During the exam itself, read the entire exam from beginning to end, and find out how much time should be allotted to each individual problem. Once writing the exam, should more time be taken for a problem, it should be abandoned, in order to begin another problem. If there is time at the end, the unfinished problem can always be returned to and completed.

Read the instructions very carefully - twice - so that unpleasant surprises won't follow during or after the exam has ended.

When writing the exam, pretend that the situation is actually simply the completion of homework within a library, or at home. This will assist in forming a relaxed atmosphere, and will allow the brain extra focus for the complex thinking function.

Begin the exam with all of the questions with which the most confidence is felt. This will build the confidence level regarding the entire exam and will begin a quality momentum. This will also create encouragement for trying the problems where uncertainty resides.

Going with the "gut instinct" is always the way to go when solving a problem. Second guessing should be avoided at all costs. Have confidence in the ability to do well.

For essay questions, create an outline in advance that will keep the mind organized and make certain that all of the points are remembered. For multiple choice, read every answer, even if the correct one has been spotted - a better one may exist.

Continue at a pace that is reasonable and not rushed, in order to be able to work carefully. Provide enough time to go over the answers at the end, to check for small errors that can be corrected.

Should a feeling of panic begin, breathe deeply, and think of the feeling of the body releasing sand through its pores. Visualize a calm, peaceful place, and include all of the sights, sounds and sensations of this image. Continue the deep breathing, and take a few minutes to continue this with closed eyes. When all is well again, return to the test.

If a "blanking" occurs for a certain question, skip it and move on to the next question. There will be time to return to the other question later. Get everything done that can be done, first, to guarantee all the grades that can be compiled, and to build all of the confidence possible. Then return to the weaker questions to build the marks from there.

Remember, one's own reality can be created, so as long as the belief is there, success will follow. And remember: anxiety can happen later, right now, there's an exam to be written!

After the examination is complete, whether there is a feeling for a good grade or a bad grade, don't dwell on the exam, and be certain to follow through on the reward that was promised...and enjoy it! Don't dwell on any mistakes that have been made, as there is nothing that can be done at this point anyway.

Additionally, don't begin to study for the next test right away. Do something relaxing for a while, and let the mind relax and prepare itself to begin absorbing information again.

From the results of the exam - both the grade and the entire experience, be certain to learn from what has gone on. Perfect studying habits and work some more on confidence in order to make the next examination experience even better than the last one.

Learn to avoid places where openings occurred for laziness, procrastination and day dreaming.

Use the time between this exam and the next one to better learn to relax, even learning to relax on cue, so that any anxiety can be controlled during the next exam. Learn how to relax the body. Slouch in your chair if that helps. Tighten and then relax all of the different muscle groups, one group at a time, beginning with the feet and then working all the way up to the neck and face. This will ultimately relax the muscles more than they were to begin with. Learn how to breathe deeply and comfortably, and focus on this breathing going in and out as a relaxing thought. With every exhale, repeat the word "relax."

As common as test anxiety is, it is very possible to overcome it. Make yourself one of the test-takers who overcome this frustrating hindrance.

Practice Test and Additional Bonus Material

Due to our efforts to try to keep this book to a manageable length, we've created a link that will give you access to all of your additional bonus material.

Please visit http://www.mometrix.com/bonus948/parcchsalg2 to access the information.